Confluence
HARPERS FERRY AS DESTINY

Confluence
HARPERS FERRY AS DESTINY

Dennis E. Frye

Catherine Mägi Oliver

Harpers Ferry Park Association
P.O. Box 197
Harpers Ferry, WV 25425
info@hfpawv.org
www.harpersferryhistory.org

Copyright ©2019 Harpers Ferry Park Association
PO Box 197
Harpers Ferry, WV 25425
info@hfpawv.org
www.harpersferryhistory.org

Cover design by Victor Curran. Image courtesy of Linda and Ron Rago, photographed by Eric Long. Back cover includes art from the Rago collection, photographed by Eric Long, and the Harpers Ferry National Historical Park Historic Images Collection.

The Harpers Ferry Park Association is a nonprofit cooperating association supporting the education and interpretive programs of Harpers Ferry National Historical Park. Proceeds from the sale of this publication benefit park programs.

All rights reserved, including the right to reproduce this work in any form whatsoever without permission in writing from the publisher, except for brief passages in connection with a review. For information, please write Harpers Ferry Park Association at the above address.

Library of Congress Control Number 2019905692

ISBN 9780967403359

Printed in the USA at HBP, Hagerstown, MD

From Dennis E. Frye:

I dedicate this book to my National Park Service mentors. Each contributed in countless ways to my growth and evolution; and they provided me with a superlative career as a professional historian, manager, supervisor, writer and park ranger. Their presence blessed me every day in every way, and they encouraged my dreams into reality.

To Donald W. Campbell, Superintendent, for inspiring me with his vision and guiding me with prudent demeanor;

To Rebecca L. Harriett, Superintendent, for sharing her font of compassion and her vibrancy for life;

To Paul R. Lee, II, Chief of Interpretation & Cultural Resources Management, for entrusting me to lead and enabling me to create and challenge risk;

To Arnold W. Schofield, Supervisory Park Ranger, for teaching me interpretive skills and nourishing my development as a park ranger;

To Edwin C. Bearss, Chief Historian, National Park Service for granting me recognition at the highest levels and partnering with me on preservation; and finally,

To Stephen R. Potter, Regional Archeologist, National Capital Region, for enabling my research discoveries and being a kindred spirit in searching for meanings from the past.

From Catherine Mägi Oliver:

My work is forever dedicated to my paternal grandfather Alfred, a World War 2 Estonian refugee, who instilled in me an abiding passion for the American story, and inspired me to live my life in a way that is truly, as Mr. Jefferson would say, "worth a voyage across the Atlantic."

Treasures of Harpers Ferry, top to bottom: 19th century ceramics discovered in local resident's garden; park ranger speaking with visitors at Jefferson Rock; souvenir porcelain boot with view of the Harpers Ferry gap.

Contents

Welcome, Reader
    Why Harpers Ferry?................................xi

Notes on the State of Virginia, excerpt
    Thomas Jefferson Falls in Love with the Ferry xii

Chapter 1: Terror's Tentacles
    John Brown Launches War............................1

Chapter 2: Making Might
    The Armory and George Washington's Legacy of Defense...14

Chapter 3: Slavery's Storm
    The Tornado Strikes the Ferry 33

Chapter 4: Motion Matters
    Canals, Railroads, and the Transportation Revolution 47

Chapter 5: Fury and Fire
    Portent to Civil War................................62

Chapter 6: War Wounds
    Civil War on the Border 77

Chapter 7: Redeemers, Resisters
    From Emancipation to Civil Rights 109

Chapter 8: Renaissance Repelled
    Rivers as Blessing and Curse 133

Chapter 9: History's Harness
    Birth of a National Park 159

Chapter 10: Sparks Still Smolder
    John Brown's Challenge to the National Park Service 171

Chapter 11: Meaning's Master
    Evolution of a National Park 181

Epilogue *201*

Timeline *203*

Further Reading *210*

Index *211*

Acknowledgements *221*

About the Authors *225*

"When you come leisurely to examine, you find that there is grandeur in it—there is the serene majesty of nature—there is that which touches the soul, and soothes it in calm contemplation!"

Eli Bowen
Visit to Harpers Ferry
Rambles in the Path of the Steamhorse, 1855

A soul reflects on Harpers Ferry's mysteries.

Welcome, Reader...

To tell the story of Harpers Ferry is to tell our own stories.

In this book you will read about many struggles—some of Man's making, some of Mother Nature's—and how they have collided again and again at one small, scintillating juncture of rocks and rivers: *Harpers Ferry*.

Famous names rush through the gap in a whirlwind: Washington and Jefferson. John Brown and Robert E. Lee. Frederick Douglass and W. E. B. Du Bois. Dark words lurk, too: Insurrection. Slavery. War. Flood. The very mountains seem to reverberate with challenges. A landscape dotted with ruins hints that change has not come gently to Harpers Ferry.

Perhaps you, yourself, have fought a great battle. Maybe you have been beating against some impossible wall, or screaming beneath the suffocating ceiling of injustice. Perhaps you have won, and perhaps you have lost. Perhaps you are yet down deep in the middle of your quest—uncertain.

Have you felt the waters rising over your head?

Have you known the lurch of solid earth swept out from under you?

Then you are not so different from the Ferry, and this story belongs as much to you as to this village.

Doubtless, you have been inventing and innovating; raising proverbial bridges and roads; building your way out of broken. You have been terrified and proud. You have dreamed, and you have almost forgotten to dream. And somehow you have found yourself again, so alive, and staring at shapes now rising in the mist: lush mountains, quaint buildings, silver-flecked rivers. *Harpers Ferry*. And because you are holding this book, a particular question must have sparked in your mind.

What happened here?

A marvelous question—and how appropriate that you have arrived at this very moment to ask it.

In 2019, Harpers Ferry National Historical Park marks its 75th year as caretaker of this special place and its saga of struggle and resilience. To honor the occasion, the Harpers Ferry Park Association offers this volume as testimony to the dedication, dreaming, and defiance of the generations who have come before, whose destinies have turned together at Harpers Ferry—at the Confluence.

Harpers Ferry belongs to you. And in many ways, is within you.

"The passage of the Patowmac through the Blue Ridge is perhaps one of the most stupendous scenes in Nature."

You stand on a very high point of land. On your right comes up the Shenandoah, having ranged along the foot of the mountain a hundred miles to seek a vent. On your left approaches the Patowmac in quest of a passage also.

In the moment of their junction they rush together against the mountain,
    rend it asunder and pass off to the sea.

The first glance of this scene hurries our senses into the opinion that this earth has been created in time,
    that the mountains were formed first,
        that the rivers began to flow afterwards,

that in this place particularly they have been so dammed up by the Blue Ridge of mountains as to have formed an ocean which filled the whole valley;
    that, continuing to rise, they have at last broken over at this spot
        and have torn the mountain down
            from its summit to its base.

The piles of rock on each hand, but particularly on the Shenandoah, the evident marks of their disruptions and avulsions from their beds by the most powerful agents in nature, corroborate the impression.

But the distant finishing which nature has given the picture is of a very different character. It is a true contrast to the former. It is as placid and delightful as that is wild and tremendous.

For the mountains being cloven asunder, she presents to your eye, through the cleft,

> *a small catch of smooth blue horizon,*
>> *at an infinite distance in that plain country,*
>>> *inviting you, as it were,*
>> *from the riot and tumult roaring around*
> *to pass through the breach and participate in the calm below.*

Here the eye ultimately composes itself; and that way, too, the road happens actually to lead. You cross the Patowmac above the junction, pass along its side through the base of the mountain for three miles, the terrible precipice hanging in fragments over you, and within about 20 miles reach Frederictown and the fine country around that.

This scene is worth a voyage across the Atlantic.

*Thomas Jefferson,
Notes on the State of Virginia (1785)*

Thomas Jefferson visited Harpers Ferry in 1783 and fell in love at once with the wild beauty of the scene. His poetic endorsement would endure for generations.

Harpers Ferry children outside the town jail on Shenandoah Street.

Chapter 1
TERROR'S TENTACLES

Danger lurked outside the school. No one knew its presence.

A miserable Monday morning awaited schoolmaster Lind Currie and his nearly 30 students as they awakened at their homes. A cold rain had fallen much of that October night in the mountains of western Maryland, chilling the Blue Ridge and the Potomac River valley, dropping temperature in their one-room schoolhouse to a raw and cutting frost.

As Mr. Currie shivered on his horse during his four-mile trot from home, he watched his transporter snort steam in the damp autumn air, and pondered his first important task. He must start the school stove. Cold kids, he reasoned—who themselves walked up to two miles every morning and evening to and from school—expected their teacher to provide comfort and warmth in their log-cabin lyceum.

The road to the mountain school was narrow and steep, and its dirt pathway had transformed into sticky glue. Mud-caked shoes and boots printed the floor boards as the boys and girls arrived. Mr. Currie watched an assortment of pants and skirts scamper in through the door, stained with red-clay ooze. Waterlogged wool coats and rubber ponchos doggedly dripped, creating their own metronome rhythm. Quite a Monday morning mess.

Despite the weather, Mr. Currie beamed as his students strolled in. The Aults arrived almost as a clan, with brother and sisters and cousins as a van. The Peachers packed a short trip from their mountain farm—just fine with Cudelia, who could almost see the school up the deep ravine. Christian Smith's five kids came the furthest, led by sixteen-year-old Thomas and younger brother John, and sisters Eugenia and Catherine, with Jasper (age eight), in tow. And there appeared John Unseld's "little boy," nine-year old George, who soloed to school along mysterious forest paths.

Lessons commenced, eventually, once Mr. Currie deemed all warm and in comfort. It was time to learn; time to engage the education routine. The clock ticked toward 10 a.m.

Then hell detonated.

Strangers with rifles burst through the door.

A man darted toward the teacher. Two revolvers bulged from his belt. A Bowie knife flashed from inside his coat. He brandished a Sharps Rifle in his hand. He demanded possession of the schoolhouse.

The traumatized teachers and students were hostages—captives —entrapped.

What was happening?

As Mr. Currie struggled to calm and quiet his startled students, more men entered with more guns. Their mission then was announced.

CONFLUENCE

John Cook, leader of the fearsome band, informed the terrified teacher that he intended to occupy the schoolhouse as "a depot for their arms . . . and implements of war."

War?

"It is our design to use every effort," explained Cook, "to disseminate our sentiments in regard to the institution of slavery."

Cook confidently presented the plan. A war against slavery had just launched. Mr. Currie and his kids were witnessing the opening salvo. A paramilitary guerilla force, armed with its own constitution, intended to invade the Southern states, exact freedom for the enslaved, and enact justice for the bondsmen.

THE SCHOOL-HOUSE IN THE MOUNTAINS, USED BY BROWN AS AN ARSENAL.
[SKETCHED BY PORTE CRAYON.]

Cook was an officer in this army. At this moment, he revealed other men had captured nearby Harpers Ferry, seizing weapons from the U.S. Arsenal located there. Cook conveyed that any slaveholder who gave up their slaves voluntarily would "meet with protection." But those who refused to give them up "would be quartered upon and their property confiscated."

As Cook's commandoes commenced moving long boxes into the school house, each loaded with Sharps Rifles, Mr. Currie did his best to settle his frightened students. "The children were then very much alarmed, and I could not do anything with them." While moving about, he spied a loaded wagon outside a school window. Around it he witnessed

some black men, armed with a peculiar weapon, which appeared to be a war-like spear, or pike. The pugilistic sight staggered Currie. He, himself, a Virginia farmer, owned slaves. What did this mean for him?

Cook's continued expressions offered Currie no comfort. "We, as a little band, may perish in this attempt," Cook informed the teacher, "but there are thousands ready at all times to occupy our places, and to step into the breach."

As Cook supervised the moving of weapons into the school, he made a startling proclamation. He was following the orders of Captain John Brown.

John Brown.

TERROR'S TENTACLES

Mr. Currie recognized the name. No abolitionist had earned greater notoriety as a battlefield warrior against slavery. Brown had become famous in the North and infamous in the South only a few years before. Fighting in Kansas Territory, he had defied the extension of slavery westward into the expanding nation. Brown garnered a reputation as a violent, and sometimes ruthless, assailant of opponents of freedom. Brown's exploits as a guerilla fighter had earned him front-page newspaper coverage, but that was some years ago. Little had been heard of him recently.

Now suddenly, abruptly—and with terror—John Brown's war had invaded Mr. Currie's school room.

As Brown's forward man, Cook had spent the past year quietly collecting intelligence on the Ferry.

Terrence Byrne knew nothing of an invasion.

Just before dawn on Monday, October 17, 1859, he saddled his horse and began riding south toward Harpers Ferry, along the same Maryland road that led by the schoolhouse.

As dim light began to edge over Elk Ridge, he encountered something unusual for that early hour—an unknown black man driving a large empty freight wagon in the opposite direction. Thence came a command.

"Mr. Byrne, stop."

It was John Cook. Byrne recognized him immediately, even in the dimness of dawn. Cook had been living in the vicinity for more than a year now, and had become pretty well known. Byrne reined up his horse, as Cook approached.

"I am very sorry to inform you that you are my prisoner."

Byrne, incredulous, looked at Cook and smiled. "You are certainly joking."

"I am not."

Byrne then noticed the barrel of a rifle protruding from under Cook's coat. A second unknown man aggressively approached, with his gun pointed.

"No parley here, or I will put a ball in you," the second assailant threatened.

Now a hostage, Byrne received demands to take the insurgents to his Maryland home and to turn over his slaves. When the armed party arrived at the Byrne home a few minutes later, the captive whispered to his startled brother, "civil war."

The Byrnes owned six slaves, a fact well known to Cook. Unbeknownst to the Byrnes, John Brown's headquarters was right in their midst, less than two miles up the road from their farm. Brown and his "army of liberation" had been living amongst them. Who knew?

While en route to the Byrne farm, Cook proposed a deal: give up the Byrnes' slaves voluntarily, and enter into an article of agreement with his "Captain" (Brown) for the protection of the Byrnes and their property. Byrne adamantly refused. "That was something

CONFLUENCE

I would not do," exclaimed Byrne. "I looked to the state government, or, if that failed, to the federal government to protect me."

Since negotiation failed, and the three male slaves "had left home the Saturday evening preceding, and had not returned yet, Monday morning," Cook retained Terence Byrne as his hostage. Meanwhile, the freight wagon had traveled to and from the nearby Kennedy Farm— Brown's secret headquarters. It returned loaded with boxes of Sharps Rifles— contents unknown to Byrne, but certainly ominous. Fearful of a bloody civil war, Byrne stood amazed. How had this happened right under his nose?

A few minutes later, a horrified and helpless Byrne witnessed the seizure of the schoolhouse. He had no children there, but he knew neighboring families that did. Soon his captors commenced transferring the mysterious boxes into the building. As the work progressed, he saw a distressed Mr. Currie wander into the school yard.

"I whispered across the fence to him . . . that I was a prisoner," remarked Byrne. "You have nothing to fear; you are not a slaveholder."

"I am," whispered Currie.

Soon thereafter, as Cook continued operations at the schoolhouse, he detached Willie Leeman, instructing him to escort Byrne to Harpers Ferry, about one mile distant from the schoolhouse. Young Willie was John Brown's most youthful recruit. At twenty, he already was experienced in guerilla warfare, having joined Brown in Kansas when only seventeen. The native of Maine "smoked a good deal and drank sometimes," but overall came across as "very handsome and very attractive." Among Brown's men, he was "only a boy," but a youth committed to the cause.

"I am now in a Southern Slave State," Leeman wrote his mother from Brown's Maryland hideaway, just four miles from the schoolhouse. "[B]efore I leave it, it will be a free State, Mother. . . . Yes, mother, I am war[r]ing with Slavery the greatest Curse that ever infested America."

Byrne knew the boy meant business. The barrel of his Sharps Rifle protruded from his coat as they briefly interrupted their journey to Harpers Ferry to seek shelter from the miserable rain. It was here, for the first time, that Byrne learned the true identity of Leeman's chieftain.

"Our captain is no longer John Smith, or I. Smith, or J. Smith, or something like that," Leeman revealed, referring to various neighborhood aliases familiar to Byrne. "He [is] John Brown, of Kansas notoriety."

My mind was busy with the future . . . . I was fearful of a bloody civil war.

~Terrence Byrne

TERROR'S TENTACLES

In Harpers Ferry, twelve hours earlier on Sunday night, Daniel Whelan's shadow danced in the lamp light within the U.S. Armory fire engine house.

No need to be out patrolling that evening, mused the 39-year old night watchman. Whelan primarily served as a fire-alarm, monitoring the buildings within the U.S. government's weapons complex. A steady rain, however, had dampened the brick buildings of the Musket Factory; and since it was a day off for the armorers, the interior forging fires either were banked or extinguished. Even sparks along the adjacent railroad from a coal-burning locomotive figured an improbable danger. A good evening to relax, it seemed.

Little light existed in Harpers Ferry that night, or on any night. Under cloud cover, the river town especially was dark, masking even the mountains whose towering edifices hovered overhead. A few lamp posts inside the Musket Factory cast an eerie yellowish glow in the mist, complimented by wicks flickering within the nearby train depot and the town's best accommodation—the Wager House Hotel. Other than the expected east-bound passenger train, and the incessant roar of the rapids within the Potomac and Shenandoah rivers, all was poetry in Harpers Ferry that Sunday evening, October 16, 1859.

About an hour before midnight, the rhythm ruptured.

The rumble and rattle of a wagon stopped abruptly at the armory entrance. In the shadows, Whelan saw two men at the gates striving to open the padlock.

"Hold on," barked Whelan, as he strode toward the heavy iron gates.

"Open the gate!" retorted the strangers.

Half a dozen men then rushed Whelan, thrusting rifles against his breast as he was

6

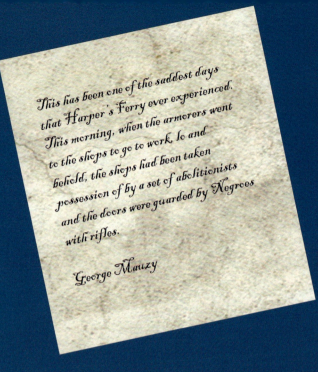

This has been one of the saddest days that Harper's Ferry ever experienced. This morning, when the armorers went to the shops to go to work, lo and behold, the shops had been taken possession of by a set of abolitionists and the doors were guarded by Negroes with rifles.

George Mauzy

frozen tight against the locked gate. "I was nearly scared to death with so many guns about me," the watchman recalled. "I did not know the minute or the hour I should drop." Whelan held his ground and refused to cooperate. "They told me to be very quiet and still and make no noise or else they would put me to eternity."

Despite his desperation, Whelan refused to give up the padlock key. Not amused, the intruders retrieved a large crowbar from the wagon and twisted and broke the gate chains. The wagon then pulled in, and soon afterward, the leader of the operation approached Whelan.

"I came here from Kansas," stated John Brown. "This is a slave State. I want to free all the Negroes in this State."

Whelan shivered at Brown's next pronouncement:

"I have possession now of the United States Armory," declared Brown, "and if the citizens interfere with me, I must only burn the town and have blood."

The ease in capturing the armory and arsenal at Harpers Ferry—a federal weapons factory and depot—did not surprise John Cook.

He knew only *one* watchman was stationed at the entrance gate. He knew the watchman was not a security guard, but principally a fireman. He knew the government employed no armed guards to protect its property. For almost a year, in fact, Cook had been gathering intelligence on Harpers Ferry and its environs. He was working as Brown's advance spy.

Cook had arrived as a stranger, but no one much noticed. Strangers were a usual occurrence at Harpers Ferry, as two intersecting railroads brought unknown passengers into town daily. Youthful, attractive, spirited, and well-educated (he had studied law in New York City), Cook commenced circulating in neighborhood social circles. He bonded well within the community, and he married local woman Virginia Kennedy. The two were soon to have a baby. Cook found employment as a lock tender on a nearby canal, and occasionally did some teaching. He feigned his real job, however, was a book agent; and he began meeting with leading personages in the Harpers Ferry vicinity to tell their stories.

As Cook conducted interviews at area estates and farms, no one knew that he was a guerilla war veteran from Bleeding Kansas. No one knew he was an ardent disciple of John Brown. No one knew that Cook was Brown's antenna, collecting information on the area's enslaved population and monitoring daily routines at Harpers Ferry.

No one knew that John Cook was a precursor of war.

Colonel Lewis Washington certainly knew nothing of Cook's background. The stately Virginia gentleman, and the great grand-nephew of George Washington, resided at his Shenandoah Valley estate about four miles west of Harpers Ferry. He encountered Cook, for the first time, in a chance meeting on a Harpers Ferry street.

"I believe you have a great many interesting relics at your house," an intrigued Cook inquired. "Could I have permission to see them if I should walk out some day?"

Washington, ignorant of Cook's real motives, assented. When Cook soon visited, he arrived with two revolvers strapped to his belt, explaining "he was in the habit of carrying them in his occupation." Washington thought little of it, and enjoyed some target practice with Cook, using his weapons. At some point, the gracious host displayed two remarkable artifacts associated with General Washington: a pistol presented by Lafayette and a sword given to him by Frederick the Great.

"They descended from my father and from him to me," Washington remarked. "My grandfather had the first choice of five swords left by the general." Frederick the Great's gift was used by General Washington as his personal dress sword.

Cook, most impressed with these artifacts of American independence, parted after an amicable stay. His next visit was not so friendly.

A month passed. On Monday, October 17, about an hour and half past midnight, a disturbance awakened Colonel Washington. Something was wrong outside his bedroom. Believing he heard someone calling his name, he opened the door. The next few seconds seared into his soul. A flaming torch blinded him. Four armed men, each with a rifle and two revolvers, confronted him with guns drawn.

"You are our prisoner."

Startled, Washington struggled to make sense of the moment. He focused his eyes.

"I looked around, and the only thing that astonished me particularly was the presence of this man Cook."

More astonishment awaited Washington. His captors permitted him to dress, then escorted him to his horse-drawn carriage, where he discovered an unknown African American, a fighter nicknamed "Emperor" (Shields Green), controlling the driver's seat. More shocking, however, was what Washington witnessed behind him. There stood his freight wagon and its four-horse team, ready for transport, and occupied by Jim, Sam and Mason—three of his male slaves.

"Possibly you will have the courtesy to tell me what this means," inquired Washington. "It is really a myth to me."

Above: Lewis Washington, great grand-nephew of President George Washington, was one of several locals taken in by Cook's charm prior to the attack. Eventually, Washington would find himself a hostage of John Brown. Background: John Cook's spyglass, recovered after the raid.

CONFLUENCE

"We have come here for the purpose of liberating all the slaves of the South," retorted an assailant, *"and we are able to do it."*

Indeed they were. And Washington's capture proved only the beginning. Ninety minutes later, Cook's party proved its capabilities, striking again. En route to Harpers Ferry with hostage Washington, the conspirators captured slave owner John Allstadt, along with his son, who resided about two and a half miles from the Ferry.

"They bursted the door open with a rail," recalled Allstadt. "I saw five or six men with arms, rifles, standing right at the door."

"Get up quick, or we will burn you up!"

Allstadt and son were soon crammed into Washington's freight wagon, along with seven of Allstadt's male slaves (Henry, Levi, Ben, Jerry, Phil, George and Bill). Never had Jefferson County, Virginia, experienced such a night. Cook likely mused over the irony—the war to end slavery commenced in a county named after the author of the Declaration of Independence.

As Cook's detachment returned to Harpers Ferry just before Monday dawn, he beamed proudly of his accomplishments. He had captured three slave owners. More important, perhaps, he had delivered ten Virginia slaves to Captain Brown for liberation. Brown, himself, distributed spear-like weapons to each of the slaves once they arrived within the armory, with instructions to watch over the hostages, including their "owners."

Cook exuded pride in one other achievement, as well. Prior to departing Washington's estate, he retrieved the coveted pistol and sword—now symbols of a new American revolution—and presented them as prizes of war to Brown at the armory. The Captain then awarded Lafayette's pistol to Shields Green, one of five African American soldiers accompanying him on this mission. The sword Brown kept for himself, strapping it onto his waist belt.

Successes, indeed, buoyed Cook's spirits. Triumph thus far. But Cook could not rest upon his early-morning laurels. The plan of operation required additional urgent work. Weapons must be brought closer to the front. To achieve this next assignment, Cook proceeded across the Potomac River bridge into Maryland, employing Washington's freight wagon and most of the newly liberated slaves. Their jobs: gather up the boxes of Sharps Rifles at the Kennedy Farm headquarters and forward them to the schoolhouse.

Meanwhile, at the armory fire engine house, John Brown met Colonel Washington.

"I wanted you particularly for the moral affect it would give our cause, having one of your name as a prisoner."

Not all was going well for Captain Brown.

A passenger train had disrupted his plan.

Brown knew the Baltimore & Ohio eastbound was scheduled to arrive at Harpers Ferry at 1:25 a.m. on Monday. The Wheeling to Baltimore express chugged into the depot at the same time every day. Though Brown's master plan sliced the telegraph lines east and west of the Ferry—thus eliminating rapid dissemination of warnings about his plot—it

TERROR'S TENTACLES

did not design for detention of the train. In fact, to ensure all sense of normalcy, the train had to proceed. Someone, certainly, would come in search of a missing train.

Right on time, the B & O locomotive and cars screeched to a halt outside the depot. The engine hissed and spitted steam, and its locomotive light illuminated the entrance to the Potomac River bridge, only about 60 yards distant. Neither the engineer nor the conductor noticed anything extraordinary. No one knew that John Brown's provisional army was just outside launching a war.

Then . . . the routine ruptured.

Baggage porter Heyward Shepherd sensed something wrong. Where was the bridge watchman? William Williams never failed to meet the passenger train. Where was he?

Shepherd, curious, walked down the railroad platform toward the mouth of the covered bridge.

"Halt!"

Startled, Shepherd scanned his environs, illuminated by the locomotive's light. When he spied two men with rifles at the bridge entrance, Shepherd turned and hurried back toward the train depot.

"Halt!"

Then shots. Two of them. From two rifles.

Gunshots from Brown's soldiers that soon doomed John Brown.

Shepherd fell. A bullet pierced his back, entering just beneath his heart. The wound would kill him. His destiny, forever irony—the first man to die in Brown's war against slavery—a *free* African American.

Around the same moment (about 1:30 a.m.), Patrick Higgins rushed toward train conductor Phelps. Arriving to relieve watchman Williams, he had encountered Brown's armed men on the bridge. "Halt!" barked an assailant. Higgins ran instead. "I didn't know what halt meant any more than a hog knows about a holiday." A bullet then grazed his skull, plowing a furrow in his scalp. Higgins' hysterical escape ensured conductor Phelps that the bridge was a hazard zone. The train would not proceed.

What was happening? Perhaps a drunken mob had seized the bridge. Were disgruntled workers striking against the railroad? More ominous, were these ruffians here to steal from the train's passengers? No one gave thought to a slave war.

A hard dilemma now confronted Captain Brown. By accident, and through the overzealousness of his soldiers, an entire passenger train had become hostage. Two choices presented themselves; neither promised benefit. Either allow the train to proceed (and sound an alarm); or hold the train, relegating it to missing in action (and sound the alarm).

By 3 a.m. the train already had delayed ninety minutes. Brown made his decision. He dispatched an emissary (a captive) to move forward the train. "The parties who have arrested me allowed me to come out on condition that I would tell you that you might cross the bridge with your train," said Albert Cross, a bystander seized earlier. "I [will] not cross the bridge until daylight," Phelps responded, "that I might see whether it is safe."

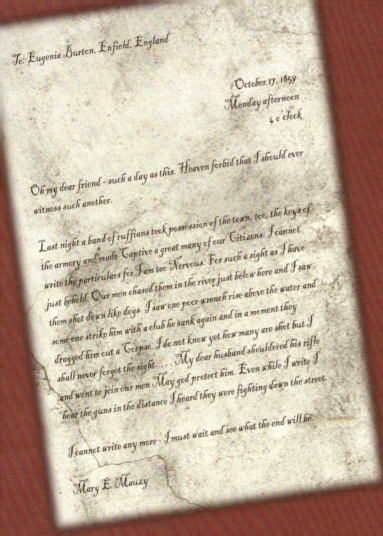

To: Eugenia Burton, Enfield, England

October 17, 1859
Monday afternoon
4 o'clock

Oh my dear friend - such a day as this. Heaven forbid that I should ever witness such another.

Last night a band of ruffians took possession of the town, too, the keys of the armory and made Captive a great many of our Citizens. I cannot write the particulars for I am too Nervous. For such a sight as I have just beheld. Our men chased them in the river just below here and I saw them shot down like dogs. I saw one poor wrench rise above the water and some one strike him with a club he sank again and in a moment they dragged him out a Corpse. I do not know yet how many are shot but I shall never forget the sight. . . . My dear husband shouldered his rifle and went to join our men May god protect him. Even while I write I hear the guns in the distance I heard they were fighting down the street.

I cannot write any more - I must wait and see what the end will be.

Mary E. Mauzy

Meanwhile, the early morning gunshots had awakened Dr. John Starry. "I jumped out of my bed," explained the 35-year old physician. "My room is nearly opposite the railroad bridge." Looking out his chamber window, he noticed considerable confusion around the train, and he witnessed armed men passing from the bridge toward the armory entrance. "In a short time I was in the street."

Starry's first stop was the railroad office. Here he discovered the wounded baggage porter Shepherd, lying on a plank between two chairs. He had been shot, "the ball entering from behind, through the body, nearly on line with the base of the heart, a little below it." Shepherd would suffer nearly twelve hours before he expired about noon on Monday.

Bewildered, Starry sought answers. He strode right to the armory entrance and confronted the intruders. No good responses. He then approached the railroad bridge, where his inquiries met equivocation. "Never mind," said an invader. "You will find out in a day or two." Starry continued observing for the next three hours, growing in frustration and anger. About 5 a.m., he discerned a four-horse wagon enter the railroad bridge, heading for Maryland, with "three men standing up in the front part, with spears in their hands."

Starry could take no more. "[A]s these strangers seemed to have possession of the public works, I determined to get on my horse and go out and notify [the authorities] of the condition of things."

In a Paul Revere-like tale, Starry informed high-ranking armory officials at their homes; galloped to the nearby village of Bolivar (home to many armorers) and "roused up some of the people." He ordered the Lutheran church bell rung in the upper town of Harpers Ferry to sound an emergency and "to get the citizens together to see what sort of arms they had." Then he galloped to Charles Town, the county seat eight miles distant, to stir up the local militia. "When I returned . . . I found that the citizens had gotten some arms out of one of the workshops . . . and were pretty well armed."

John Brown's war against slavery now mutated into a war against John Brown.

Conductor Phelps was anxious to proceed with his train. He now was four hours behind schedule. As daylight approached on Monday morning, he walked to the armory seeking answers. "There is Captain Smith," an armed guard gestured. "He can tell you what you want to know."

Phelps then met Brown for the first time. The reticent conductor explained his concerns in taking the train across the bridge in the midst of so many men with rifles.

"You doubtless wonder that a man of my age should be here with a band of armed men," queried Brown. "If you knew my past history you would not wonder at it so much."

"You will not be hurt," pledged the Captain. As further assurance, Brown accompanied Phelps on a walk across the 300-yard long bridge.

Satisfied with safe passage, conductor Phelps ordered the locomotive forward. It rumbled off, soon a distant echo within the bowels of the Potomac valley. It was not the last sound to be heard from this train.

About one hour later, a telegraph operator at B & O headquarters in Baltimore read these frantic words from Phelps: "They say they have come to free the slaves and intend to do it at all hazards."

The telegraph operator never had seen words like this.

Shots fired. Train retained. Bridge seized. Armed men. Baggage porter fatally wounded. No more passage of trains permitted. Insurrectionists 150 strong!

"Your dispatch is evidently exaggerated and written under excitement," responded one of the railroad's top executives, the master of transportation.

"Why should our trains be stopped by Abolitionists, and how do you know they are such [?] . . . Let me know at once before we proceed to extremities."

"My dispatch was not exaggerated," fired back Phelps. "I have not made it half as bad as it is."

As Phelps' messages circulated up to railroad president John W. Garrett, he wasted no time challenging their credibility. At half-past ten on Monday morning, he telegraphed the President of the United States, the Governor of Virginia, and the commander of an infantry division of Maryland volunteers that an insurrection was in progress at Harpers Ferry. Each responded by ordering troops to the troubled town. A martial net, from every direction of the compass, commenced closing on Brown.

About the same time Garrett's distress telegrams were finding their targets, John Cook was seizing the schoolhouse—and numerous pint-size prisoners.

*To Mrs. Eugenia Burton, sister
November 7, 1859*

I arose about 6 o'clock as near as I can judge, made the fire and sat down to wait the tap of the first bell (the 6:30 a.m. signal bell at the U.S. Arsenal) that I might start the clock for it had stopped sometime during the night.

I waited and waited but the bell didn't ring. I got up and walked out to the gate. I then saw some of the neighbors running down towards the armory yard. I asked what the trouble was and was told the abolitionists had come in from the north, taken possession of the armory and were going to liberate the slaves.

Then came down the street three or four citizens in a pretty fast dog-trot and reported that there were at least 500 abolitionists down at the ferry. They had possession of the armory there and there was a part of them on their way up here to take possession of the rifle works.

We looked down the road, and sure enough, the hill by the graveyard and opposite Herr's Mill and down the road were black with people, making their way towards us as fast as they could. Of course we could not tell who they were and took it for granted they were enemies.

There was then a movement in our little crowd and all appeared to have particularly important business up the road and with one consent we moved in that direction [away from the ferry] – didn't exactly run but walked right fast.

Soon our town was alive with soldiers and such firing I never heard before.

I was on my feet from Monday morning until Tuesday night, completely drenched with the rain and with only the few mouthfuls of breakfast I had eaten on Monday morning before I left home.

~Joseph Mauzy

Cook quickly discovered he could withstand guerilla warfare, but terrified kids unnerved him. "Their manner of acting, their expressions…indicated the greatest alarm," observed Mr. Currie. "[Cook] tried to pacify them as much as he could, but it was impossible to do it." Overwhelmed by the students' persistent fear, Cook finally agreed to release the captive kids—not for humanity, but for his own relief.

Oblivious to any problems at the Ferry, Cook methodically supervised the movement of the heavy boxes of Sharps Rifles into the school. Since Brown's army of liberation comprised only twenty-two men—and the inventory of Sharps equaled nearly 200 rifles—reinforcements were expected.

"With how many men did you commence this foray?" inquired Mr. Currie.

"I do not know how many men are there now," responded Cook. "[T]here may be 5,000 or there may be 10,000 for aught I know."

Later, Currie particularly remembered Cook's faith in the outcome of his mission. "[H]e had no doubt that the efforts would be strong now and unfailing in order to extirpate the institution of slavery from the entire land."

Hours passed in the solace of the school. By mid-afternoon, the unmistakable staccato of gun shots echoed off the mountains, originating from Harpers Ferry.

"Mr. Cook, what does that mean?" asked Currie, anxious about the crescendo of firing.

"Well," said Cook, "it simply means this: that those people down there are resisting our men, and we are shooting them down."

Chapter 2
MAKING MIGHT

"This spot affords every advantage that could be wished for water works... and no place is more capable of complete defen[se] at a small expense."

George Washington envisioned Harpers Ferry as a seat of war; not a war zone.

Sixty-five years before John Brown launched his revolution against slavery, the original hero of the American Revolution garnered big plans for Harpers Ferry.

"From my own knowledge, I can speak of the eligibility of this situation for a public Arsenal," declared Washington while serving his second term as President of the United States.

Washington, indeed, had a personal familiarity with Harpers Ferry. While serving as a colonial Virginia major at the outset of the French and Indian War (104 years before John Brown's arrival), the twenty-three-year old Washington drew a rough sketch map of the Harpers Ferry rapids of the Potomac, envisioning the river as a possible avenue of military supply to the western frontier of Ohio. Thirty years later, following the American Revolution, Washington served as president of an entrepreneurial enterprise called "The Patowmack Company," designed to establish the river as the principal and foremost west-to-east navigation artery in the fledgling nation.

As president, Washington's vision for the Potomac expanded. With establishment of the new federal capital on

George Washington, *1772. Charles Willson Peale (1741 - 1827), Washington and Lee University Special Collections.*

CONFLUENCE

> "If we desire to avoid insult, we must be able to repel it....
>
> "[I]f we desire to secure peace, one of the most powerful instruments of our rising prosperity, it must be known that we are at all times ready for war."
>
> President Washington to Congress, 1794

the river, about sixty miles downstream from Harpers Ferry, Washington deemed Harpers Ferry essential for weapons' manufacturing and the defense of the new country.

Washington understood the United States would fail if it could not protect itself. Concerned by "the reputation of weakness," Washington asked the Congress to establish federal armories and arsenals to ensure the nation's self-defense.

The government thence established two federal armories in the last decade of the eighteenth century. Springfield, Massachusetts, became the site of the Northern weapons manufactory. Washington himself demanded that Harpers Ferry be selected for the Southern armory. "From what I have heard of this site, and partly from what I know of it, it must be the most eligible spot on the whole river in every point of view."

In addition to its proximity to the new capital, Washington reasoned favoritism for the Ferry. Its water power could generate energy to torque machinery. Its nearby hardwood forests could produce charcoal for forging fires and walnut for gunstocks. Veins of iron ore and local furnaces and forges could provide metal for gun barrels and lock plates. Three mountains crests surrounding Harpers Ferry formed a triangle for elevated fortifications. And the site was too far inland (ensconced well above the Potomac River's fall lines), for an enemy's greatest power—its navies—to reach or harm.

Washington also had a commercial interest in mind. For decades he had visualized the Potomac Valley as a center of commerce for the United States. "[T]he favorite object of his heart" was connecting the country's far-flung territory from the Mississippi and Ohio rivers to deep water Potomac ports and the Chesapeake Bay.

Washington and his extended family also held property interests throughout the Potomac Valley region. A federal largesse at Harpers Ferry would stimulate economic development up and down the Potomac corridor, transforming the region into a commercial catalyst at the epicenter of the original colonies.

Washington died at Mount Vernon in December 1799, before his Harpers Ferry endeavor produced many weapons. But his foundation eventually germinated, with the first full-scale musket manufacturing commencing in 1801—Thomas Jefferson's first year as president.

The same year, John Brown turned one year old.

By 1821, the armory included 20 workshops, two arsenal buildings, 86 dwellings for employees, and employed 271 workers. Image courtesy of Maryland Historical Society, 1944.1.1.

From its outset, problems plagued the Harpers Ferry Armory.

Two Secretaries of War objected to its location, stalling for nearly half a decade. Only through Washington's persistence did he overcome these obstacles. Land acquisition of the 125-acre ferry tract from the heirs of Robert Harper exacted bargaining time and a pecuniary price (almost triple the average price of adjoining acreage). Access was difficult, subject to the vagaries of river flows and rugged rural roads. Infrastructure was limited, as the Ferry was still a wilderness outpost with but a few buildings. The local iron proved excellent for stove plates but deficient for gun barrels, requiring its import from hundreds of miles distant. And a shortage of laborers to build the dam and power canal almost wrecked the project from its start. U.S. Army soldiers stationed atop Camp Hill at the Ferry eventually helped complete this tedious work.

The government, on the other hand, had little difficulty recruiting a labor force to produce rifles and muskets, attracting skilled artisans famous for their stylistic versions of the famed "Pennsylvania Rifle." Dozens of craftsmen moved from Philadelphia and other regions of the Quaker State into temporary quarters at Harpers Ferry, bringing with

CONFLUENCE

> *"I found more Difficulty in concluding the Bargain than in any Thing of a similar Kind that I ever undertook. I am peculiarly happy in having effected it as it seems an Object of the first Importance for the Public."*
>
> ~Tobias Lear, Washington's negotiator to purchase land for armory from Harper heirs.

them their experience, talents and skills to produce small arms for the defense of the United States.

They traded their local gunsmith shops for the moniker of U.S. government employees—a rare breed in America at the turn of the nineteenth century.

They soon went on strike—perhaps the *first* strike of public employees in American history.

"The seeds of sedition . . . have since sprouted into open rebellion," reported the armory's paymaster.

The armorers, upset they were being paid in rations rather than in cash (and rumored that a "dead cow" was part of their diet), "deserted the workshop on a signal being given . . . and retired to the Tavern." They strategically selected Washington's Birthday (February 22, 1799) for their walkout.

Negotiations settled the conflict, but the paymaster feared a bad precedent. "[T]hey will in future be more petulant, and ready to dispute & oppose the best regulations," complained the manager. "[T]hey will be constantly resolving themselves into Committees on every appearance of imaginary grievance."

Labor strife, indeed, became a recurring theme during the armory's six decades of operation. The craftsmen fashioned themselves as self-inspired, self-controlled and self-achievers. Efforts to impose a factory system of central control and uniform discipline often met with refusal. Tension existed between the government's demand for high productivity (the best product at the least expense) and the workers' insistence on independence (an American trait).

When the War Department introduced new methods, or new machines, or regulations, or managers, or technology—or anything new—resistance was a response.

Even rules that forbid loitering, gambling, tardiness, or consumption of alcohol on armory property garnered blow back. One armorer, dismissed for his foibles, became so distressed, he assassinated the armory superintendent! Armory workers hailed their peer

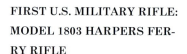

FIRST U.S. MILITARY RIFLE: MODEL 1803 HARPERS FERRY RIFLE

The style and beauty of the first rifle manufactured for the U.S. Army reflects the influence of craftsmen who designed and produced variations of the famed "Pennsylvania Rifle." The brass fittings are a particular characteristic imported to Harpers Ferry from Quaker State artisans. Though four times more accurate than a musket, it required three times longer to load a rifle (up to one minute per shot), limiting this weapon's distribution to specialized rifle companies.

Background image: Men at work in the Rifle Works.
National Park Service/HFCCAC/ Richard Schlecht.

"*It is a strange perverseness of our nature which makes us the most restless when we have the least cause to be so. The people employed here, from the Superintendent down to the apprentices, enjoy so many comforts, and know so little of the hardships of life that one would expect a universal harmony should pervade the whole community of them. But instead of this . . . they become less happy; and the causes of happiness to generous minds degenerate into sources of petulance & discontent. More discord has not distracted the French Councils in the [French] revolution than that which actuates our petty Cabals at this place.*"

~John Mackey,
Paymaster of the Harpers Ferry Armory, 1799

(executed for his crime) as a folk hero, extolling him as a blunt reminder to future generations of managers of what consequences may result from too much control.

This lackadaisical craftsmen approach frustrated War Department officials, who constantly were comparing the Harpers Ferry Armory with its sister armory in Springfield. The Yankee establishment, where industriousness ruled over indolence, boasted higher rates of weapons production, lower cost per piece, and muskets and rifles of better quality. Ordnance Department inspectors pronounced the Harpers Ferry workmen "not generally so skillful" as at the Massachusetts armory; and the Harpers Ferry weapons "40 per cent inferior" to Springfield's, with "many of the parts exhibit[ing] marks of unskillful workmanship and want of rigid watchfulness and exactness."

In addition to shoddy workmanship, Ordnance Department officials identified another problem at Harpers Ferry: tenure. "The difficulty . . . is to get rid of inferior workmen who have been so long employed as to consider themselves to have a prescriptive right to work there."

Abetting these embarrassments was a succession of civilian superintendents appoint-

CONFLUENCE

ed not for their military acumen, but for their loyalties to political parties. Commissioners of cronyism and corruption, these superintendents and their subordinate supervisors often enabled the workers to control the workplace.

FIRST U.S. MILITARY PISTOL: MODEL 1805 HARPERS FERRY PISTOL

"[W]orkmen came and went at any hour they pleased, the machinery being in operation whether there were 50 or 10 at work," reported one exasperated inspector.

"[T]he shops were made places of business. I have seen four farmers at one time in one shop with paper and pencil in hand, surrounded by more than a dozen workmen, who were giving orders as to the number and weight of hogs they were to receive at killing time." The inspector concluded the shops were "a more convenient place of meeting than the houses of the workmen, and arrangements of all kinds whether for politics, pleasure or business were concluded there."

This single-shot flintlock pistol—the only pistol ever manufactured at the Harpers Ferry Armory—was issued to officers as a sidearm. Its stylistic grace and brass highlights reflected the early influence of craftsmen at Harpers Ferry schooled in the "Pennsylvania Rifle" genre. Its production was short-lived, with production of only about 4,000 pistols in two years (1807-1808). Today it is among the rarest of Harpers Ferry weapons. More than a century after its creation, the U.S. Army Military Police Corps reinvigorated this model, adopting it as its official insignia in 1923. It is popularly known as the "Crossed Pistols."

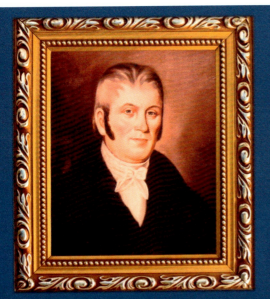

Armory Superintendent James Stubblefield, and his wife, Mary Beckham Stubblefield. Stubblefield's twenty-two-year tenure (1807-1829) was the longest of any superintendent—nearly one-third of the armory's existence. He more than tripled the number of employees and factory buildings. Corruption, cronyism and corporate ineptitude plagued Stubblefield's administration, and following investigation by the War Department, he was forced to resign.

As superintendent's wife, Mary wielded prestige and influence in Harpers Ferry society, with the armory fueling her clan's prosperity. Her brother worked for the superintendent as master armorer, while two other brothers received lucrative government contracts, also via the superintendent. These unethical associations eventually helped in the demise of her husband's career.

JOHN HALL & THE REVOLUTION OF PRECISION

"I have succeeded in an object which has hitherto completely baffled ... all the endeavors of those who have heretofore attempted it—I have succeeded in establishing methods for fabricating arms exactly alike, & with economy, by the hands of common workmen."

~John H. Hall to Sec. of War John C. Calhoun, December 30, 1822

Every one of the tens of thousands of U.S. small arms produced at either Harpers Ferry or Springfield lacked one thing: replacement parts. Technology did not exist that permitted the easy replacement of broken parts.

Since each musket or rifle was hand-crafted, any damage or defect required human hands to craft every new part. This proved cumbersome, labor-intensive, wasteful and expensive. It was easier to throw away a broken gun than to replace its parts.

John Harris Hall devised a solution. The ingenious inventor from Maine convinced the War Department he could utilize machines, rather than men, to produce weapons with perfect parts. So perfect, in fact, that he could disassemble 100 rifles, toss the parts into a pile, and reassemble each weapon—a new technology known as *interchangeability*.

The War Department, always searching for newer, better and less expensive weapons, issued Hall a contract. He subsequently established shops on a couple of islands along the Shenandoah River, about one-half mile from the main armory complex on the Potomac.

There he developed and utilized a vast array of machines to cut and shape iron and woodwork to manufacture lock, stock and barrel for his rifle.

Here Hall created a miracle . . . and here he launched a revolution.

"Captain Hall has formed and adopted a system, in the manufacture of small arms, entirely novel & which no doubt, may be attended with the most beneficial results to the Country," effused a War Department report. "By no other process known to us . . . could arms be made so exactly alike, as to interchange."

Hall's ingenuity in creating machines that could "perfect uniformity" spawned the *American System of Manufacturing*—a revolution literally born in Harpers Ferry.

But the traditional craftsmen at the Harpers Ferry Armory viewed Hall and his machines as intruders of evil. This Yankee ingenuity and industriousness could doom their jobs, replacing them—artisans—with artifices of the trade. Hall, himself, earned this reputation when he boasted he could fabricate rifles "in the perfect manner." Commenting on his system of mechanical apparatus, Hall gleamed. "A large portion of these operations—with the machinery—is effected with the aid of Boys, each of whom can perform as much & as good work, with those machines . . . as a man."

"[O]ne boy by aid of these machines can perform more work than ten men with files, in the same time, and with greater accuracy."

The cost of new technology.

FIRST U.S. MILITARY BREECHLOADER:

MODEL 1819 RIFLE

The War Department contracted with John Harris Hall to develop a weapon designed to increase the loading speed of a rifle. Inserting a projectile in the rear or "breech" of a rifle achieved a loading rate similar to a musket (up to three shots per minute). This eliminated the time-consuming steps of "ramming a charge" down a barrel after its insertion from the muzzle (or top). Though technologically advanced and produced with machine precision, its production proved expensive. Heavy and cumbersome—and faulted with hot gases exploding in a soldier's face on every discharge—the Hall Rifle proved unpopular and saw limited use by front-line rank and file.

"The reduction will take place immediately following the rolls for July. Selections for discharge to be those least valuable to the Public Service. It is expected that this notice will be sufficient to induce those coming within its range to prepare for this inevitable result.   ~Col. Henry Craig, Armory Superintendent, July 16, 1841

HIGH PAY. NO PAY.

Armorers at Harpers Ferry received a government salary that far exceeded wages in the private sector. The average American worker earned $1 a day in the decade prior to the Civil War, or about $300 in one year. Most armorers were paid double that amount. They were, after all, manufacturing weapons for the defense of the United States.

Most of the armory workers had a specialty, and pay depended upon the complexity of work. Barrel welders, for example, earned more than a man pounding large slabs of iron in the tilt-hammer shop. A machinist overseeing a stock-making machine received less salary than a filer fitting a lock. Inspectors and supervisors could earn over $1,000 per year, commensurate to their responsibilities. Slaves received no pay, but their owners did. Slave owners would rent their "property" to the U. S. government, usually as laborers.

The number of enslaved who worked at the armory during its six decades of operation remains undetermined, but it is certain that slaves performed services on behalf of the government.

The armory workforce fluctuated, dependent upon times of war and peace. As the new nation anticipated its second war with Great Britain (the War of 1812-1815), the armory payroll nearly tripled—rocketing from 82 to 210 employees. During the Mexican War period, employment rose almost one-third (from 199 to 301 workers). Production of new model weapons—the original "arms race"—also increased workforce.

The government strived incessantly to replace antiquated firearms technology with improved, more efficient and modern accurate weaponry. Only once did the armory employ 400 workers (1858), during production of the most advanced rifle-musket in antebellum history.

One other factor influenced armory payrolls—"panics" and deficits. Panics referred to economic downturns. In a recession environment, the government collected less revenue; and a consequence could be layoffs of federal employees, including at the armory. Deficit spending seldom occurred prior to the Civil War, and to balance its books, the government would reduce its workforce or withhold pay. During one four-year period, the payroll reduced by nearly fifty percent (1851-1855).

Periods of no pay—where armorers continued their jobs with expectation of deferred pay—cycled through the decades, always inflicting misery. On one occasion, seven months passed with no pay.

"You have no idea the distress of the people at this place," the superintendent informed the War Department, "in consequence of the want of money and the high prices of all the Necessities of life." The superintendent pleaded for his workers, noting that "many of them have large families, and no other means but their pay to subsist on." He further explained "the time is now at hand, when they must lay in their Pork Food for the Winter, which cannot be obtained without money."

MAKING MIGHT

Model 1841 lockplate

The War Department finally ended this liaise fare circus in 1841 when it abruptly replaced civilian authorities with trained military officers.

At the Ferry, in particular, the military enacted, exacted, and enforced strict regulations, attempting to overthrow four decades of a decadent work culture.

The workers, of course, fumed, and refused to be flummoxed. "The Armorers may attempt to disguise or hide the truth under a thousand clamors," reported an Ordnance Department official, "but this is the *real cause* of their objections to a Military Superintendent. He enforces the Regulations which lay bare their secret practices (frauds—for I can use no better term). They can control a civil Supt. and have often done it! They have occasionally ousted one, and they have shot one.'

But a new ruler had arrived. No worker would intimidate the U.S. military.

> **FIRST U.S. MILITARY PERCUSSION RIFLE: MODEL 1841 RIFLE**
>
> *A weapon's ignition system was most prone to failure. The traditional flintlock, in use for nearly 200 years, used a rock, striking against metal, to generate sparks to ignite gun powder. This clumsy procedure demanded exactness and high maintenance and added considerable time to the loading process. It also was weather sensitive. Powder exposed to moisture from rain, snow or humidity (hence the term "keep your powder dry") made it difficult to utilize flintlocks in poor weather. The percussion cap evolved as a tiny brass cylinder, with a self-contained explosive, that ignited when struck by the gun hammer (the "percussion"). This dramatically reduced "misfires" due to weather, permitting warfare in most conditions.*

"We say to the Armorers—here are our Regulations; if you will not abide by them—go elsewhere."

The "Clock Strike" of 1842 sounded the objection to this oppression.

The military superintendent had instituted a mandatory ten-hour work day, six days each week. This particularly infuriated workers used to a six-hour day, who sometimes failed to work for a week at a time. Certain their rights had been infringed, and positive

Military supervisors kept close watch on Armory operations.

CONFLUENCE

in their power of appeal, the armorers determined to impress the highest authority in the land. They subsequently leased a canal boat, floated to Washington, and marched to the White House. Here they held a private conference with the U.S. President—their ultimate boss, as federal employees.

President John Tyler listened patiently to their grievances. The armorers stated they were demoralized. They had been degraded into "mere machines of labor." Military control must be banished. Tyler promised he would investigate, and he assured no retribution would result from the uprising.

But the president's decision was disheartening: "[G]o home and hammer out [your] own salvation."

That settled, the military managed the armory with an iron rule during the next decade. Now that it had impressed discipline, it also wrought revolution in impression.

The War Department launched a construction program that transformed the armory's civilian appearance into a massive military base. "Every workshop of this armory . . . was found unfit for use, and not worth repair, and has been removed." The military razed virtually every building along the Potomac, replacing a hodgepodge of thirty-five decaying and disorderly structures in the musket factory.

Twenty decorative brick buildings, boasting uniform design and utilitarian function, soon stretched for 600 yards astride the pleasing Potomac. Powerful cast iron waterwheels and new technology turbines replaced decrepit and decaying energy infrastructure. Antiquated machines were tossed, superseded by advanced arms-manufacturing equipment. The government purchased property along Potomac Street to further separate it from the commercial district (and the taverns). A beautiful, but formidable, iron and brick wall soon enclosed the works.. Hovering over this military domain was Old Glory, atop a ninety-foot flag pole, featuring the garrison flag (twenty feet hoist by thirty-six feet fly) version of the Stars and Stripes. No one doubted who was in charge at Harpers Ferry.

The military even provided insurance against its biggest enemy—fire—installing hydrants and pumping apparatus to respond to an emergency. So important was this function, the first building one witnessed upon entering the revamped Musket Factory was

THREE-FIRSTS RULE: MODEL 1855 RIFLE

Innovation at Harpers Ferry reached an apex with this weapon. It was designed to overcome three issues: loading speed, ignition speed, and accuracy. Perfection of the "Burton Bullet" (a.k.a. "Minie Ball") at Harpers Ferry permitted, for the first time, the loading of a rifle at a rate equal to a musket (three shots per minute). This revolutionized warfare, as the longer-distance rifle became the principal weapon for infantry for the first time in history. This occurrence produced deadly results during the Civil War—the bloodiest war in American history.

Ignition speed increased through adoption of the "Maynard Tape Priming" magazine system. This placed percussion explosives on a paper strip that advanced as part of the trigger mechanism (like a modern-day cap gun). It thus eliminated the extra steps of a soldier fumbling and setting individual caps drawn from a box on his belt, saving valuable loading time. The imperfect paper strip proved susceptible to damage and moisture and jamming, however, and had limited practicability in the field.

A rifle's accuracy enabled the soldier to "aim" at his target rather than point at a nebulous mass (as with a musket). A rear sight was added to this weapon (a folding leaf graduated out to 900 yards) that permitted ranging targets at long distance.

the armory's fire engine house. **N**o one conceived it later would ignite a fire storm of national import as "John Brown's Fort."

FIRST EXPANDING BULLET: THE BURTON BULLET

James Henry Burton, Master Armorer at Harpers Ferry in the early 1850s, perfected a bullet design that expanded a lead projectile into the grooving of a rifle. Burton accomplished this by hollowing out the base of a cone-shaped bullet, leaving just enough edging so that when ignition occurred, the hot gases enlarged the bullet's base so that it fit snugly into the rifling. This eliminated the requirement to "pound" an oversized bullet into a muzzle and down the barrel, a hammering process that required considerable time.

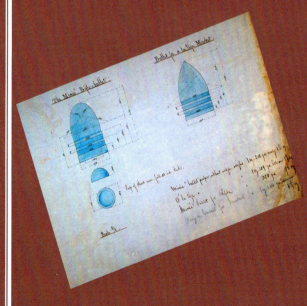

With the Burton Bullet, a conical projectile could be dropped in the barrel with the same ease as a musket ball. This tripled the speed of loading a rifle, making the rifle—for the first time in history—the weapon of choice for infantry tactics.

One of Burton's many technical drawings of bullet designs.

"[W]e were introduced to all the mysteries in this wonderful assemblage of contrivances for death... We learned that a musket consists of 49 pieces, and that the number of operations in completing one... amount to 346...

[W]ith but little turn for mechanical science, most of these complicated machines were rather surprising than comprehensible... [I was] rather grieving than glorying in the inventive skill that had been lavished on their construction under national auspices. It may be considered more sentimental than practical in the present belligerent state of mankind, to doubt the wisdom of making military preparations under the amiable name of 'defense,' yet I have never been able to understand why it should not be 'constituted' to create as well as to kill, and to make a sickle as well as a sword. . .

How much more beneficially would these hundreds of workmen be employed, if government devoted their labor to the manufacture of such unpicturesque instruments as hoes, spades, rakes, axes, pitchforks, plows, and reaping machines; and if the army, which is to wield the perilous weapons that are strewn in every direction, were transmuted, under national patronage, into cultivators of 'homesteads.'

But, alas! [T]he soldier is epic, and the farmer only pastoral, and pageantry beats homeliness all the world over."

~Brantz Mayer, *Harper's New Monthly Magazine*, 1857

> *I visited the armoury, which is a magnificent establishment, replete with all that is required for the destruction of the human family.*

> "Yesterday, I shot my guns and examined the several articles which had been manufactured for me at this place; they appear to be well executed."
>
> Meriwether Lewis to President Thomas Jefferson
> July 8, 1803

The Harpers Ferry Armory helped supply one of the most famous expeditions in American history.

Soon after Thomas Jefferson completed the acquisition of the Louisiana Territory from the French, explorer Meriwether Lewis arrived at the Ferry in March 1803 with instructions from the Secretary of War to obtain "such arms & Iron work, as requested." Six weeks later, Lewis departed with fifteen rifles, fifteen powder horns, thirty bullet molds, thirty ball screws (for rifles), extra rifle and musket locks, gunsmith's repair tools, several dozen hand-forged tomahawks, and twenty-four large knives.

His biggest prize was a collapsible boat frame, comprised of two iron sections that came apart, over which stretched a covering of hide. Lewis designed this strange contraption, improved and built by the armorers, and tested it successfully on the Potomac. His intention was to carry the 176-pound vessel—it could hold 8,000 pounds—several thousand miles, deep into the wild interior of the country, and use it on the Missouri River.

The Lewis and Clark transcontinental expedition proved one of the great explorations of its day, but the collapsible boat sank at the Great Falls of the Missouri two years after its construction at Harpers Ferry.

CONFLUENCE

Harpers Ferry's population swelled over the first half of the nineteenth century as the armory operation expanded.

The number of residents grew to nearly 3,000 about the confluence by 1850; and the once primitive ferry lot became an enterprising intersection of two railroads, three turnpikes, two river bridges, and a thoroughfare canal. Commercial businesses thrived, though crammed into a six-acre reservation retained by the powerful and wealthy Wager family (heirs to Robert Harper). Town citizens enjoyed a world of modern conveniences and delicacies, such as stylish ready-made (manufactured) men's clothing and fresh oysters from the Chesapeake Bay, arriving daily via the B & O Railroad. Almost fifty different stores and businesses operated in the town during the decade before the Civil War.

Private industry also spurred economic prosperity. The water power of the Shenandoah transformed the wilderness of Virginius Island into a booming industrial center, featuring two cotton mills, a saw mill, a foundry and Abraham Herr's flour mill—the largest producer of flour in the Shenandoah Valley.

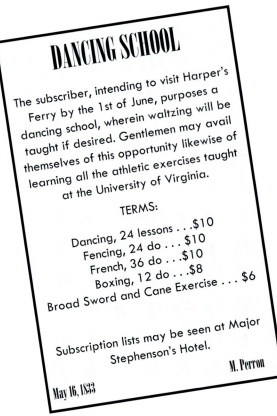

Local newspapers like the Virginia Free Press were packed with notices of modern offerings that mid-19th century Harpers Ferrians could enjoy.

Deemed "the Lowell of Virginia," the cotton mill owners hired and housed dozens of young women to operate their looms and weaving machines, an experiment in the South, patterned after the Lowell, Massachusetts, model.

But this cosmopolitan life leached with problems.

Health was a significant concern.

The scene had deteriorated from Jefferson's "worth a voyage across the Atlantic" to an "abominable village" cloaked in the sooty blackness of coal smoke—pouring forth from the factory buildings, train locomotives and home stoves—chocking the confluence's air. Local springs strained to provide drinking water, and sewer sanitation consisted of chamber pots, slop jars and outhouses. Open-window ventilation helped some, but since germ theory had not yet been discovered, people believed a principal source of disease was foul-smelling air.

MAKING MIGHT

Bad water, actually, provided a principal source of disease, with typhoid and dysentery particularly prevalent. Pest-borne diseases, especially malaria from menacing mosquitoes habituating the river valleys, generated misery during the "sickly season."

A frightening scare occurred in 1832 with an outbreak of Asiatic Cholera, an incurable plague that spread gradually south from Canada into the eastern U.S.

"Imagine the panic produced by a man's turning black and dying in twenty four hours," reported a C & O Canal official, whose workers were especially devastated by the contagion. "[U]nfortunately for the cause of humanity, nearly every person who has been with the dead bodies or who has assisted in burying them have paid the forfeit with their lives: and now it is scar[c]ely possible to get the dead buried."

Sanitation proved an ubiquitous ugliness in the crowded village. "It is hereby declared to be a nuisance and to endanger the health of the town, for dirt, filth, water, manure or rubbish, to remain in the streets . . . [or] in any cellar, vault, stable, or other out-house," decreed the town's ordinances. Property owners could be fined up to $3.00 per day (equal to three full days' pay for many) if "said nuisance be unremoved."

"We were pleased to find on a recent visit to Harpers Ferry that the very efficient members of the Corporation have commenced a thorough cleansing of the place," reported an area newspaper. "The streets are now as pure and clean as any town in the Union."

The same could not be said about race relations.

Slave or Free Black.

That's how U.S. census takers categorized African Americans residing in Harpers Ferry during the decades before the Civil War.

The slave, by legal definition, was *not* a human being, but property belonging to humans. Slave population schedules indicated this debasement by listing slaves only by sex and age, *but not by name.* Slaves were enumerated by individual owners (the latter were, of course, identified by name).

> *Robert Harper's heirs were the earliest and largest slave-owning family at the Confluence at the turn of the nineteenth century.*

The 1829 will of Catherine Wager, Harper's niece, estimated values and dictated destinies of several enslaved persons: "I devise to my said Son James B. Wager the following Negro slaves to wit, Henry, Ned, James and Charles. I devise to my Son Gerard B. Wager my two Negro boys Lewis and John. I devise to my Daughter Sarah Ann Wager, my Negro woman Betty and her daughter Philistia."

28

> **Trustees' Sale Of Valuable Property.**
>
> BY virtue of a Deed of Trust from Philip Coons and his wife, dated October 22d, 1855, and duly recorded—the undersigned, Trustees therein mentioned, will sell at public auction for cash in front of United States Hotel, Harpers Ferry, On Saturday, the 9th Day of August, 1856, several valuable SLAVES—namely, a woman named Mary, aged about 22 years—a girl named Mary, aged about 10 years—a boy named Howard, aged about 7 years and a woman named Annette, aged about 28 years with her child Lucy, about 3 years old.
>
> Sale to take place between 1 and 2 o'clock, P.M.
>
> ANDREW HUNTER,
> A. M. KITZMILLER, Spr.
> Trustees.
>
> July 24, 1856
>
> *Sale of slaves posted in the* Virginia Free Press, *July 24, 1856.*

John Wager, Jr., and his wife Catherine, who moved to the Ferry from their native Philadelphia, quickly acclimated to the Southern slave culture, owning as many as eight enslaved persons.

A slave named "Black Tom," owned by Harper's heirs, transported travelers and freight as the ferryman for nearly twenty years after Harper's death. He "purchased" his own freedom in 1805 at age fifty-six and was "fully emancipated, he having paid the amount of the sum he was sold for at the sale of the effects of his late master John Wager senior."

The slave population grew as Harpers Ferry expanded. It reached its zenith by the Census of 1850 when it recorded 155 enslaved humans (about five percent of the population) living in the combined communities of Harpers Ferry, Bolivar and Virginius Island.

All men of power managing the armory owned slaves, including the superintendent, paymaster and master armorer.

Women who owned and operated hotels or boarding houses habitually ranked among the top slave owners. Professionals like doctors, lawyers and railroad officials possessed slaves, as did prominent business entrepreneurs. Though history does not identify slave occupations, most at the confluence were called "domestics"—meaning they principally conducted cooking, cleaning, and washing activities, and often resided with the white owner family.

Strict laws governed a slave's existence.

Since human bondage defied the instinctive desire for freedom, slave insurrection was a constant fear in Southern society. Controls and slave patrols particularly hardened following the 1831 Nat Turner slave uprising in southeastern Virginia. Blacks could not congregate, attend religious services, or preach; and if discovered with a firearm or any weapon, could be subject to 39 lashes.

Free Blacks fared little better. Though technically not "owned," and able to pursue places of employment, paid occupations, and travel, Southerners feared Free Blacks nearly as much as slaves.

> **TOWN OF HARPERS FERRY**
>
> **ORDINANCE 14**
>
> If any slave commit any offence against the laws or ordinances of the corporation punishable by fine, and the fine be imposed, and be not promptly paid or secured to be paid, he or she may be punished by whipping, with any number of stripes, not exceeding thirty-nine provided no trial of any slave be had before notice of the time of said trial be given, to his or her master or mistress, if a resident within the limits of the corporation.

No Free Black could reside in Virginia without the sponsorship of a white person.

Travel within the South required written permission of a white sponsor. Free Blacks were required to carry papers on them at all times, validating their sponsorship.

ORDINANCE 3

Sec. 1. It shall be the duty of the town Sergeant to lodge in the jail each and every colored person, whom he may find upon any streets, lanes or alleys, after ten o'clock at night, unless such colored person be on urgent business; and if a slave, have a written order from the master or mistress. On or after the following morning, and not before, the party thus lodged in jail may be released by the payment of 25 cents to the jailer.

Sec. 2. If the fees are not paid, the party shall be confined in jail forty-eight hours and no longer.... [I]f the party committed be a slave, he or she shall be whipped by the jailer, ten lashes, provided notice has been previously given to the master or mistress. The Sergeant, for any neglect of duty imposed by this ordinance shall be fined two dollars.

CONFLUENCE

Free Blacks in Virginia could own property, but after the Turner rebellion, they could not own slaves. Nor could they purchase slaves, even if attempting to buy their own family members, unless bought through a white intermediary.

Isaac Gilbert (enslaved himself) desired to purchase his wife, Sarah, and their three children, owned by Dr. James Logie. Gilbert worked for years, saving $1,400 (more than three years pay for an average white American). But he could not carry on the transaction himself. He thus sought a middleman, in this case, Harpers Ferry Mayor Fontaine Beckham, who agreed to arrange the deal.

Even the judicial system proved unequal for African Americans. A slave, as property, had no standing to pursue any claim whatsoever. Free Blacks, meanwhile, could not testify in their own defense, nor assert a claim against another—*unless they had a white witness to speak for them.*

John Butler, an African American veteran of the U.S. Navy during the War of 1812 and a decades-long resident of Harpers Ferry, was assaulted in town by a white bully. Butler "called upon me," affirmed the white constable, "scarring upon his head, face, and other parts of his body, evidence that he had been cruelly and inhumanely treated."

And here was the problem: criminal charges against a white person could not be filed where the only witness was Black.

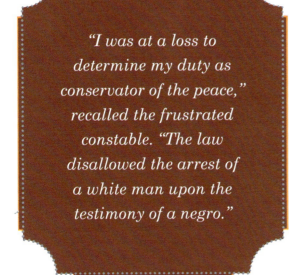

"I was at a loss to determine my duty as conservator of the peace," recalled the frustrated constable. *"The law disallowed the arrest of a white man upon the testimony of a negro."*

But the constable believed he must act. "I had no doubt that an outrage had been committed upon the person of an inoffensive individual of character and credit in the community."

Through diligence, the constable discovered a white man who witnessed the attack, and who agreed to testify against the perpetrator. The assailant "was arrested upon the testimony of his equal in colour," contended the constable, "and in every other respect, recognized by the laws, and upon that testimony, aided by his admissions, he was committed [to jail]."

Free Blacks lived throughout the towns of Harpers Ferry and Bolivar, many making a living through craft trades. Though the two towns combined boasted the largest municipal population in Jefferson County, the Free Black population comprised only 147 individuals (five percent of the residents).

At least the census gave them names.

MAKING MIGHT

As the Harpers Ferry Armory entered its sixtieth year of operation, trouble brewed within the country it was constructed to defend.

Southerners worried more about abhorrent abolitionists than British invasions. Northerners concerned themselves more with detested slave catchers than intrusions from Canada. South Carolina seemed anxious to declare war on Massachusetts. The new Republican Party was threatening the power of Southern Democrats. Never had the rift grown so extreme over the divisive issue of slavery.

Yet the "peculiar institution," as Southerners termed it, continued to grow and thrive. Virginia, in fact, became the largest slave-trading state in the South. It was a rich business to purchase slaves in the Old Dominion, then sell them at even higher prices in areas of demand such as Mississippi, Louisiana, Texas and Arkansas. Slave prices had reached new heights by the 1850s, with a skilled male laborer attracting $1,600 on the auction block (more than five times the average worker's pay).

Harpers Ferry discovered itself within a sea of slavery by the mid-nineteenth century. Almost 11,500 humans in bondage surrounded the town within the three counties touching the confluence.

A target ripe and rich for John Brown.

Chapter 3
SLAVERY'S STORM

I can imagine your feelings at receiving such news from your home—poor doomed Harpers Ferry. We little dreamed that our quiet peaceful streets should ever be the scene of Battle.

George and Mary Mauzy to daughter Eugenia

John Brown ruminated upon slavery long before he launched his war at Harpers Ferry.

The fifty-nine-year-old Connecticut native, born the year Thomas Jefferson was elected president, had committed most of his adult life to the abolition of black bondage.

Believing that God had chosen him as His instrument to destroy slavery in the United States, Brown depended upon prayer for his guidance and the Bible for his direction. A favorite verse, *Remember them that are in bonds, as bound with them,* he recited and preached over and again. Brown committed himself only to God; and Brown's faith assured him that God had committed him to the purpose of freedom.

Slavery's abolition had become a crusade by the 1830s. New England reformers, convinced that human enslavement was immoral, commenced using their pulpits, their pupils, their press and their publications to pressure the Southern slave culture toward emancipation. Growing ranks of abolitionists, and their persistent efforts, produced consequences at the polls.

Over the next two decades, more and more elected officials from the North expressed antislavery sentiments. So successful became the politics of abolition, it created a new national organization: the Republican Party.

This doctrine of abolition infuriated Southerners. "Be it good or bad, [slavery] has grown up with our society and our institutions, and is so

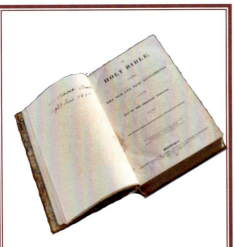

John Brown's Bible, inscribed "John Brown's Book." Brown's antislavery fervor, inseverable from his religious code, both inspired and terrified his contemporaries. Henry David Thoreau likened Brown to the Puritans: "men of simple habits, straightforward, prayerful; not thinking much of rulers who did not fear God, not making many compromises[.]"

SLAVERY'S STORM

interwoven with them that to destroy it would be to destroy us as a people," proclaimed U.S. Senator John C. Calhoun of South Carolina, a former vice president of the nation. Calhoun, the South's most ardent defender, defined abolition as "a systematic design of rendering us hateful in the eyes of the world, with a view to a general crusade against us and our institutions."

Calhoun predicted a dire outcome:

"[Northerners] will have been taught to hate the people and institutions of nearly one half of the Union," Calhoun lamented. "It is easy to see the end…. we must become, finally, two peoples."

"Abolition and the Union cannot coexist," declared a prescient Calhoun.

John Brown rejected any notion of a Union coexisting with slavery. Unlike most abolitionists who fashioned a powerful, but peaceful resistance, Brown advocated for the violent overthrow of slavery. "I don't think the people of the slave states will ever consider the subject of slavery in its true light," he opined, "till some other argument is resorted to other than moral persuasion."

> "I have only a short time to live, only one death to die, and I will die fighting for this Cause," pledged Brown. "There will be no peace in this land until slavery is done for."

American constitutional democracy particularly piqued Brown. He tired of congressional compromises that extended slavery into western territories. He opposed a balance of power that added new slave states in exchange for an equal number of Free states. He bristled at laws that required the return of escaped slaves to their former owners. He detested courts that ruled against the freedom of the enslaved. Even the Constitution offended Brown, decrying the failure of the founders to eradicate slavery at the formation of the republic.

"Talk is a national institution," decreed Brown, "but it does not help the slave."

Brown's first militant effort at defeating slavery occurred in 1851. Residing then in Springfield, Massachusetts, he organized the United States League of Gileadites—his attempt to protect freedom seekers from slave catchers—a lucrative profession, emboldened by the national Fugitive Slave Act, a federal law that required the return of escaped slaves.

Advocating collective and armed self-defense for formerly enslaved African Americans, Brown instructed his adherents: "Should one of your number be arrested, you must collect together as quickly as possible so as to outnumber your adversaries." Then followed Brown's permission for his followers to use violence:

"Do not delay one moment after you are ready [to attack]; you will lose all your resolution if you do. Let the first blow be the signal for all to engage; and when engaged do not do your work by halves; but make clean work with your enemies."

CONFLUENCE

Pro-slavery "border ruffians" enter Kansas to influence the local decision on whether or not to permit slavery.

Brown's first opportunity to war aggressively against slavery came soon afterward in Kansas.

In yet another compromise, Congress had determined the best response for slavery's expansion was not by Washington's fiat, but instead, by the will of local settlers. "Popular sovereignty," it was termed; bloody butchery, it evolved. This policy permitted people moving into a territory (like Kansas) to adopt their own preference with regards to slavery.

Soon Kansas found itself engulfed in a violent guerilla war between "Free Soilers" (settlers opposed to slavery) and "Border Ruffians" (those in favor). "Bleeding Kansas" became the talk of the country. As opponents battled for supremacy and influence in establishing the state's constitution, recruits representing both factions rushed into the territory.

John Brown arrived in Kansas in 1855. Five of his sons preceded him, staking out farms and boosting the ranks of the anti-slavery settlers. When Brown ventured west himself, another son, as well as a son-in-law, joined the patriarch in the family's venture to stifle slavery.

Threatened by pro-slavery militias, "Captain Brown" soon established a military company in southeastern Kansas along the Missouri border. He designated his company the "Liberty Guards," and his leadership attracted aspiring anti-slavery devotees, along with New York newspaper reporters anxious to journal the action to a craving public. Brown soon attained fame for battles near Lawrence (at Black Jack and Osawatomie), where he outfoxed superior forces. He also gained infamy for ordering a mutilating massacre along Pottawatomie Creek, where five settlers were hacked into pieces with artillery broad swords. Afterward, the very utterance of "John Brown" generated terror.

SLAVERY'S STORM

Now notorious, Brown became a wanted man, with a price fixed on his head by the U.S. government. This notoriety did not injure Brown, but instead vaulted him to near martyrdom in abolitionist circles.

> One journalist, so impressed with Brown as a fighter and his devotion to his mission, marveled that he "had seen the pre-destined leader of the second and the holier American Revolution."

Following Kansas, Brown returned east and socialized openly in the circles of New England and New York's intelligentsia, as well as among leading abolitionists. Though a wanted man, no one dared arrest the "chieftain hero of Kansas." Brown preached in historic churches; dined with philanthropists; mesmerized intellectuals; and often argued with "pacifist" abolitionists who expressed discomfort at his penchant for violence.

Brown retained hope and his faith, however, and he never questioned his guidance. "God had created [me] to be the deliverer of slaves," he believed, "the same as Moses had delivered the children of Israel."

Perhaps nothing infuriated John Brown more than the Supreme Court determination that a slave was not a citizen, but rather an object of private property (as defined by U.S. and Southern state laws).

The 1857 Dred Scott decision denied the enslaved Mr. Scott citizenship. It also nullified nearly forty years of previous Congressional compromises limiting the expansion of slavery. And it explained why. Scott represented "beings of an inferior order," the Court surmised, "altogether unfit to associate with the white race, either in social or political relations."

The Court concluded that African Americans "were so far inferior, that they had no right which the white man was bound to respect; and that the negro might justly and lawfully be reduced to slavery for his benefit."

Ad for pamphlet explaining and supporting Dred Scott opinion, Harper's Weekly, July 23, 1859.

36

CONFLUENCE

Brown exploded. "Our Servants, or Law makers, are totally unworthy the name of Half Civilized Men," he declared. "All their National acts (which apply to slavery) are false, to the words, Spirit, and intention, of the Constitution of the United States, and the Declaration of Independence."

Brown then defined, more clearly than ever, his vision, issuing a proclamation entitled: *A Declaration of Liberty, by the Representatives of the Slave Population of the United States of America*:

PROVISIONAL CONSTITUTION & ORDINANCE

WHEREAS, Slavery throughout its entire existence in the Unites States, is none other than a most barbarous, unprovoked, and unjustifiable war of one portion of its citizens upon another portion, the only conditions of which are perpetual imprisonment and hopeless servitude or absolute extermination; in utter disregard of those eternal and self-evident truths set forth in our Declaration of Independence:

THEREFORE, We, citizens of the United States, and the Oppressed People, who, by a decision of the Supreme Court are declared to have no rights which the White Man is bound to respect; together with all other people degraded by the laws thereof, Do, for the time being ordain and establish for ourselves, the following

PROVISIONAL CONSTITUTION and ORDINANCES,

the better to protect our Persons, Property, Lives and Liberties; and to govern our actions.

"When in the course of Human events, it becomes necessary for an oppressed People to Rise, and assert their Natural Rights as Human Beings…and break that odious yoke of oppression."

The *Declaration of Liberty* recited "the enormous sin of slavery found in the General History of American Slavery…a history of repeated injuries, of base hypocracy [sic]; A cursed treasonable, usurpation; The most abominable provoking atrocities….Such cruelty, tyranny, and perfidy, has hardly a parallel, in the history of the most barbarous ages."

Convinced that war was the only answer, Brown proposed his most bold action yet—a plan to create his own government in occupied slave territory. For this purpose, Brown organized his own constitutional convention. He held the conference in Canada, at a town of six thousand residents called Chatham, where one-third of the population comprised escaped slaves.

Thirty-four African Americans participated, including Martin Delany. Delany, a physician who had attended Harvard Medical School before expulsion due to his race, was a native of Jefferson County, where Harpers Ferry is located. He ranked as a leader of black abolitionists and was a contemporary of Frederick Douglass. Delany recalled

SLAVERY'S STORM

Brown revealing his scheme to make Kansas, rather than Canada, the terminus of the Underground Railroad. Here Brown would establish his own state, with its own constitution, to prove the right of freedom could be maintained. To provide for the defense of this state, the convention elected Brown as its "Commander-in-Chief." At no time did Delany hear the words "Harpers Ferry" mentioned.

Few, in fact, knew of John Brown's Harpers Ferry plan.

But Frederick Douglass did.

John Brown summoned his friend Frederick Douglass to an urgent meeting in August, 1859.

He must come quickly, and secretly.

Fifteen months had passed since the Chatham Convention, and Captain Brown was anxious to launch his war upon slavery. Not in Kansas, but at Harpers Ferry.

Their rendezvous occurred in an abandoned quarry near Chambersburg, Pennsylvania. Over the past dozen years, the two had become close associates in their fight against slavery. "[O]ur relations were friendly and confidential," revealed Douglass. So confidential, in fact, that Captain Brown divulged his master plan to America's most famous escaped slave.

The plan, in short, expanded upon the Underground Railroad concept, with a significant improvement. Brown's scheme provided armed soldiers to protect those seeking freedom. To this point, the Underground Railroad, as a physical route of escape, was a hazardous journey. Southern states offered minimal safe-houses and shelters, and families seldom could flee together. Large groups of slaves almost never escaped in concert, making detection too easy. And in case of discovery, the freedom seeker had no form of self-defense.

Brown meets Douglass in Chambersburg quarry.

Brown's strategy corrected these shortcomings. Armed and trained guerilla soldiers, stationed upon mountain ridges at fortified refuges along the Appalachians, would protect all escapees as they journeyed from slave country into the sanctuary of the North. The Appalachians stretched 1,500 miles from Alabama into Canada, and offered an avenue to freedom, passing through eight Southern slave states.

38

CONFLUENCE

> *"The mountains and swamps of the South were intended by the Almighty,"* conferred John Brown, *"for a refuge for the slave, and a defense against the oppressor."*

Implementation would commence in Maryland and Virginia, slave states adjacent to the Mason-Dixon Line—the symbolic barrier between bondage and freedom. The first target must be Harpers Ferry and the U.S. Arsenal—the principal source of weapons for Brown's army of liberators.

Douglass defined Brown's plan not as slave insurrection (i.e., an uprising that results in mass killing of white masters); but instead, as slave migration. And this, in turn, served a larger strategic purpose: economic warfare against the slave owner.

"I readily saw that this plan could be made very effective in rendering slave property in Maryland and Virginia valueless by rendering it insecure," approved Douglass. "Men do not like to buy runaway horses, nor to invest their money in a species of property likely to take legs and walk off with itself."

Investment in slaves as property could prove a costly proposition. A male slave, age eighteen, designated as a laborer, averaged $1,600 at auction by the 1850s. Since most Americans earned only $300 annually, the purchase of just one slave required five years of savings for a typical Southerner. If that investment "vanished," or dozens of slaves at an estate disappeared one night, or hundreds of slaves on a plantation escaped to the mountains, one word pummeled the slave owner: bankrupt.

In Maryland, evidence supported this principal of slave devaluation caused by self emancipation. "[Slave owners] are not so foolish as to bring slaves here, the most insecure State for such property in the whole Union," reported a Hagerstown newspaper.

> "We believe that these influences consist of a set of prowling missionaries, of both races, who under the cloak of religion, contrive to avoid suspicion, and thus reach and poison the mind of the slave with their worse than foolish doctrines of liberty and freedom. Inducements and promises, such as never can be realized are held out to him to desert the comfortable home of his owner, and to make his way into those States which guarantee to him the free and uninterrupted enjoyment of the blessings of liberty and equal rights—blessings, by the by, which both nature and education render him incapable of appreciating."
>
> *Hagerstown Herald of Freedom,*
> *February 13, 1846*

"[A] greater number of slaves have absconded from their masters in this State and Virginia, than at any former period for years. Runways are advertised almost daily, and it is very evident to our minds, that the abolitionists of the North have some sort of secret influences at work amongst the slaves in Maryland and Virginia."

Another factor that weighed in favor of Brown's plan was the composition of the African American population in Maryland. Free Blacks comprised nearly half of the state's racial minority (84,000), the largest Free Black population in the South. Baltimore's Free Black population was the most of any city in the U.S.

This so alarmed Maryland's aristocracy that it called a "Slave Owners Convention" in June 1859—only three weeks prior to Brown's unknown arrival—to "devise some plan for the better regulation of the free negro population . . . which is regarded by many persons as an evil of no small magnitude, but it is evidently one that cannot be remedied easily, and which ought to be approached with the utmost caution and wisdom."

Both Brown and Douglass envisioned assistance from three African American communities: enslaved fleeing from the South; escaped slaves living in the North; and the Free Black population. "[B]rown proposed to add to his force in the mountains any courageous and intelligent [blacks] who might be willing to remain and endure the hardships," recounted Douglass. "These, he thought, if properly selected, on account of their knowledge of the surrounding country, could be made valuable auxiliaries."

Brown understood that western Maryland, in particular, served as a logical corridor to freedom because of its *geography*. Sandwiched between North and South, the narrowest slice of the state (about two miles wide) offered a short passage to the free territory of southern Pennsylvania. Hagerstown and Washington County, located within the thinnest segment, especially served the interests of the Underground Railroad network, and had become a magnet for escaping slaves. Slave owners knew this, and adopted measures to interdict. "There is evidently a secret influence at work . . . which, if not discovered and frustrated, will, ere ten years elapse, effect a total abolition of Slavery."

John Brown knew the "runaway" reputation of the tri-state region surrounding Harpers Ferry. He was aware of the sizable Free Black population in Maryland and in southern Pennsylvania that potentially could render assistance. He had requested intelligence, in fact, from his son, John Jr., about the names and residences of "every person and family of the reliable kind," meaning the operators and infrastructure of the Underground Railroad net-

> **LAW OF VIRGINIA!**
>
> Whenever any slave is arrested in the counties of Allegheny, Washington, and Frederick in the State of Maryland . . . escaping to a nonslaveholding state, the person making the arrest of such slave, and delivering him unto his owner or his agent, or to the jailer of any county of this Commonwealth, shall be entitled to demand of the owner of such slave . . . a reward of fifteen per centum on the value of such fugitive slave.

Recognizing the region's popularity as a route to freedom, Virginia law encouraged actors outside its borders to assist in capturing slaves running through Maryland to freedom.

work stretching from the Harpers Ferry vicinity north nearly 90 miles to Carlisle, Pennsylvania.

Brown, too, was aware the Quaker State counties of Franklin and Adams (where Gettysburg is located)—both bordering the Mason-Dixon Line—were aggressively active in Underground Railroad operations. As important, a rail head at Chambersburg in central Franklin County connected with railroads throughout the Northeast, permitting Brown the rapid and secret transport of weapons and munitions and a steady supply of recruits.

At Chambersburg, in a secluded and abandoned stone quarry, Brown and Douglass conferred the third week of August 1859. Brown already had established his forward base at the Kennedy Farm, five miles from Harpers Ferry. He offered Douglass an update.

"He had completely renounced his old plan," Douglass reported. "The taking of Harpers Ferry, of which Captain Brown had merely hinted before, was now declared as his settled purpose."

This change in strategy alarmed Douglass.

"[Brown] thought that the capture of Harpers Ferry would serve as notice to the slaves that their friends had come, and as a trumpet to rally them to his standard." Douglass objected.

> "To me, such a measure would be fatal to running off slaves (as was the original plan), and fatal to all engaged in doing so. It would be an attack upon the federal government, and would array the whole country against us."

Brown spent a weekend trying to persuade the famous black orator, writer and aboli-tionist to join him. "Come with me, Douglass. I will defend you with my life," promised Brown. "I want you for a special purpose. When I strike, the bees will begin to swarm, and I shall want you to help hive them."

Douglass refused.

Despite Brown's dispassionate pleas, Douglass remained resolute. He would not join him. Turning to an African American companion who had joined him at the meeting, Douglass asked Shields Green what his future would be: "I b'leve I'll go wid de old man."

> "All [Brown's] arguments, and all his descriptions of the place, convinced me that he was going into a perfect steel-trap, and that once in he would never get out alive."
>
> - Frederick Douglass

Nearly two months passed before Brown launched his war against slavery. Though discouraged by Douglass' absence, he was encouraged by his war preparations. Conducting business under the alias

SLAVERY'S STORM

> "The people of our quiet [community] could hardly realize the fact that a plot of such villainy could have been concocting almost in their midst without even a suspicion of its existence... [S]o adroit were they in their nefarious scheme, that at no time, we believe, was suspicion cast upon their movements."
>
> ~Hagerstown Herald and Torch Light, *October 1859*

"Isaac Smith and Sons," Brown began importing his implements of war. Boxes marked "Furniture," and containing 200 Sharps rifles, had arrived at Chambersburg via the railroad and been forwarded to the Kennedy Farm undetected. Nearly one thousand disassembled spears or pikes were delivered, also secretly. Pistols, knives, and kegs of gunpowder also showed up at the front without notice. Brown's soldiers began massing too, twenty-one guerrilla fighters in sum, most arriving under cover of darkness at the Kennedy Farm hideaway.

The army of liberation included three of his sons, all veterans of the Kansas battles, and five African Americans. To prevent detection, the men cooped up in two log cabins on the farm during the daylight, with Brown's daughter Annie and his daughter-in-law Martha as sentinels.

Annie recalled one particularly poignant conversation with her brother Owen, outside in the yard of the Kennedy Farm headquarters. "Owen remarked as he looked up at the house: 'If we succeed, some day there will be a United States flag over this house. If we do not, it will be considered a den of land pirates and thieves.'"

"I was there to keep the outside world from discovering that John Brown and his men were in their neighborhood. I used to help Martha with the cooking all that she would let me.

Father would often tell me that I must not let any work interfere with my constant watchfulness. That others could help do the housework, but he depended on me to watch.

When I sat on the porch or just inside the door . . . when I washed the dishes . . . while carrying the victuals across the porch, from the kitchen, and while sweeping and tidying the rooms. My evenings were spent on the porch or sitting on the stairs, watching, and listening."

Recollections of Annie Brown, who was just sixteen when she lived at the Kennedy Farm with her father and his army.

CONFLUENCE

As October arrived, Brown sent the girls home to North Elba, New York, knowing the moment had come. Everyone sensed the launch was near. Son Watson Brown, thinking of his wife and infant son (named after his brother Frederick, killed in action in Kansas), wrote his beau: "Oh Bell, I do want to see you and the little fellow very much but must wait. There was a slave near where we live whose wife was sold to go South the other day, and he was found hanging in [an] orchard, dead, the next morning. I cannot come home as long as such things are done here."

Two weeks later, on the raw and rainy Sunday evening of October 16, Captain John Brown gathered his men in the yard of the Kennedy Farm, and announced his first orders:

"Men, get on your arms. We shall proceed to the Ferry."

"I want you to buy me as soon as possible, for if you do not get me some body else will . . ."

~Harriet Newby, wife, August 16, 1859

Dangerfield Newby was born a slave

in Fauquier County, Virginia. He was thirty-nine when he arrived with Brown at Harpers Ferry. His white father moved to Ohio and freed Newby when he was a child. Newby first met Brown in Oberlin, Ohio. Newby himself married an enslaved Virginia woman, and he desired to purchase her freedom. The owner agreed to sell her and one of Dangerfield's six children for $1,000; but when Dangerfield raised the amount, the owner refused the sale. Newby's wife and children eventually were sold to a planter in Louisiana.

Newby's Death

"One of the armorer's . . . got an opportunity at a shot at him from an upper window of Mrs. Stephenson's house at the corner of High and Shenandoah streets, and killed him on the spot. I saw his body as it was yet warm as it lay on the pavement in front of the arsenal yard; and I never saw, on any battlefield, a more hideous musket wound than his. For his throat was cut literally from ear to ear, which was afterwards accounted for by the fact that the armorer, having no bullets, charged his musket with a six-inch iron spike."

~Alexander Boteler

SLAVERY'S STORM

John Cook knew something was wrong.

He had received no communication from the Ferry for some hours. At his schoolhouse post, he could hear an increase in intensity of gunfire, echoing off the mountains. He determined to investigate.

"I met a negro woman a short distance below the schoolhouse who informed me that they were fighting hard at the Ferry," recounted Cook. Along the Potomac River, he encountered two boys he knew, who explained that local militias had "hemmed in" the insurgents. Cook hurried down to opposite the Ferry, where he ascended Maryland Heights for a better view.

"I saw that our party was completely surrounded." *What had happened?*

Brown was trapped, besieged within the armory's fire engine house, with most of his soldiers now dead or wounded.

After Mr. Beckham, who was my grand uncle, was shot, I was much exasperated, and started with Mr. [George Chambers] to the room where the man Thompson was confined, with the purpose of shooting him. We found several persons in the room [at the Wager House Hotel], and had leveled our guns at him, when Mrs. Foulke's sister threw herself before him and begged us to leave him to the laws. We then caught hold of him and dragged him out by the throat, he saying: "Though you may take my life, eighty [thousand] will rise up to avenge me, and carry out my purpose of giving liberty to the slaves." We carried him out to the bridge, and two of us, leveling our guns in this moment of wild exasperation, fired, and before he fell, a dozen or more balls were buried in him. We then threw his body over the tressel work....[W]e concluded to start after the others, and shoot all we could find; had just seen my beloved uncle and best friend I ever had, shot down by those villainous Abolitionists, and felt justified in shooting any that I could find; felt it my duty, and have no regrets.

   Harry Hunter, Testimony at John Brown's trial,
   October 28, 1859

William Thompson

To Daughter Eugenia~   Monday, October 17, 1859

Oh every face is so terror stricken. Those wretches that were killed lay in the street until the hogs began to tear them up.... God only knows what will become of us all.

*   Mary Mauzy*

CONFLUENCE

Charles Town's Jefferson Guards militia company had responded with alacrity. The citizen soldiers, dressed in the dark blue U.S. Army regulation uniform, had seized the Potomac River bridge from the Maryland side about noon, cutting off Brown's route of escape and his communications with the school house and the Kennedy Farm headquarters. Additional civilian militia also arrived from Charles Town, occupying lofts overlooking the armory and arsenal yards, showering the insurgents with a hail of lead bullets from above. Citizen militia also sealed the Rifle Factory compound along the Shenandoah, snaring Brown's fighters there in a death trap.

Dangerfield Newby, retreating from the railroad bridge toward the armory entrance, fell first among the invaders, shot through the neck and killed instantly. Residents enraged by the death of two of their own citizens on Shenandoah Street, and by Newby's black race, abused his corpse, slicing off his ears and allowing hogs to masticate his remains. "No one seemed to notice him particularly more than any other dead animal," reported a local newspaper.

Brown's situation was desperate. More troops had arrived. Militia companies from the nearby towns of Martinsburg and Frederick disembarked via the B & O Railroad, and the "Hamtramck Guards" marched in from Shepherdstown. The rails were bringing more reinforcements from as far away as Winchester and Baltimore, with the Baltimore militia boasting nine companies and 225 men. Hundreds of armed soldiers now encircled Brown's "fort."

Rev. Charles White had preached in Harpers Ferry at the Presbyterian Church on Sunday, October 16, only hours before Brown's arrival. He spent the night, unknowing of events unfolding around him. On Monday, he witnessed a detachment of Brown's soldiers routed from the Rifle Factory along the Shenandoah River. Among them was one of John Allstadt's enslaved men. White recites what happened.

"When Alstadts [sic] man who ran towards us came up—I asked him how came he there & what he was doing with the pike—he said they had taken him and his master the night before— brot [sic] them down—& told him if he didn't keep guard at Rifle factory they would kill him. I believe he was innocent. While talking a reckless fellow came up—leveled his musket at the negro's head within an inch or so—and was about to pull the trigger. I ask him not to fire as did others. He swore he'd kill him & that he had orders from the Captain of the Charlestown Company. I told him no matter what the Capt. said we had the man prisoner—perhaps he was innocent—he was ours—and stepping between the two,

I ordered him not to fire. Several then took hold of his gun & saved the negro. . . . [S]o enraged were the multitude that it was with difficulty they were restrained from hanging & shooting several on the spot. I did all I could to prevent it."

The bullet that killed Mayor Fontaine Beckham freed four slaves.

The only slaves John Brown freed during his Harpers Ferry invasion oc-curred at 2 p.m. on Monday, October 17, when a rifle slug fired from the fire engine house ended Beckham's life, assuring the liberation of Isaac Gilbert's family.

Beckham had agreed to assist Isaac Gilbert purchase his wife and three children. Gilbert, a slave himself, owned by Miss Susan Harding (residing in Harpers Ferry), was earning and saving money to obtain his family's freedom. But Virginia law prohibited an African American from paying for people's release from bondage, even if close kin. So Gilbert arranged a deal with his friend Mayor Beckham. He paid Beckham $1,400 in installments so that the mayor could purchase the freedom of his family. Beckham codified this arrangement in his personal will, guaranteeing the release of Gilbert's relations, should he pass before consummating the purchase.

Only four of Brown's 18 men, who had seized Harpers Ferry 20 hours earlier, still stood to fight.

Captain Brown had one bargaining chip: hostages. Eleven prominent citizens—including Colonel Lewis Washington and John Allstadt and Terrance Byrne—as well as four armory top executives (the acting superintendent, paymaster's clerk, master armorer, and master machinist) were confined within the fire engine house with Brown. When asked to surrender, Brown presented his terms: "Permit me, my hostages and my men to depart into Maryland unmolested; and I will release the hostages once I deem safety attained."

Brown's offer received no positive response. Negotiation ceased, and impasse ruled. A Monday of terror ended with the advent of darkness.

Then arrived Robert E. Lee and the United States Marines.

CONFLUENCE

Chapter 4
MOTION MATTERS

"The railroad is bringing an empire to our doors."
Baltimore News American, *1828*

The railroads doomed John Brown.

Three and one-half hours, via rail lines, rushed U.S. Marines from Washington to Harpers Ferry. Some years earlier, that same journey of sixty-two miles along the Potomac would have taken three and one-half *days*.

Unlike remote, undeveloped Kansas, where Brown had ample time to plot, prod and pluck the pro-slavery forces, his Harpers Ferry target was not isolated. Railroads east, west and south connected the Ferry to three corners of the compass. Travel from the Ohio River to the Chesapeake Bay had once demanded fifteen days; now, it could be completed in less than one.

Traditionally, the most reliable means of overland transportation had been the horse-drawn stagecoach, illustrated in this Virginia Free Press *clipping. Travelers could access major points of interest for a fee via a network of regularly-scheduled trips.*

Perhaps Brown's gravest strategic error was his failure to calculate the railroads into his Harpers Ferry formula. Captain Brown conceived only that the Harpers Ferry junction offered him no advantage: no train passing through town went due north. Since of no value, he determined the railroad could simply be ignored.

But Brown did not understand the power the railroads offered an aroused and enraged population. Nearly 500 civilian militiamen—riding the rails from nearby towns of Frederick and Martinsburg, and from points afar at Winchester and Baltimore—arrived within hours of the alarm. The express use of the railroads by the military disrupted and foiled Brown's enterprise.

Brown knew his war upon slavery would make history. He did not, however, anticipate that for the first time in American history, railroads would enable a shockingly rapid response to a military crisis.

Opposite: Robert Harper's ferry operation

47

MOTION MATTERS

The water gap at Harpers Ferry has been a beacon for human travel from prehistoric periods.

Archeological evidence suggests that humans habituated the area at least from 10,000 B.C., no doubt drawn to the site by the hole in the mountain. The gap in the Blue Ridge, carved by the combined powers of the Potomac and Shenandoah rivers, can be seen for miles, tantalizing travelers through its wild but appealing aperture. The gap offered an invitation for the indigenous inhabitants to discover the secrets behind a mountain fortress.

English explorers first viewed the breech in the Blue Ridge about a century after the Jamestown settlement. Literally labeled "The Hole," indicating its utilitarian purpose, this inglorious title was tone-deaf to the majestic poetry of native names, "Shenandoah" (daughter of the stars), and "Cohongoroota" (river of wild geese).

For early Europeans, the opening in the mountain provided a doorway into the vast and fertile Shenandoah Valley. Robert Harper ventured this way in 1747, choosing this passage along his route into the heart of the valley. The architect from Philadelphia had been commissioned to build a Quaker meeting house at the fledgling village of Winchester. Following this assignment, Harper returned to "The Hole," recognizing his own opportunities at the confluence. The starry-eyed entrepreneur arranged to take over a primitive ferry operation established fourteen years earlier by a local squatter, and successfully petitioned Virginia's colonial government for a charter to operate his own business—"Mr. Harper's Ferry."

George Washington was only fifteen when Harper established his ferry operation. The youthful lad first viewed the water gap in his late teens while serving as a surveyor for the English Baron Thomas Lord Fairfax. Fairfax's "Northern Neck" land grant included more than six million acres of the Virginia colony, and it was Washington's job to survey its gargantuan boundary. The impression Harpers Ferry forged upon a young Washington would later change not only the confluence, but a nation's destiny.

As world war erupted between the English and French in the middle decades of the eighteenth century (waged, in part, over colonial dominance in North America), Washington visualized the gap not for its beauty, but as a necessity—a military necessity.

Now a major in the Virginia militia fighting aside the British, Washington had just been whipped at Fort Necessity (June 3, 1754) in southwestern Pennsylvania. Blemished by this ignominious defeat, one month later the twenty-two-year-old officer was canoeing down the Potomac. He was seeking a sustainable route for military troops, equipment and supplies to Fort Cumberland, Maryland, 124 miles upriver from Harpers Ferry, and the western-most outpost of the British Empire in America.

Washington discovered rapids covering a river distance of nearly six miles about Harpers Ferry. Just above the Ferry was termed "Shenandoah Falls." In the heart of the gap was the notorious "Spout." Downstream the river roared into "Bull Ring Falls" and "Payne's Falls."

48

CONFLUENCE

The waters proved so rough that Washington nearly capsized. "[T]he canoe I was in, which was not new, had near sunk having received much water on both sides."

The Potomac never developed into this avenue of supply during the French and Indian War. But the venture provided Washington with invaluable insights into its navigation, its rapids and its falls—knowledge he would later use to fulfill his entrepreneurial spirit.

Three decades later, following his triumph as Revolutionary War hero, Washington again turned his attention to his Potomac navigation dream. Losses by the French and British in two wars had opened territory for expansion of the United States from the Ohio River to the great Mississippi. The problem: accessing these vast areas from the eastern seaboard.

No good roads existed connecting east and west. More problematic were the mountains. The Appalachians, "the endless mountains" so familiar to indigenous natives, stretched from Alabama into Canada, forming a natural wall inhibiting entrance into the "Northwest Territory" (as the new nation termed it). Part of this range included the intimidating Alleghenies, 100 miles wide and an average 3,000 feet in elevation, guarding approaches to the west for at least 500 million years.

What could overcome this obstacle?

The Potomac River, according to Washington. Though other routes existed through upstate New York via the Hudson, or through Pennsylvania via the Susquehanna, or through Virginia via the James, Washington promoted the Potomac as the geographic center of the original thirteen colonies. His home river—along which he had accumulated vast property interests—was, argued Washington, "the shortest, easiest & least expensive communication with the invaluable & extensive Country back of us."

> "The River Potomac, shall be considered as a common highway, for the purpose of navigation and commerce to the citizens of Virginia, Maryland and of the United States, and to all other persons in amity with Aid states..."
>
> Mount Vernon Compact
> March, 1785

From the mouth of Patterson's Creek [seven miles below Cumberland] to the Shannondoah Falls you encounter no other obstacles but shallow Water (in places, & this only at certain Seasons) but from hence there is Rocky, Swift & consequently uneven Water for near Six Miles in which distance there are 4 falls. The first is shallow and pretty clear of Rocks which may be avoided by opening a Channel on the Maryland side—Abt 2 Miles from this & half a one below the Mouth of Shanh Iyes [Shenandoah] what is commonly called the Spout which indeed is the principal difficulty. I might almost add the only difficulty of the whole. The water is confined to narrow bounds & having pretty considerable fall at the same time shoots thro, with great rapidity—the risk of passing this sluce [sic] is somewhat increased by the Rockyness [sic] of the bottom which occasioning dry uneven surface. Subjects small Vessels to the danger of filling—I passed it in a Canoe & was near sinking here[.] may likewise be had a passage on the Maryland Shore thro, which Vessells [sic] with ease may be hauled up, after removing some Rocks at a moderate expence [sic].

George Washington, "Remarks I made upon the Navigation of Potomack in the year 1754"

Washington, in his enthusiasm for promoting the Potomac, expressed eagerness to minimize one detail—the Potomac did not slice through the mountains to a direct connection with the Ohio.

This seemed a small matter for the Revolutionary War general, who had success overcoming odds. Washington solved the issue by suggesting the solution was improvement of an existing road between Cumberland and Pittsburgh.

Washington subsequently was elected president of the Patowmack Company. In his August, 1785 inspection visit to view the work at the "Shenandoah Falls" on the Potomac—stretching for about one mile above the confluence—he reported with optimism, "We have got the Potomac navigation in hand—Workmen are employed, and the best Manager and assistants we could obtain."

But persistent problems plagued the Patowmack Company construction effort. In building the "Long Canal" along the Maryland shore to bypass or "skirt" the "Shenandoah Falls," and blasting sluiceway channels through other nearby Harpers Ferry rapids, the company suffered.

Work was dangerous, and the shortage of laborers proved an unending frustration. The company considered "renting" slave labor; but even this option failed for the Harpers Ferry section, as slave owners considered the risk of damage to their human chattels too great for pecuniary return. Furthermore, the company lacked equipment and machinery to remove rocks and boulders from river channels. Not one professional engineer supervised the work. And bad weather and heavy rains made a predictable construction schedule impossible. Nearly a decade would pass before the Harpers Ferry section along the Potomac was completed. By that time, Washington was entering his second term as President of the United States.

Despite the hardships and delays, the Patowmack Company navigation route opened from Cumberland to the port of Georgetown in 1802—fourteen months after Washington's death. A marvelous system of locks allowed travelers to safely bypass the Potomac's ferocious Great Falls, looming just above the nation's capital. Products and goods such as flour, whiskey, iron and coal commenced shipping down the Potomac. The U.S. Armory at the Ferry particularly benefited, receiving iron and coal from upriver suppliers. As many as fifty boatloads of coal arrived in the best years, each boat carrying up to nineteen tons of the burning black rock. The economic effect was immediate. The cost of transporting materials via the water *reduced by one-half* shipping costs via land.

George Washington envisioned opening the Shenandoah River for navigation to complement his Patowmack Company vision.

"In a word, the Shannondaoh which runs thro' the richest tract of country in this State . . . may, with great ease be made navigable 100 miles," Washington declared. It will *"induce hundreds & thousands of [farmers] to cultivate articles from the growth of which they have been entirely discouraged by the length & expence [sic] of land transportation."*

Washington was wrong. No "great ease" existed in opening or maintaining the Shenandoah for shipping. The river rapids above the Harpers Ferry confluence proved especially troublesome. In the river's last eight miles, it dropped dramatically as it plunged its way toward the Blue Ridge gorge, requiring four bypass canals and a river sluice for navigation.

Most burdensome was "Saw Mill Falls" (named after Robert Harper's mill) that commenced one-quarter mile upriver from the Ferry. In this section, the Shenandoah dropped a dramatic seventeen feet, requiring construction of two 100-foot long granite locks and a near mile-long skirting canal. These projects commenced in 1803, but required four years to complete.

Though upriver improvements eventually allowed shipment of goods from more than 100 miles distant, navigation of the Shenandoah never proved prosperous. The canal and locks at Harpers Ferry eventually converted into a source of power for Hall's Rifle Works and later the U.S. Rifle Factory.

ARKS ON THE POTOMAC, GONDOLAS ON THE SHENANDOAH

> *The boats were chiefly flat bottom, though some of them were keeled. They were about seventy feet long and ten feet wide and were covered with tarpaulin stretched over hoops—the top resembling that of a Conestoga wagon, and were manned by a crew of four men, a steersman, a head oars man and two side oars men. The current was usually strong enough to take them down the river, when it was only necessary to steer them, so as to keep them in the channel and off the shoals and rocks. The trip down usually took three days, but the trip back was tedious and laborious, propelling loaded boats against the current with long sweep-oars and pushpoles, and it generally took from eight to ten days.*

Thomas J. C. Williams, History of Allegany County (MD)

Three men guide a batteau down the river. Courtesy of the Library of Virginia.

Subsequent Presidents Continued to Rally for Canals.

"The great object of . . . civil government is the improvement of the condition of those who are parties to the social compact. . . .
Roads and canals, by multiplying and facilitating the communications and intercourse between distant regions and multitudes of men, are among the most important means of improvement. . . .

[W]hile foreign nations less blessed with freedom than ourselves are advancing with gigantic strides in the career of public improvement, were we to slumber in indolence or fold up our arms and proclaim to the world that we are palsied by the will of our constituents, would it not be to cast away the bounties of Providence and doom ourselves to perpetual inferiority?"

~ President John Quincy Adams

Background image: The C & O Canal approaching Harpers Ferry. At right, the C & O at the base of Maryland Heights.

But water itself—or lack thereof—ultimately doomed the Patowmack Company.

"The average duration of the boating time . . . does not much, if at all, exceed eight or ten days passable water for full loaded boats [in fall] and from twenty-five to thirty-five days in the spring," cited a gloomy company report in 1823. "[P]roduce and goods can be stream-borne, in the course of one entire year, from thirty-three to forty-five days."

"[T]he remains of wasted mountains, scattered thickly, and in some places rising over the entire bed of the river, and leaving no passage for loaded boats, impelled by the rapid and impetuous current. . . . By these dangers many boats and cargoes are destroyed."

~ Patowmack Company Commissioners, 1823

Low waters, flood waters, ice-jammed waters and rock-strewn waters condemned the Patowmack Company. Use of the river for only one-eleventh of a year was not a sustainable business model.

"The evils attending the present state of navigation lessen the benefits," its officers sadly reported, and George Washington's company ceased operation.

His dream, however, resuscitated anew through a grander and bolder Potomac vision.

The Patowmack Company spawned one descendent: the Chesapeake & Ohio Canal.

"[T]he improvement of the navigation of the river Potomac, by a canal from the seat of government to the great Cumberland road . . . is an object of inestimable importance . . . to the commercial and political prosperity of the United States," bellowed Charles Fenton Mercer, the first president of the C & O Canal Company.

Perhaps wary of the Patowmack Company's experiences, Mercer's plan differed significantly from Washington's. The C & O would be a "continuous canal," an excavated ditch from beginning to end that would parallel, rather than paddle, the Potomac. Mercer believed that a "slack water" canal with no current, filled with a steady volume of water, would conquer the natural elements that so doomed its predecessor.

The concept of the continuous canal had proven itself. New York proudly boasted the success of the just-completed Erie Canal—a 363-mile wonder that connected the riches of the Midwest, via a Great Lake, with the harbors of New York and Brooklyn, America's two largest cities. The seven-year project, featuring eighty-two lift locks and 550 feet in elevation change, reduced freight rates 95 percent. Its grand opening in 1825 featured ten days of wild celebrations, including marches, balls, fireworks and artillery salutes. New York was proud; America was prouder.

"[We've] created a new era in history," proclaimed the New York governor, "to erect a work, more stupendous, more magnificent, and more beneficial, than has hitherto been achieved by the human race."

The C & O's Mercer intended to outdo the Erie Canal. Concerned its northern rival would draw economic wealth from the heartland—bypassing the Potomac ports of Georgetown and Alexandria, and diminishing the influence of the fledgling capital at Washington—Mercer proposed a canal from Georgetown to Pittsburgh, connecting the Ohio River directly with the Potomac.

This was ambitious, indeed: not for its length, but for its elevation. The effort would demand conquering the Alleghenies—an elevation change nearly two and one-half times that of the Erie Canal. It would require innumerable locks and several tunnels, combating mountain peaks and valleys, and leveling still water into no current. Possible, yes; but improbable—not because engineering did not exist, but because the cost seemed nearly unfathomable. Projected expenses topped $22 million; the Erie, in contrast, had been constructed for $7 million.

CONFLUENCE

> *"To subdue the earth is pre-eminently the purpose of this undertaking. . . . [We pray for] this joint effort of our great community . . . that He would make it one of His chosen instruments for the preservation, prosperity, and perpetuity of our Union."*
>
> President John Quincy Adams
> On occasion of ground-breaking for the C & O Canal at Georgetown
> July 4, 1828

A rival business had a similar vision—not with a canal, but a railroad.

On the same day President Adams was shoveling the first spade of earth for the C & O Canal, just over forty miles to the north, Maryland's Charles Carroll of Carrolton Manor—the last surviving signer of the Declaration of Independence—was laying the cornerstone of the Baltimore & Ohio Railroad.

"We are in fact commencing a new era in our history....[We are] fully prepared to commence the construction of the Great Road," pronounced an elated B & O director.

But this was not a road, not in the traditional sense.

> *"I consider this among the most important acts of my life, second only to my signing the Declaration of Independence, if even it be second to that."*

Charles Carroll of Carrolton
Cornerstone Ceremony, B & O Railroad
Baltimore, Maryland
July 4, 1828

Charles Carroll of Carrollton was an early advocate for American independence—and innovation, despite being initially barred from holding office in colonial Maryland because of his Catholic faith. Carroll lived to a robust age of 95, witnessing extraordinary change: two wars with Britain, the birth of a nation, the ratification of a Bill of Rights affirming his religious freedom, the legal closure of the transatlantic slave trade, and the advent of the steam-powered revolution.

Image: Portrait by Rembrandt Peale (American, 1778-1860). Charles Carroll of Carrollton, ca. 1815-1820. Oil on canvas, 23 x 19in (58.4 x 48.3cm). The Baltimore Museum of Art: Bequest of Ellen Howard Bayard, BMA 1939.180

MOTION MATTERS

The *railroad* was a new-fangled invention, never before tried in America as a means of travel or transport or commerce. Successful short experiments in England showed promise. But the idea of investing in this unproven upstart business, versus the tried and dependable canal, seemed risky at best and crazy at worst.

Yet speculative investors rushed for the railroad stock. "Public excitement [went] far beyond fever heat and reached the boiling point," reported an overjoyed railroad attorney. "Everybody wanted stock.... Parents subscribed in the names of their children... Before a [land]survey had been made—before common sense had been consulted, even, the possession of stock in any quantity was regarded as provision for old age."

The gamble was great. Not only was the railroad untried and untested, it lacked locomotion. No locomotive existed that could climb a mole hill, much less an Allegheny Mountain. Locomotive technology was in its infancy, with some successful testing in England. But in America, no builder existed; no factories produced these futuristic pistons of power. Many sarcastically argued traditional horsepower, featuring actual horses, could outrace a steam locomotive.

Steam power was ascending in the industrial world early in the nineteenth century. The problem was making steam power *mobile*. How does one take a multi-ton engine, fill it with gallons of scalding water, carry along the fuel to heat the boiler, attach it to wheels, and make it move? A question for inventors... and ultimately conquered by American ingenuity, spurred by the innovative B & O Railroad.

Both the B & O and C & O launched with élan.

Headliners like a U.S. president and the last living signer of the Declaration of Independence showed the enthusiasm and promise for these separate ventures. Their propulsion westward soon aborted, however, as both stunningly stalled to a halt. It seemed each enterprise faced the same problem: not enough room along the Potomac River.

Three mountain ranges—Catoctin, South Mountain and the Blue Ridge (from east to west)—protruded as natural enemies against both companies. Vertical walls of clinging cliffs constricted passage through these narrow Potomac gaps, and both the railroad and the canal claimed they had the single lane right of way. Legal spats like this required lawyers, of course; and for three years, the two rivals waged

> **THE SPLENDID PACKET BOAT**
> *The President,*
>
> Has been placed upon the CANAL, to run *daily* between *the Point of Rocks and Harpers-Ferry*, to meet the Rail-Road CARS, running to and from Baltimore.
>
> The PRESIDENT will leave Harpers-Ferry on Tuesday, Thursday, and Saturday, at 5 o'clock, A.M.; and on Monday, Wednesday, Friday, and Sunday, at 11 o'clock, A.M.; and return daily, on the arrival of the Cars from Baltimore.—FARE, One Dollar.
>
> PARTIES of PLEASURE can be accommodated on reasonable terms, by the owner and captain.
>
> Z.M. OFFUTT

This 1833 newspaper ad hints at the complex juncture of canal and railroad at Harpers Ferry..

> "The time will come when people will travel in stages moved by steam engines from one city to another almost as fast as birds can fly, fifteen or twenty miles in an hour ... a carriage will set out from Washington in the morning, the passengers will breakfast in Baltimore, dine in Philadelphia, and sup at New York the same day."

The words of inventor Oliver Evans, spoken in 18[??] portended the revolution in speed that would transform American life as the century progress[ed]. The advertisement at right was published less than twenty years later in the *Virginia Free Press*. Even with disjointed system of transfers from coach to canal to train car around Harpers Ferry, travel time overall had decreased significantly.

From Winchester to Baltimore.

THROUGH IN ONE DAY!

In order to extend still further the facilities extended to travelers, the undersigned have placed upon the route between Winchester and Baltimore an additional line of first rate Coaches, by which gentlemen travelling from Winchester to Baltimore will be enabled to perform the trip in one day.

This line has commenced running, and will hereafter leave Winchester on the mornings of Mondays, Tuesdays, Thursdays, and Saturdays, and arrive at Harpers-Ferry in time to catch the Cars which arrive in Baltimore the same evening.

A. HUMRICKHOSUE & CO.
April 24, 1831

combat in Maryland's courts. Despite being represented by renowned attorneys Daniel Webster (the "Great Orator" of the Congress) and Roger Brooke Taney (soon Chief Justice of the U.S. Supreme Court), the railroad eventually lost. The court ruled the C & O Canal had precedence of right-of-way since it was the successor of the eighteenth-century Patowmack Company.

Maryland, however, wanted both companies to succeed. The state had invested in both, believing each could bring commercial riches to its citizens and its coffers. And Baltimore demanded action. The fourth largest city in the country must have its connection with the Ohio. So the legislature concocted a deal. The two would share the Potomac shore from Point of Rocks (twelve miles downriver from the Ferry) to Harpers Ferry. Then their paths must split. The C & O would retain its Potomac route; the B & O *must cross the Potomac* and continue its avenue westward through Virginia.

This decision permitted the B & O's continuance, but with complications. The railroad had not planned for a bridge across the Potomac; and once across the river, where would it go?

The U.S. Armory owned the Potomac shoreline, and there seemed no place to cram a railroad into the densely-packed town at the confluence. Would the Maryland side of Harpers Ferry thus become the western terminus of the B & O?

No. The Ohio River remained the goal, and the B & O had become adept at patience and persistence in order to achieve its promise. The government drove a hard bargain. It granted the railroad a right-of-way *in the river*. It required the B & O to parallel the

MOTION MATTERS

Potomac factory, literally building a wall and filling in nearly thirty feet of river shore. This proved highly advantageous to the armory, as it provided a needed flood buffer for its musket factory.

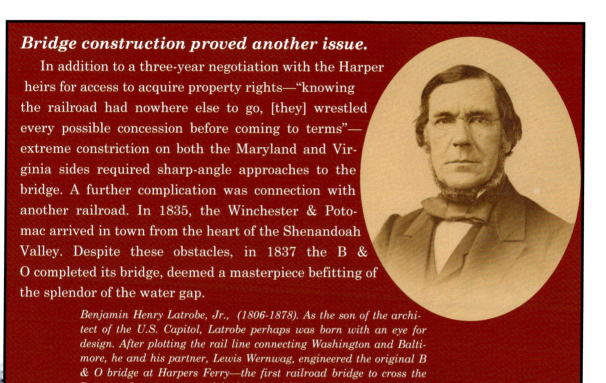

Bridge construction proved another issue.

In addition to a three-year negotiation with the Harper heirs for access to acquire property rights—"knowing the railroad had nowhere else to go, [they] wrestled every possible concession before coming to terms"—extreme constriction on both the Maryland and Virginia sides required sharp-angle approaches to the bridge. A further complication was connection with another railroad. In 1835, the Winchester & Potomac arrived in town from the heart of the Shenandoah Valley. Despite these obstacles, in 1837 the B & O completed its bridge, deemed a masterpiece befitting of the splendor of the water gap.

Benjamin Henry Latrobe, Jr., (1806-1878). As the son of the architect of the U.S. Capitol, Latrobe perhaps was born with an eye for design. After plotting the rail line connecting Washington and Baltimore, he and his partner, Lewis Wernwag, engineered the original B & O bridge at Harpers Ferry—the first railroad bridge to cross the Potomac. Image courtesy of the Maryland Historical Society.

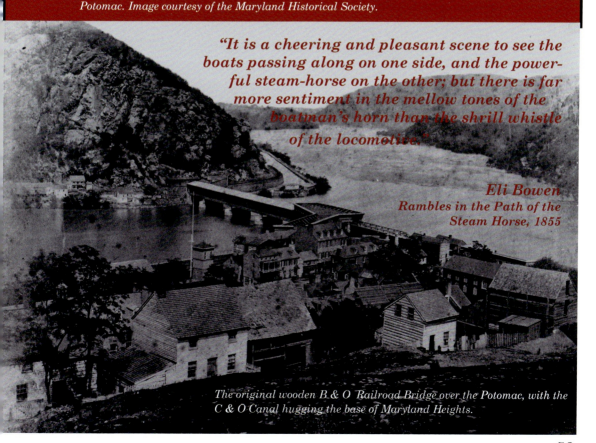

"It is a cheering and pleasant scene to see the boats passing along on one side, and the powerful steam-horse on the other; but there is far more sentiment in the mellow tones of the boatman's horn than the shrill whistle of the locomotive."

Eli Bowen
Rambles in the Path of the Steam Horse, 1855

The original wooden B & O Railroad Bridge over the Potomac, with the C & O Canal hugging the base of Maryland Heights.

58

New Industry, New Titles, New Time

The B & O Railroad, as a nascent technology, created hundreds of new jobs, new occupations, and new sounds. "Engineer," "Conductor," "Brakeman," and "Porter" had new dictionary meanings, along with "Fireman"—the worker shoveling coal into a locomotive's boiler. "Cars" now referred to vehicles conveying coal or freight or passengers. The "Baggage Master" had a particular function, not only to "receive, check, handle and dispose of baggage, carefully asking its destination," but also to be "perfectly good humored and civil to all, and even when passengers are otherwise."

The steam-engine whistle, never before heard in Harpers Ferry, began echoing off the mountains. One sharp blast indicated the engineer's readiness to begin, and was the signal for the brakemen to release the brakes. Two sharp blasts, in quick succession, meant apply the brakes—"and conductors and brakemen, on hearing it, [must] exert themselves vigorously, avoiding the loss of time caused by looking to see what [was] the matter." A continuous blast of the whistle signaled the approach of road crossings, stations and curves.

Since train schedules depended upon time—and no universal time-keeper existed in the United States when the railroads commenced (nor could time be communicated easily)—clock accuracy became an imperative. "[E]ach passenger train conductor must inspect the clocks which he had opportunity to see," read the B & O's operating manual. He must "notify the agents on every outward trip of their error, if any; and on his return to Baltimore report the state of each clock as he found it, by entering it with the date and his name in the ticket office." The manual required agents of stations to regulate their clocks in conformance with the master clock at Mount Clare station (in Baltimore), "kept in conformity with the standard."

The railroad also created "Rolling Stock"—heavy contraptions never before conceived by human kind. Twenty years after the B & O's arrival on the Maryland shore opposite Harpers Ferry, its equipment inventory included 2,200 "burthen cars, nearly all of eight wheels, and of an average capacity of about eight tons each." Of these, about 500 were used exclusively to transport coal. The B & O also sported 160 passenger cars and 110 locomotives. The passenger locomotives had "4-drive wheels," capable of riding the rails "with the swiftness of the tempest." Freight locomotives had eight-drive wheels, powered by coal, with capability of "pulling the load of 400-500 horses."

MOTION MATTERS

> *"Railways have been constructed, and are in progress, in all parts of the civilized world, and philosophers have already begun to speculate on the astonishing effects which such a means of rapid locomotion must have on the character and prospects of the whole human race, and the only question is, where will this railway impulse end? [I]nto what strange condition of humanity is it leading us?"*
>
> Eli Bowen, *Rambles in the Path of the Steam-Horse*, 1855

For all its innovations, the B & O Railroad did not welcome all travelers.

A concern existed, in fact, that it could become incorporated into the Underground Railroad, assisting enslaved persons with escape to freedom. The B & O's original western terminus at Wheeling sat on the edge of the Pennsylvania and Ohio borders—both Free states. The speed and ease of the railroad could facilitate fleeing slaves frequenting free soil. The threat of the railroad abetting fugitive slaves clamored into the Maryland legislature, producing this law (abridged beside) in 1839, a time that witnessed the rise of abolitionism.

AN ACT TO PREVENT THE TRANSPORTATION OF PEOPLE OF COLOR ON RAILROADS

WHEREAS it has been represented to this General Preamble Assembly that the owners of slaves in this State have suffered great loss by the facilities of escape, afforded to slaves by means of Rail Roads and Steam Boats, therefore for remedy of said evil.

Section 1. **Be it enacted by the General Assembly of Maryland,** That it shall not be lawful for any slave to be transported on any rail road . . . without a permission in writing from the owner of such slave, under the penalty of five hundred dollars for every violation of this act, to be recovered in the name of the State, from the president, directors and company of said rail road.

Sec. 2. **and be it enacted,** That if any slave or slaves shall escape from his or their owner or owners, by being transported on said rail roads, the master or mistress, or owner or owners thereof, shall and may recover the value of such slave or slaves from the president, directors and company of said rail road.

Exception . Sec. 3…**And be it enacted,** That the provisions of the first section of this act shall not be construed to extend to any slave travelling in company with his, or their master or mistress, his, her or their agent, or as the servant or attendant of any white person or persons, bonafide employed for that purpose.

TRAVELLING ON THE WINCHESTER & POTOMAC RAIL-ROAD

The Cars leave the depot at Winchester at 7 o'clock in the morning—
Will pass Stevenson's at half past 7, where passengers can be taken up or set down—
Thompson's depot at 15 min. past 8—
Cameron's do. at half past 8—
Charlestown about 9—and
Halltown half past 9—
Arriving at Harpers-Ferry in time for passengers to take the morning cars to Baltimore.

RETURNING
They leave Harpers-Ferry at 4 o'clock in the afternoon;
Arrive at Halltown at half past 4—
At Charlestown about 5—
Cameron's 15 minutes past 5—
Thompson's about half pat 5—
Stevenson's about 6—and
Reach Winchester about 7 o'clock in the evening.
JOHN BRUCE.

Winchester, March 31, 1836

Left: Winchester & Potomac Railroad Schedule. Via horse carriage, this journey could take two days. Above, a china plate depicting an early locomotive on the B & O.

Nine years had passed since the railroad and canal had kicked off their construction.

During that decade, the revolution of railroads had become apparent, antiquating the slower plodding canal. Advances in locomotive technology guaranteed twenty miles per hour—ten times faster than a mule-driven barge. It became far easier and cheaper to build railroad grade than to excavate canal prisms; and railroads became "rivers of rails" rather than canals dependent upon rivers. Railroads, as well, could go where no water existed; and even mountainous slopes were tamed by the rails. "Scientific power [will] conquer space," wrote a railroad advocate, "and even the Alleghenies sink . . . beneath the pressure of unconquered steam."

These advantages brought the B & O triumph. It reached the Ohio River at Wheeling, its first train chugging into that targeted town on New Year's Day, 1853.

A dream of George Washington's had been fulfilled—with an innovative technology impossible for Washington to dream—nearly a century after his inaugural vision.

Nor had Washington visualized the coming of John Brown.

Chapter 5
FURY AND FIRE

No night in Harpers Ferry had been more miserable.
Four civilians dead. Nine militiamen wounded. Six of John Brown's soldiers killed; three more wounded; two captured. Two of Brown's sons dying on the cold brick floor of the armory's fire engine house. Eleven prominent citizens held hostage. More than 500 soldiers around town.

What would the morrow bring?

United States Marines.

Inside the engine house

President James Buchanan had received wild reports of slave insurrection at Harpers Ferry. Sources estimated up to 750 abolitionists and slaves had seized the U.S. government's armory and arsenal and declared full scale war. The White House had little for response. The U.S. Army was small, with most of it scattered 2,000 miles away on the western frontier. In Washington, few officers resided; and the Department of War, during a period of peace, was stagnating. The commander-in-chief had limited resources for this national emergency.

Fortunately for Buchanan, the U.S. Marines maintained a barracks within the Washington Navy Yard, just over three miles distant from the White House. Orders ar-

CONFLUENCE

rived at 1 p.m. on Monday, October 17, for the ninety marines stationed there to embark immediately for Harpers Ferry.

Just as fortunate for the President, a veteran U.S. Army officer—a former West Point superintendent with wartime experience—happened to be home on leave when Harpers Ferry erupted. Word arrived at Arlington House—the stately Virginia residence of Lieutenant Colonel Robert E. Lee that overlooked the capital—to rush to the War Department for orders. Soon Lee was traveling on a special train for Baltimore, and thence to the Ferry, departing so quickly that he left home without donning his army uniform. A young cavalry lieutenant named James Ewell Brown ("Jeb") Stuart accompanied Lee as his aide.

By 11 p.m. on Monday—almost exactly 24 hours after Brown had arrived—Lee, Stuart and the marines entered Harpers Ferry. Lee first relieved the militia troops, surrounding the armory fire engine house with the marines "to prevent the possibility of escape by the insurgents." He contemplated making an attack at midnight, but deferred, "for fear of sacrificing the lives of some of the gentlemen held by them as prisoners."

Meanwhile, misery and anxiety permeated the interior of Brown's "fort."

> ***Near total darkness consumed the gloom; no heat existed on the cold, damp night; and hunger prevailed, as most had not eaten in more than a day.***

At twenty years old, Oliver was the youngest of John Brown's sons to accompany him to Harpers Ferry. He had previously fought beside his father in Kansas—only a teenager at the time. Despite his youth, Oliver was also a husband and father-to-be. The baby he never met, along with his wife, died just a few months later.

Few sounds were heard, other than breathing and the agony of Oliver Brown, suffering from a mortal wound. So painful was Oliver's injury, he asked his father to shoot him to end the agony. "You will get over it," snapped his father. "If you must die, die like a man." Sometime later, Captain Brown called out to Oliver, but received no response. "I guess he is dead," said Brown.

Despite their desperation, neither Brown nor his four remaining soldiers flinched. "[N]o one of Brown's men showed the slightest fear," recalled John E. P. Daingerfield, one of the hostages and the armory's acting paymaster. "[They] calmly awaited the attack, selecting the best situations to fire from upon the attacking party, and arranging their guns and pistols so that a fresh one could be taken up as soon as one was discharged." Portholes through the brick walls had been chiseled, and the two fire engines barricaded the doors to prevent easy entry.

At one point during the endless night, Daingerfield conversed with Brown, citing his war an act of treason.

FURY AND FIRE

"Are we committing treason against our country by being here?" asked two soldiers of their leader.

"Certainly," answered Brown. "We thought we came to liberate the slaves, and did not know that was committing treason."

Hours passed.

Just before dawn, Stuart drew near the fire engine house with a surrender demand from Colonel Lee. "I approached the door in the presence of perhaps 2,000 spectators," recorded Stuart. "[B]rown opened the door about four inches, and placed his body against the crack, with a cocked carbine in his hand."

"Are you ready to surrender and trust to the mercy of the Government?" inquired Stuart.

"No!" Brown replied. "I prefer to die here."

After an extended discussion in which Brown demanded that he, his men, and their prisoners be permitted safe passage in exchange for eventual release of his hostages in Maryland, Stuart ceased negotiating. He backed away from the door. Then, he waved his cap—the signal for attack.

The marines vaulted into action. Three sprang forward with sledgehammers, attempting to bash through the barricaded doors. "Those inside fired rapidly at the point where the blows were given upon the door," remembered Lieutenant Israel Green, the marine commander; but "very little impression was made with the hammers."

CONFLUENCE

Frustrated by this failure, Green spotted a nearby ladder. He ordered 12 marines to use it as a battering ram. In a hazardous operation, the marines stormed the door. The first strike failed to break through. A second attempt hurled forward. It shattered "a ragged hole low down in the right hand door, the door being splintered and cracked some distance upward." Through this opening—so small that only *one* man could crawl through at a time—sprang Lieutenant Green.

Seconds later, Private Luke Quinn climbed head-first through the hole and was shot with a mortal wound to the abdomen. Private Matthew Ruppert stepped forward next and received a bullet in his face. More marines barged through the widening gap

"Quicker than thought I brought my saber down with all my strength on [Brown's] head. He was moving as the blow fell, and I suppose I did not strike him where I intended for he received a deep saber cut in the back of his neck. He fell senseless on his side, then rolled over on his back. He had in his hand a short sharp cavalry carbine...

Instinctively as Brown fell I gave him a saber thrust in the left breast. The sword I carried was a light uniform weapon, and either not having a point or striking something hard in Brown's accoutrements, did not penetrate. The blade bent double.

By that time three or four of my men were inside. They came rushing in like tigers, as a storming assault is not a play day sport. They bayoneted one hiding under [a fire] engine, and pinned another fellow up against the rear wall, both being instantly killed. I ordered the men to spill no more blood. The other insurgents were at once taken under arrest, and the contest ended. The whole fight had not lasted over three minutes."

~Lt. Israel Green

in the doors. They spied combatant Jeremiah Anderson, immediately bayoneted and dragged him out vomiting gore. He died in minutes. Dauphin Thompson, whose brother had been unceremoniously executed the previous day, was pierced with a bayonet and pinned against the wall, killed instantly. Captain Brown was prostrate; alive, but in a bloody heap. Green ordered a halt to further combat, saving fighters Edwin Coppoc and Shields Green from similar fates. Brown's men never turned upon their prisoners; not a single hostage was injured.

By 7:30 a.m. on Tuesday, October 18, 1859—thirty-four hours after Brown's arrival at Harpers Ferry—the government had reclaimed complete possession of the armory.

John Brown's war had ended.
Or had it just begun?

An interrogation of Brown as a prisoner commenced the afternoon of his capture.

Bruised, bandaged and bloodied, Brown answered that he was "glad to make himself and his motives clearly understood."

The notoriety of his attack attracted a high-powered audience of questioners, including the governor of Virginia, a U.S. senator from Virginia, the congressman representing the lower Shenandoah Valley, and a congressman from Ohio. Also in the room were Colonel Lee, Jeb Stuart, and a curious press reporter representing the *New York Herald*—among the top circulating newspapers in the country.

"Mr. Brown, who sent you here?" inquired Congressman Clement Vallandingham of Ohio.

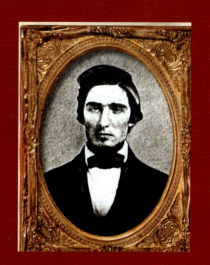

Jeremiah Goldsmith Anderson was a 27-year old native of Indiana who was killed in the fire engine house during the final stance against the U.S. Marine attack. One day after Independence Day, July 5, 1859, he wrote of his determination to continue fighting with John Brown for freedom:

"Millions of fellow-beings require it of us; their cries for help go out to the universe daily and hourly. Whose duty is it to help them? Is it yours? Is it mine? It is every man's, but how few there are to help. But there are a few who dare to answer this call, and dare to answer it in a manner that will make this land of liberty and equality shake to the centre."

"No man sent me here," retorted Brown. "[I]t was my own prompting and that of my Maker, or that of the devil, which ever you please to ascribe it to. I acknowledge no man in human form."

CONFLUENCE

"How do you justify your acts?" asked Senator James Mason of Virginia.

"I think, my friend, you are guilty of a great wrong against God and humanity," responded Brown. "[I]t would be perfectly right in any one to interfere with you so far as to free those you willfully and wickedly hold in bondage."

"Did you expect a general rising of the slaves [insurrection] in case of your success?" queried Vallandingham.

"No, sir; nor did I wish it. I expected to gather them up from time to time and set them free."

> November 10, 1859
>
> To Daughter Eugenia
>
> I tell you some of these fellows are as hard to kill as any grisly bear, even old Brown, he is cut and hacked all to pieces within yet he is as fierce as a lion. They are a hard set of customers, they are all perfect Infidels having no faith in the Bible, and are all imbued with free loveism, Socialism, Spiritualism and every other ism that was ever thought of by man or Devil, & hence this recklessness of Character.
>
> George Mauzy

As the three-hour interview labored toward a conclusion, the reporter for the *New York Herald* commented: "I do not wish to annoy you, but if you have anything further you would say I will report it."

"I claim to be here carrying out a measure I believe perfectly justifiable, and not to act the part of any incendiary or ruffian, but to aid those suffering great wrong."

Brown then issued this warning:

"[Y]ou had better—all you people of the South—prepare yourselves for a settlement of that question that must come up for settlement sooner than you are prepared for. . . . You may dispose of me very easily. I am nearly disposed of now. But this question is still to be settled—this negro question I mean—the end of that is not yet."

Brown's admonition did not go unnoticed. Concerned additional abolitionists would follow Brown's model, security at the armory and arsenal increased dramatically. "I was one of the twenty-four who stood guard for twenty-three nights employed . . .

> **To Daughter Eugenia**   **November 10, 1859**
>
> "I made [your brother George] a blue jacket with gilt buttons, on Saturday evening he wore it and the boys called him Captain of the Marines. He says tell sister I've a pistol and I am going to shoot N—ers with it. His paps gave him a double barrel Pistol and sometimes he will hold it and let him shoot it off. Everyone children and all seems to have a warlike feeling."
>
> — Mary Mauzy

at $1 a night," beamed Joseph Mauzy in a letter to his sister Eugenia. "I am now a regular night watchman at the rifle works."

Harpers Ferry, and most of Jefferson County, assumed a war-like appearance as Brown and his captured comrades were imprisoned in Charles Town's jail the day following the marine assault.

Town citizens caught off guard now transformed into vigilantes. "I have a rifle and pistol at my house and [the armory superintendent] promised me more," boasted George Mauzy to his daughter Eugenia. "So you see I have quite an armory, even one of Hall's rifles . . . they have the advantage of the bayonet."

Governor Henry Wise assembled the largest military force in Virginia since the War of 1812 when he ordered nearly 2,000 Old Dominion militiamen into Jefferson

Although the prime suspect was severely crippled by his wounds, a veritable army guarded Brown's passage between jail and courthouse during his trial.

CONFLUENCE

County. They guarded the jail house, the court house, the county seat, Harpers Ferry, and the county border along the Potomac. Alarmed by Brown's stunning surprise and his residency in their midst, the Virginians determined they would not be fooled again.

The fear of slave insurrection spread far beyond the confines of Harpers Ferry. "Virginia is arming to the teeth," exclaimed former President John Tyler, himself a Virginian. "[M]ore than 50,000 stands of arms already distributed, and the demand for more daily increasing."

A volcanic anger erupted as well. "All Virginia [will] stand forth as one man and say to fanaticism," declared James L. Kemper before the General Assembly in Richmond, that "whenever you advance a hostile foot upon our soil, we will welcome you with bloody hands and hospitable graves."

Hospitable graves did not honor the lives of John Brown's dead soldiers. Harpers Ferry authorities were at loss. What disposition for the bodies of the insurgents? "Sepulture in one of the village cemeteries was, in view of the excited state of the public mind, out of the question."

The answer was to bury the bodies in a remote location "in order that the place might be unknown or forgotten in a short time." Subsequently, seven corpses of Brown's men were packed into two "store boxes," carried across the Shenandoah bridge in a freight wagon, and buried in a hole near the shore, one-half mile upriver, in an un-marked grave—victims of a failed war.

The body of John Brown's son Watson suffered a worse fate. His remains were crammed into a barrel and shipped to the medical college at Winchester for anatomical exam and phrenology—the detailed study of the shape and size of the cranium as a supposed indication of character and mental abilities. Watson was placed on display in the museum of the college "well prepared for preservation" and containing "all the muscles, arteries and nerves," as a "specimen and as an object of interest and note." According to the professor responsible for Watson's corpse, "Virginia was entitled to the body as an object of warning."

Warning indeed. John Brown epitomized the most terrible of Southern fears. Brown, in fact, represented a horror worse than the Nat Turner slave insurrection nearly three decades earlier. Insurrections, led by blacks, were expected in the South. Insurrection to attain freedom, a universal human desire, was a logical anticipation that produced a cultural and racial phobia for whites throughout the South. Fear of a black slave uprising was omnipresent. But Brown was a *white man* who came to free black slaves. Brown was a Northerner—*an invader*—who came to interfere. Brown was poison.

John Avis, the Charles Town jailer, helped Brown recover from his wounds while awaiting trial and, ultimately, execution. He developed a friendly rapport with the abolitionist and grew to respect Brown as a man of principle.

WHAT BECAME OF THE SLAVES?

Eleven local enslaved males entered Harpers Ferry with John Brown's soldiers during the early morning hours of Monday, October 17, 1859. Colonel Lewis Washington owned three; John Allstadt possessed seven; and another was "hired out" to Colonel Washington. Debate exists over whether they came as volunteers or whether Brown's men forced them to join their effort. "No Negro from this neighborhood appeared to take up arms voluntarily," testified Colonel Washington. But no evidence exists—from the slaves' perspectives—that confirms or counters this notion.

According to contemporary accounts, following the capture of Brown and the end of hostilities in Harpers Ferry, nine of the 11 slaves returned to their homes. History does not record what became of them.

George Mauzy's account to his daughter, written six weeks after the attack, details what happened to the remaining two slaves:

> A colored man Jim, belonging to Dr. Fuller of Winchester, & hired to [Colonel] Washington, was with the party at the Rifle Factory, (and probably the only volunteer from this county), in attempting to cross the [Shenandoah], was drowned in A. H. Herr's millpond[.]
>
> [O]ne of J. H. Alstadt's [sic] men was with this same party, & when they all started to run, he ran too, and hid himself in some bushes, and weeds, but was taken prisoner, and in such a frightened condition that he was taken sick and in a very few days after, died in jail."

"The fruit of Satanic doctrines," recorded the Virginia *Petersburg Express*. A fruit "inculcated by the rabid and unprincipled teachers of the [abolitionist] schools."

Or was Brown, as ascribed by abolitionist preacher Theodore Parker, "one bright clear flash into the Southern ground?"

CONFLUENCE

Brown's trial began one week after his capture, with Judge Richard Parker—himself a slave owner and a slave trader—presiding.

Brown asked for a postponement due to his wounded condition and the blows suffered to his head at the hand of Lieutenant Green. "My memory don't serve me," he apprised the court. "My health is insufficient, although improving." Parker rejected a delay, and then assigned defense counsel.

Brown bristled. "The Governor of the State of Virginia tended me his assurances that I should have a fair trial; and under no circumstances whatever will I be able to have a fair trial. If you seek my blood, you can have it at any moment, without this mockery of a trial."

Despite Brown's objections, a jury was selected, court convened, and indictments levied. Brown was charged with murder, treason and inciting slave insurrection.

Brown's appointed defense lawyers, including one who had led Charles Town militia against the insurgents, first attempted an insanity plea. Brown objected. More friendly attorneys then arrived from the North to defend the fiery abolitionist. The trial lasted five days and included testimony from twenty-two witnesses—twelve for the prosecution and ten for the defense. Star witnesses included Lewis Washington, John Allstadt and his son, conductor Phelps of the B & O Railroad, the bridge night watchman, Dr. Starry, and armory officials held captive in the fire engine house.

The jury of white males, some of them slave holders, deliberated for 45 minutes. The verdicts: guilty of murder; guilty of treason; guilty of insurrection.

On November 2, 1859, Judge Parker sentenced John Brown to death by hanging.

Thirty days would pass between sentencing and execution day. One month that ruptured the nation.

"The notorious horse thief, murderer, insurrectionist and traitor expiated his guilt," declared an angry *Savannah Daily Morning News*. "There are thousands of white-cravated necks in New England and the Northern states today that are as deserving of John Brown's hempen tie."

Northerners viewed Brown differently.

Brown meets with his wife Mary just days before his execution.

"The Lord High Admiral of the Almighty," abolitionist preacher Wendell Phillips proclaimed. "[Brown] has twice as much right to hang Governor Wise as Governor Wise has to hang him." Phillips extolled Brown "as a repre-sentative of law, of government, of right, of justice, of religion."

Perplexed Southerners asked, how could this be? Brown, by judgment of a jury, broke the law (slavery was legal); created his own constitution (treason defined); attacked the government (Harpers Ferry Armory); murdered citizens (four innocent civilians dead); and claimed he was chosen by God (beware false prophets).

But many Northerners disagreed. "These men, in teaching us how to die, have at the same time taught us how to live," mused transcendental philosopher Henry David Thoreau.

Abhorred by the public opinion rift between North and South, more moderate voices cautioned against Brown's execution and instead recommended a life sentence.

"To hang a fanatic is to make a martyr of him," warned the *New York Journal of Commerce* (predecessor to the *Wall Street Journal*). "Monsters are hydra-headed, and decapitulation only quickens vitality and its power of reproduction."

Father M. A. Costello served the Catholic parish at Harpers Ferry, where he had "a very pretty little church, capable of holding between 400 and 500 persons." He administered the last Sacraments to two civilians killed who were members of his church; and he dispensed "the holy writs of the Church" to Marine Private Luke Quinn, the only marine fatally wounded in the assault against the fire engine house.

Costello described his meeting with John Brown in his jail cell:

> I visited 'Old Brown,' who was the commanding general of the invaders, some time previous to his execution, and he informed me that he was a Congregationalist. He said that he would not receive the services of any minister of religion, for he believed that they, as apologists of slavery, had violated the laws of nature and of God, and that they ought first to sanctify themselves by becoming abolitionists, and then they might be worth to minister unto him. Let them follow St. Paul's advice, he said, and go and break the chains of the slaves, and then they may preach to others. I told him that I was not aware of St. Paul's ever giving any such advice, but that I remembered an epistle of St. Paul to Philemon, where we are informed that he sent back the fugitive slave Onesimus from Rome to his master. I then asked him what he thought of that, and he said that he did not care what St. Paul did, but what he said, and not even what he said if it was in favour of slavery!"

JOHN BROWN'S SPEECH TO THE COURT ON LEARNING OF HIS DEATH SENTENCE

I have, may it please the Court, a few words to say. In the first place, I deny everything but what I have all along admitted, of a design on my part to free slaves. I intended certainly to have made a clean thing of that matter, as I did last winter when I went into Missouri, and there took slaves without the snapping of a gun on either side, moving them through the country, and finally leaving them in Canada. I designed to have done the same thing again on a larger scale. That was all I intended to do. I never did intend murder or treason, or the destruction of property, or to excite or incite the slaves to rebellion, or to make insurrec-tion.

I have another objection, and that is that it is unjust that I should suffer such a penalty. Had I inter-fered in the manner, which I admit, and which I admit has been fairly proved—for I admire the truthful-ness and candor of the greater portion of the witnesses who have testified in this case—had I so inter-fered in behalf of any of the rich, the powerful, the intelligent, the so-called great, or in behalf of any of their friends . . . and suffered and sacrificed what I have in this interference, it would have been all right, and every man in this court would have deemed it an act worthy of reward rather than punishment.

This court acknowledges, too, as I suppose, the validity of the law of God. I see a book kissed, which I suppose to be the Bible, or at least the New Testament, which teaches me that all things whatsoever I would that men should do to me, I should do even so to them. It teaches me further to remember them that are in bonds, as bound with them. I endeavored to act up to that instruction. I say I am yet too young to understand that God is any respecter of persons. I believe that to have interfered as I have done, as I have always freely admitted I have done in behalf of His despised poor, in no wrong, but right.

Now, if it is deemed necessary that I should forfeit my life for the furtherance of the ends of justice, and mingle my blood further with the blood of my children and with the blood of millions in this slave *country* whose rights are disregarded by wicked, cruel, and unjust enactments—I submit; so let it be done!

Brown, left center, still suffering from his wounds, spent most of his court time lying on a cot.

Edwin Coppoc, captured with John Brown in the armory fire engine house, was sentenced to hang in Charles Town two weeks after the execution of Brown. The 24-year-old Quaker, originally from Salem, Ohio, wrote a letter to his uncle from his jail cell just before his own execution on December 16, 1859:

I seat myself by the stand, to write for the first and last time to thee and thy family. Though far from home and overtaken by misfortune, I have not forgotten thee. . . .

Thank God, the principles of the cause in which we are engaged will not die with me and my brave comrades. . . . The cause of everlasting truth and justice will go on conquering, to conquer, until our broad and beautiful land shall rest beneath the banner of freedom.

I have hoped to live to see the dawn of that glorious day. I had hoped to live to see the principles of our Declaration of Independence fully realized. I had hoped to see the dark stain of slavery blotted from our land, and the libel on our boasted freedom erased[.] . . .

But this cannot be. I have heard my sentence passed. My doom is sealed. But two more short days remain for me to fulfill my earthly destiny. But two days between me and eternity. At the expiration of these two days, I shall stand upon the scaffold to take my last look at earthly scenes, but that scaffold has but little dread for me[.] . . .

By the taking of my life and the lives of my comrades, Virginia is but hastening on that glorious day when the slave shall rejoice in his freedom. When he can say, 'I, too, am a man, and am groaning no more under the yoke of oppression!'

CONFLUENCE

As the country raged over the meaning of John Brown, he approached his forthcoming execution with his own understanding. "I have been whipped, as the saying is," he informed his wife Mary, "but I am sure I can recover all the lost capital occasioned by the disaster by only hanging a few moments by the neck."

Six weeks after his capture, John Brown ascended the scaffold.

The hanging platform, constructed in an empty field three blocks from the Charles Town court room, stood starkly against the picturesque background of the Blue Ridge. Nearly 2,000 Virginia militiamen surrounded the execution site, firearms loaded and bayonets fixed, with artillery guarding every approach to the county seat. Many feared a last-minute rescue by Northern abolitionists. No civilians were allowed.

Brown faced his final moments with firm resolve. He also deemed satisfaction, knowing he had "stirred the sluggish blood" of both North and South over the conundrum of slavery. The first Sunday of Advent was two days away; perhaps an American advent was approaching.

At 11:30 a.m. on December 2, 1859, the rope was cut. A voice echoed in the crisp winter air. "So perish all such enemies of Virginia! All such enemies of the Union! All such foes of the human race!"

Major John T. L. Preston of the Virginia Military Institute felt assured by his pronouncement of John Brown's death. But he miscalculated. Brown's flesh died, but his soul did not perish.

In the North, on execution day, church bells clanged in Brown's honor. Ministers held special memorial services. Banks closed in memory of Brown. Communities staged parades. Newspaper editors lauded him with praise.

FURY AND FIRE

Ralph Waldo Emerson labeled Brown "a pure idealist of artless goodness"; and his younger Concord contemporary, Louisa May Alcott, worshiped Brown as "St. John the Just."

William Lloyd Garrison, among the North's most tenacious and vocal abolitionists, compared Brown's efforts at revolution with that of America's fight for independence. "Was John Brown justified in his attempt?" queried Garrison. "Yes! . . . if Washington was in his."

Southerners, infuriated by the martyrdom conferred upon Brown, demanded separation.

"Have we no right to allege that to secure our rights and protect our honor, we will dissever the ties that bind us together, even if it rushes us into a sea of blood!" decried Jefferson Davis, Mississippi's U.S. Senator, in a speech in the Senate chamber.

"The day of compromise is passed," announced South Carolina's *Charleston Mercury*. "The South must control her own destinies, or perish."

And Virginia's *Richmond Enquirer* offered this dire assessment: "The Harpers Ferry invasion has advanced the cause of Disunion more than any other event that has happened since the formation of the Government."

What just happened?

What was about to happen?

John Brown offered his own prediction. Just before ascending the scaffold, he handed his jailor a hand-written note. The man stuffed the paper away, but soon after the execution, he witnessed these final words:

"I John Brown am now quite certain that the crimes of this guilty land; will never be purged away; but with Blood."

Chapter 6
WAR WOUNDS

"*No spot in the United States experienced more horrors of the war.*"

~Joseph Barry, resident

George Washington never envisioned his beloved Potomac River as an international boundary—especially not within his own country.

Six decades after Washington's death, the land the fabled general had liberated, the country he had built, and the nation he had led was at war with itself. The great grandchildren of the parents of the American Revolution had broken their United States into the *divided states*.

"We have truly fallen upon evil times," wrote George Mauzy, as the first flames of Civil War engulfed his home industry in Harpers Ferry.

As war dawned, no one could measure its length; no one could predict its outcome. But one matter was certain—Harpers Ferry was in a precarious place.

Situated on the edge of Virginia, the Ferry teetered on the border between North and South. Maryland, its neighbor, indeed was a slave state; but Maryland remained loy-

WAR WOUNDS

al to the United States. Virginia, on the other hand, cast its future with the fledgling Confederate States of America. The federal factory town of Harpers Ferry discovered itself suddenly, secretly seceded, and in a new country.

On April 18, 1861, Armory Superintendent Alfred Barbour, fomenting with passion, returned from Richmond. Fort Sumter had surrendered the week before, attacked by Southern forces in Charleston, South Carolina. To meet the emergency, President Abraham Lincoln called upon all states to send troops to quash the rebellion. Virginia must respond.

Alfred Barbour

Barbour, a federal employee (and until now, an advocate for the Union), informed his stunned community that the armory and arsenal no longer belonged to the United States. Instead, these resources were now possessions of a seceded Virginia. The reasons were irrefutable. Virginia could not take up arms against its Southern brothers and sisters. Virginia—the largest slave population state in the country—could not break with Southern social norms. Southern culture and the Southern economy demanded Virginia. Virginians must be Southerners first, and unite against Northern aggression. And lest not forget, Virginia already had been assailed by John Brown.

Was this, however, not treason? How did this differ from John Brown's war?

"Now don't this show most clearly what the South may expect from this Abolition Administration," exclaimed Mauzy. "And yet men are crying Union, Union…but where is the Union?"

Division consumed the citizens. "The wildest excitement prevailed in the town," witnessed local resident Joseph Barry. "All business was suspended except in the barrooms, and many fist fights came off between the adherents of adverse factions."

A surreal scene rose from the chaos: a stare-down between North and South. At the telegraph office astride the B & O Railroad stood young John Burk, armed with his rifle to defend Southern honor. Fifty yards distant loomed a "gigantic Irishman" named Jeremiah Donovan, who grabbed a musket and commenced his own guard at the armory gate. As the two warily watched, the Civil War became personal.

Also watching and listening was U.S. Army Lieutenant Roger Jones. Assigned to the Ferry with a company of U.S. Regulars in January 1861 to protect the government's property, this army detachment had received initial instructions from the secretary of war to shun "making a display of your force." Any military preparations could "excite the already feverish feeling of the neighborhood." The secretary reiterated: "It is desirable to avoid all needless irritation of the public mind."

Three months later, Jones listened with alarm to Superintendent Barbour's speech announcing imminent seizure of the armory and arsenal. With less than fifty soldiers at hand, he knew his defense was inadequate.

What should he do?

Destroy the place.

Opposite: Burned and broken bridges were more than metaphor in war-era Harpers Ferry. The vital transportation link would be destroyed nine times during the Civil War, incinerating more than a century of business and family, personal and public ties woven over the Potomac.

CONFLUENCE

> "[H]aving become satisfied that an attempt would be made to seize the arsenal and workshops during the night, I made preparations for the destruction of the place, to be carried out only in the event of my being unable to defend it. I detailed twelve men of my company, and ordered six of them to get their bed-sacks, which were filled with straw, and put a keg of powder in each one of them. I proceeded in person with this party from the armory to the arsenal buildings. . . . I distributed these sacks, with powder in them, in the two arsenal buildings. . . and with the aid of shavings and bituminous coal, which I had previously carried in there . . . and with a quantity of lumber lying in the buildings, I prepared things so that a fire could be kindled in an instant."
>
> ~Lt. Roger Jones

Intelligence reports indicated a nightmare scenario. Word arrived from Washington that three trainloads of Virginia militia were approaching the Ferry, coming from the direction of Manassas. "Be on your guard," warned the army's top general. An informant learned the W & P Railroad, normally silent at night, was preparing to move trains from Winchester. A scout discovered 300 militiamen gathered at Charles Town, where veterans of John Brown's war were now marching on the turnpike toward Bolivar Heights.

Certain the enemy—how odd to call fellow Americans the enemy!—was approaching rapidly, Jones discreetly began moving powder into the two arsenal buildings. "I was surrounded by spies and persons in the interest of the rebel cause, who watched every movement and everything that was done." Transferring the powder without raising suspicion or detection proved difficult. Located in the armory magazine atop Camp Hill, and nearly 500 yards up a steep slope from the arsenals, the powder was in packages of 100 pounds, and could not be conveyed "without revealing the fact and perhaps the object."

To counter this problem, Lieutenant Jones turned up a solution: *use John Brown's powder*.

Brown had brought smaller kegs of powder to his Kennedy Farm headquarters to conduct his own war.

Following his seizure, these were retrieved and stored at the armory magazine. Jones discovered these could "easily be rolled up in the men's bedsacks without exposure."

At 10 p.m. on April 18, 1861—eighteen months to the day that Brown was captured—John Brown's powder kegs ignited the Civil War in Virginia.

Horse cavalry, leading the militia, responded with alacrity, galloping two miles into old town Harpers Ferry. But it was too late. The two arsenals burned like blow torches. Lieutenant Jones had prescribed precise work before his rapid departure into Maryland, destroying 15,000 rifles and muskets.

Concerned more explosions would erupt inside the armory, a large crowd of citizens gathered near the workshops and employed the fire engines from "John Brown's Fort" to battle additional flames. The carpenter shop and grinding mill crashed "into a perfect heap of ruins," but most of the buildings and arms-making machinery escaped serious injury.

"These are truly the most remarkable times I think I ever saw," lamented George Mauzy. And this was just the opening day. *For the next 1,452 days, Harpers Ferry would not escape the jaws of Civil War.*

"*There was seen in the direction of the armory a flash, followed by a report like the discharge of a cannon. A number of other flashes followed in quick succession, and then the sky and surrounding mountains were lighted with the steady glare of ascending flames.*"

David Hunter Strother, artist-illustrator accompanying the Virginia militia, recorded the fearsome fire in word and art, while viewing the explosions from his stage on Bolivar Heights.

FIRST OCCUPATION: APRIL 19, 1861 - JUNE 15, 1861
CONFEDERATE BEGINNINGS

Thomas Jonathan Jackson arrived in Harpers Ferry eleven days after the destruction of the arsenals. Three months before he became the famous "Stonewall," Jackson received his first command of the Civil War at Harpers Ferry.

The West Point graduate, Mexican War hero, and Virginia Military Institute professor wasted no time. He organized dozens of militia units into regiments; began arduous and daily drilling of more than 10,000 civilian soldiers; and enforced martial law upon the civilian population. He soon established and trained atop Bolivar Heights the First Virginia Brigade, forever acclaimed afterward in military annals as the "Stonewall Brigade."

Confederates occupy Bolivar Heights, spring 1861.

Most important, he dismantled and shipped south hundreds of tons of weapons-producing machinery from the armory, eliminating jobs for armory workers at Harpers Ferry. If an armorer wished to continue working with his own machines, he needed to move to Richmond or Fayetteville, North Carolina. With the Ferry on the border between North and South, Confederate authorities knew the armory's days were over.

"I am of the opinion that this place should be defended with the spirit which actuated the defenders of Thermopylae," proclaimed a zealous and confident Jackson. Jackson recognized Harpers Ferry as a gateway into the strategic Shenandoah Valley, and essential to the defense of Virginia. He was correct. But Confederate General Joseph E. Johnson replaced him and overruled him, considering the place an outpost too vulnerable on the border. The Southerners thus abandoned Harpers Ferry, destroying the armory buildings and blowing up the majestic B & O Railroad bridge. Stonewall Jackson, however, later would return.

WAR WOUNDS

"The whole structure seemed to ignite at once and was soon consumed, the incombustible parts, iron rails and metal roofing, falling into the water, the quantity of half-burned timber and there forming a dam the whole way over that one might cross upon.... As it burned, the blazing camphor poured down into the river and floated off burning upon the surface."

~David Hunter Strother
June 14, 1861

Before abandoning the Ferry in June 1861, Confederates determined to leave nothing that could aid federal troops. The B & O Railroad was a prime target for eradication.

CONFLUENCE

Life in Harpers Ferry during the Civil War was hazardous at best; deadly at worst.

Bullets did not discriminate between men and women, children and adults. Projectiles did not question whether one was soldier or civilian. Cannon shells cared not about one's occupation or social status. Blood from blacks and whites alike would soak streets, gutters and floorboards.

Houses became headquarters, hospitals and hovels. Church pews morphed into operating tables and sick beds. Factory buildings became warehouses, corrals and prisons. Business owners first shuttered, and then shuddered. Everything changed. A daily terror reigned.

Army occupations supplanted daily existence. Martial law stripped away constitutional rights. No one was trusted; everyone was feared. In Harpers Ferry, little was "civil" during the Civil War. A candle of light, even, could kill you.

Mary Louisa Roeder met the war.

"Well, we have got rid of that [Confederate] lot, but what will the next party that comes do with us?" — *Frederick Roeder, Spring 1861*

Her father Frederick ran a successful confectionary business on High Street, just one block from the arsenal. An immigrant from Saxony, Roeder still voiced his German accent when selling his baked pies, breads and candies, assisted by his seven children. Tragedy had struck recently (one month before the destruction of the arsenals) when Mary's mother suddenly died. Mary, age 17, now was the family matron. Three of her siblings were age eight and under, including her one-year-old sister.

Mary knew her father was a staunch Union supporter. Despite the hazards of living in the Confederacy, her family determined to remain in Harpers Ferry. On July 4th, three months into the war, her father went for a stroll toward the railroad and the confluence of the rivers, perhaps to celebrate Independence Day. Rifle fire suddenly reverberated from Maryland Heights. Roeder collapsed, with "a ghastly hole in his groin through which his intestines protruded." He crawled 100 yards back to his home and died in Mary's arms.

Irony, once again, branded itself into Harpers Ferry's destiny. The first man to die in John Brown's war was a Free Black man. The first Harpers Ferry civilian killed in the Civil War was a defender of the United States, stricken by a U.S. bullet, fired by a U.S. soldier.

Frederick Roerder's confectionary today.

WAR WOUNDS

> *"Few were more uncomfortably situated during the Civil War than the people who lived on the border where the power of one Army ended and the authority of the other began. Where sometimes one had control; sometimes the other; and often times neither."* ~Annie Marmion

Annie Marmion met the war.

Just nine when the strife commenced, she lived with her father Nicholas at the top of the Stone Steps in a stately row of stone and brick buildings adjacent to the original Harper House. Situated high above the rooftops of the town, Annie cherished her views of the mountains and confluence—one of the best vistas in Harpers Ferry—from her home windows.

But her windows became portals of danger. Her father, a physician and owner of three slaves, pledged allegiance to the Southern cause. This was disloyalty in the eyes of U.S. troops stationed in the area. Certain Dr. Marmion was a spy, they kept a vigilant watch on all movements about "Marmion Row," with their rifles targeting the house from Maryland Heights.

"Lights of every kind [were] regarded as signals to the Rebels [and] were usually greeted by a volley of guns," recorded a terrified Annie. "The great objects in life were to procure something to eat and to keep yourself out of sight by day, and your lamps or rather candle lights hidden by night."

For four years, grade-schooler Annie encountered fear and terror. Every day, the darkness of the Civil War consumed her.

Annie Marmion.

SECOND OCCUPATION: JULY 21, 1861 - JULY 28, 1861
THE FIRST NORTHERN INVASION

"Many curiously examined every place famous for John Brown's footsteps. . . . Chief in interest was the engine-house. I recognized it from the pictures then published.....The long lines of noble [armory] shops were mainly in ghastly ruins; the very trees of that once beautiful spot, scorched to death. By some chance, the only building of that vast series which still remains uninjured, is the engine-house . . . and over it still wave the green trees, unhurt. Is it a prophetic emblem?"
Alonzo Quint, Chaplain, 2d Massachusetts Infantry

"Until Harpers Ferry is occupied and fortified, I should fear the return of the rebels," opined General Robert Patterson, commander of the first U.S. force to invade Harpers Ferry. Subsequently, 6,000 Northerners flooded the town on the same day the first major battle of the Civil War occurred at Manassas, fifty miles distant.

"We were welcomed with joy," reveled a Massachusetts chaplain accompanying the "Harvard Regiment." The patriotic women of Harpers Ferry had secretly made the Stars and Stripes during the Rebel occupation, hiding it with hopes they could present it to the first Union regiment that entered the town. "Thankful that you have come here to protect our homes and firesides," rejoiced the loyal ladies, "we . . . take pleasure in presenting you this banner."

The U.S. colors, planted upon seceded slave soil, also encouraged enslaved persons to seek refuge and freedom behind Union lines at the Ferry. Slave masters protested, and Patterson (adhering to law at that time) ordered their return and no slave harboring. "The slaves were turned out of camp in obedience to the order," remembered a Wisconsin soldier, "but were supplied with provisions and started northward to the Pennsylvania border."

Patterson was replaced soon after his arrival by an ardent Republican politician and former governor of Massachusetts (politicians often elevated to generals during the Civil War). General Nathaniel Banks determined "[20,000] men is the least force that can hold this place against a probable attack." Banks promptly withdrew to Maryland Heights and the Maryland shore. After only seven days, the first U.S. occupation ended.

WAR WOUNDS

Herr's destroyed mill, right center, as seen from Jefferson Rock.

Abraham Herr met the war.

A vocal Unionist from Pennsylvania, the 45-year old Herr was the wealthiest man in Harpers Ferry. So rich, in fact, he was four times wealthier than his nearest competitor. Owner of the most prosperous private industry in the Ferry—the flour mill on Virginius Island—Herr lived on the island with his wife and five children; and even though a Northerner from the Quaker State, he owned four slaves.

Wheat from local Shenandoah Valley farmers continued to arrive at Herr's mill after the war erupted. But with the railroad bridge destroyed, and ties to Baltimore severed, no flour could be shipped. Herr thus accumulated hundreds of barrels of flour and thousands of bushels of wheat. Both Union and Confederate armies salivated over this prize. The Yankees struck first, removing 700 barrels of flour on August 17, 1861, and destroying nearly 25,000 bushels of wheat and 15,000 bushels of horse feed. Three days later the Federals returned, vandalizing the shafts, belts and machinery, to ensure "Herr's famous flour-mills were useless for the war."

Another irony. The first destruction of private industry in Harpers Ferry—at the hands of United States soldiers—affected an entrepreneur who was a "Union man at heart."

THIRD OCCUPATION: FEBRUARY 24, 1862 – SEPTEMBER 15, 1862
THE STRATEGIC SHENANDOAH VALLEY

Ten months into the Civil War, a 20,000-man army crossed the Potomac on a pontoon bridge at Harpers Ferry. Located at the entrance into the Shenandoah Valley, Union authorities agreed the Ferry offered a launch pad for invasion into Virginia. The B & O Railroad could provide a line of transport and supply, and with its Potomac bridge reconstructed, an umbilical cord to the North. The abandoned and partially destroyed armory buildings could be repurposed as an army depot. On a grander scale, a U. S. presence at Harpers Ferry could hinder Confederate invasion of Maryland or Pennsylvania. Just as important, because the Ferry was situated northwest of Washington, it could shield the capital from potential enemy incursions, coming via a "backdoor."

"The spirit of the troops is most excellent," beamed General George B. McClellan, general-in-chief of all Union armies at the time, as he witnessed the invasion from the Potomac shoreline. "This we regarded as an event of great importance," recalled an Indiana soldier. "We were at last upon insurgent soil. . . . When the boundary of a state which had declared its separation from the Union was crossed, it was understood to mean that hostilities had begun."

For the next seven months, Harpers Ferry supported Federal troops campaigning in the Shenandoah Valley. Christened the "Railroad Brigade," and headquartered at the Ferry, a detachment remained to guard and protect nearly 350 miles of rail lines, stretching from Baltimore deep into northwestern Virginia.

This Yankee presence garnered the attention of Stonewall Jackson, who attacked Harpers Ferry in May during his famous "Valley Campaign." But his demonstration was foiled—the only Union position that did not collapse to Stonewall's speed and stealth. Jackson soon would return.

> *"Harpers Ferry was a fitting place to begin an advance against the rebellion. It was a rebellion solely in the interests of slavery."*
>
> Edmund Brown
> 27th Indiana Infantry
> February 1862

Hector Tyndale met the war.

The major of the 28th Pennsylvania Infantry had been to Harpers Ferry before. He came as the personal escort of Mary Brown to retrieve the body of her executed husband, John Brown. Tyndale, a wealthy Philadelphia merchant of china, glass and pottery, and an ardent Republican, volunteered for this mission, despite "grave fears for the personal safety of those who dared accompany her."

A bullet whistled by Tyndale, in fact, as he awaited Brown's body, and he felt "exposed to the dangers of assassination from an unseen enemy." When the rude coffin finally arrived, Tyndale insisted the lid be removed and the body identified. This caused "an outburst of anger" from the locals, and "imprecations and threats were made against him." Tyndale would remember.

Twenty-two months later, in August 1861, Tyndale was responsible for guarding ten miles of the U.S. border along the Potomac, with Harpers Ferry the central nest of Rebel nuisance. "[S]ome small and unimportant, but not infrequent" skirmishing occurred for months, but one day the Confederates went too far.

A favorite Union scout of Tyndale's named George Rohr was lured to the Ferry and ambushed by Confederate snipers. His death so incensed the Union command, Tyndale was ordered to burn all the buildings along the river used by Confederates for concealment. On February 7, 1862, Tyndale arrived with his torches, "ruthlessly destroying with fire [the] hotel and all the town between the armory and the railroad bridge." The commercial heart at the confluence was incinerated.

"The killing of Rohr was the cause of another calamity to the hapless town."

Joseph Barry

Camp and illustrations of the 22d New York State Militia, summer 1862. This regiment formed part of the occupation force encamped on Camp Hill. After ninety days service, the men returned to New York City the first week of September 1862. They just missed impending disaster.

SEPTEMBER 12 - 15, 1862
STONEWALL'S BRILLIANT VICTORY

Thomas Jonathan "Stonewall" Jackson

Robert E. Lee encountered a problem.

The Confederate chieftain had launched an invasion of the North. Pennsylvania was his target, but Harpers Ferry impeded his passage. The U. S. garrison there of 14,000 men, now located in the rear of the advancing Confederates, threatened Lee's line of communication and supply. Something must be done.

General Lee devised his plan. Split his army into three separate columns. Seize the three mountains overlooking Harpers Ferry. Entrap the Yankees and eliminate the Union menace. Lee selected Stonewall Jackson to lead the arduous and complex assignment. Stonewall knew Harpers Ferry well.

The Federal commander, Colonel Dixon Miles, was aware the Rebels were coming. Cut off from communication, isolated from reinforcement, and outnumbered two to one, Miles clutched his final orders: "[D]efend all places to the last extremity. . . . There must be no abandoning of post, and shoot the first man who thinks of it."

Jackson's Confederates seized Maryland Heights, after a battle, and Loudoun Heights without firing a shot. But Miles made a stand upon Bolivar Heights, frustrating Stonewall. "The position before me is a strong one," he complained. Jackson brought forward his artillery, pounding the surrounded Yankees with more than 50 cannon. Still no surrender. Miles stood firmly.

Finally, on the third day of the siege, Jackson ordered General Ambrose Powell Hill to conduct a daring flanking maneuver along the steep slopes of the Shenandoah. It worked. A surprised and stunned Miles discovered his position untenable, and he ordered white flags waved.

The largest surrender of U. S. soldiers during the Civil War occurred on September 15, 1862. Jackson captured more than 12,700 Federals along with 73 Union cannon. A remarkable Confederate victory.

But the Harpers Ferry venture delayed and despoiled Lee's drive into Pennsylvania. Instead, he waited nervously for Stonewall and two-thirds of his army to reunite with him along the Antietam Creek in Maryland.

WAR WOUNDS

> *"The infernal screech owls came hissing and singing, then bursting, plowing great holes in the earth, filling our eyes with dust, and tearing many giant trees to atoms."*
>
> **James H. Clark,   115th New York Infantry,   Bolivar Heights**

Situation at Harpers Ferry, Sept 15- 1862, 7 A.M.
White - 12,500 Union
Confederates Jackson - 25,000

The three mountains surrounding Harpers Ferry were the key to Confederate victory. If the Rebels failed to seize any of the mountains, an escape valve existed for the Union army. Fortunately for Jackson, his forces converged about the same time, forcing the Union army into the Harpers Ferry hole. With the Confederates holding the high ground, and the United States forces completely surrounded and outnumbered, surrender became the Union option.

CONFLUENCE

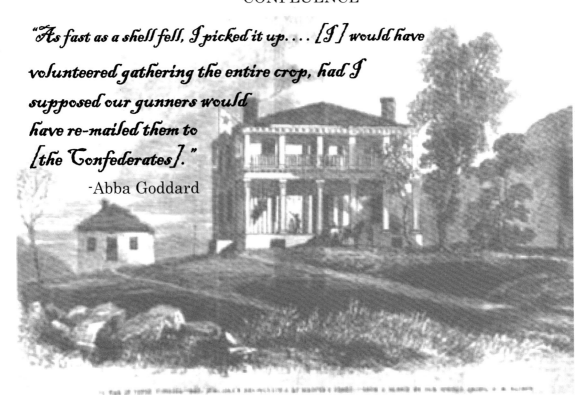

"As fast as a shell fell, I picked it up.... [I] would have volunteered gathering the entire crop, had I supposed our gunners would have re-mailed them to [the Confederates]."
-Abba Goddard

Abba Goddard met the war.

The "Matron from Maine" accompanied a regiment from the "Down East State," first arriving at the Ferry in the spring of 1862. Her job was to make the base hospital as comfortable as possible, and she busied herself seeking donated money and charity boxes from friends and families in Portland. She also made weekly trips into Baltimore, purchasing food for the hospital, including barrels of potatoes, onions, ginger cakes, boxes of lemons, and 100 pounds of codfish.

"It is no vanity in me to say that [through] the efforts of the last month the very lives of many of our men have been preserved."

Then occurred disaster. Thousands of Rebels under Stonewall Jackson surrounded the Ferry in mid-September, 1862, and commenced a blistering bombardment. Matron Goddard's hospital was not exempt. "They peppered us," she exclaimed. Undaunted, the brave woman *ran toward*, not away, from unexploded sizzling shells.

Mrs. Goddard faced another emergency after the Confederates forced U.S. capitula-tion. The Rebels set about rounding up hundreds of escaped refugee African Americans, with intention of returning them to slavery. When the Confederates arrived at the Matron's hospital, she refused to allow seven of her most intimate black companions to be seized. She greeted the Southern soldiers with her pistol. "I am almost tired of night-watching, and my revolver begins to grow heavy," she wrote. "It holds but five balls, but before secesh gets my seven ebonies, my body will pay for the two balls wanting. Oh, this traffic in human flesh!"

FOURTH OCCUPATION: SEPTEMBER 15 - 18, 1862
CONFEDERATE VICTORY

"They hoisted the bars and stars where one hour before our glorious old star-spangled banner floated proudly in the breeze," lamented an Ohio soldier, now a prisoner of Stonewall Jackson's capture of Harpers Ferry. "Boys, [Jackson's] not much for looks," wrote another Northerner, "but if we'd had him we wouldn't have been caught in this trap."

Poorly clothed and emaciated, one Union soldier labeled his captors "a mongrel, barefoot crew." A New York private starred at "the poverty of their clothing and equipments, their sallow, hungry faces, their long, tangled hair and slouched hats, and their gaunt frames which seemed nothing but bone and muscle covered with a bronzed skin."

This sharply contrasted with the appearance of the Federal army. "[I]n their luxurious garrison life they looked as if they had come out of a bandbox, with their untarnished uniforms, white shirt collars, and polished boots," observed one Rebel. The Confederates gorged. "We fared sumptuously," declared a South Carolina veteran. "In addition to meat, crackers, sugar, coffee, shoes, blankets, under-clothing, etc., many of us captured horses roaming at large, on whom to transport our plunder."

Explosions rocked the water gap 72 hours after Stonewall's victory. Flames scorched the sky as the railroad was blown up and the pontoon bridge and the government storehouses in the old armory buildings burned. "All the property the Rebels could not move from Harpers Ferry they have destroyed," observed one civilian. "They finished up by burning carload after carload of rice and beans; the air even now is full of the odor of burning beans."

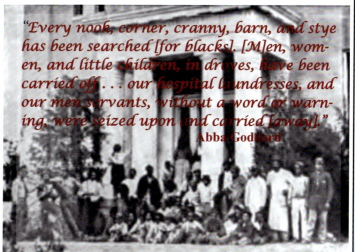

"Every nook, corner, cranny, barn, and stye has been searched [for blacks]. [M]en, women, and little children, in droves, have been carried off . . . our hospital laundresses, and our men servants, without a word or warning, were seized upon and carried [away]."
— Abba Goddard

Part of the plunder included confiscating escaped refugee slaves. Some estimates surmised up to 2,000 African Americans seeking freedom and shelter behind Union lines were returned into slavery.

FIFTH OCCUPATION: SEPTEMBER 19, 1862 - JUNE 30, 1863
FROM ANTIETAM TO GETTYSBURG

U.S. forces reoccupied Harpers Ferry two days following the Union victory in the Battle of Antietam. General Lee's army withdrew into the Virginia country surrounding the Ferry, and for nearly six weeks, the enemy armies engaged in a stare-down.

During this lull in fighting, General McClellan determined Harpers Ferry never again would be burdened with inadequate defenses. Convinced the occupation of the Ferry "was a military necessity," McClellan ordered fortification of the position "in order to avoid a similar catastrophe" as what happened with Stonewall Jackson's capture. Earthworks soon stretched across vulnerable Bolivar Heights, and tree-clearing on Maryland and Loudoun Heights denuded the mountain tops. "Sometimes there would be as many as twenty or thirty fine trees falling at once," recalled a temporary lumberjack from Massachusetts. "[T]hey reminded me of men falling in battle, that same dead, helpless fall." Soon massive fortifications of earth and stone, bolstered by rifled cannon that could fire accurately over two miles, crowned the crests.

Activity buzzed all around. The B & O railroad bridge was rebuilt; the pontoon bridge replaced; several burned armory buildings promptly reroofed and prepared for quartermaster and commissary supplies; and nearly 60,000 men—two-thirds of McClellan's Army of the Potomac—stationed about Harpers Ferry. It was the post's largest military occupation of the war.

President Lincoln traveled to Harpers Ferry via train to review and congratulate his troops for their Antietam victory. He arrived on October 1, and witnessed an impressive military stage. "The sight was a grand one as the great army encamped over these hills and the view at night of thousands of campfires illuminated the hills from base to summit." Bugles and drums and fifes and officers' orders, combined with the conversations of thousands of men, orchestrated into a "hum of voices like that of an immense city."

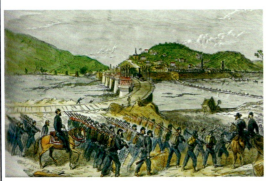

This military city virtually vanished by November 1 as the Union army launched a new offensive to Richmond. Several thousand soldiers remained around town to man the forts and artillery; but for months, the war felt far away. That ended abruptly. As General Lee drove his Confederates toward Pennsylvania in the summer of 1863, the dormant Ferry sprang to action.

WAR WOUNDS

"[I]t really seem[ed] too lovely to be the seat of a horrid war . . . a paradise too sweet for the Devil to enter with his polluting presence. But the devil of war is a mighty fiend, and he is laying his strong hand of desolation heavily on this particular region."

                     Dunn Browne
                     14th Connecticut Infantry
                     October, 1862

Harriett Dada met the war.

The young nurse arrived at the Ferry from Washington, soon after the Battle of Antietam, not to treat wounded, but the sick. Almost twice as many soldiers died of disease during the Civil War than from bullets and shells. With nearly 60,000 men surrounding Harpers Ferry in the fall of 1862, the base required a substantial hospital to treat the ill. Union authorities commandeered the tallest building in town for the purpose: the abandoned cotton mill on Virginius Island.

Christened "Island Hospital," Nurse Dada went right to work. "The fourth story was the first to be filled with sick," she recorded as she helped organize the hospital's opening. "There were iron cots, straw beds, and good new blankets, but pillows, sheets, and even stoves we did not have for some days." As the cold chill of fall consumed the confluence, Nurse Dada recalled "we were obliged to heat bricks and carry them up to those who could not otherwise keep warm."

> *"Some of the patients were so covered with vermin that their clothes had to be destroyed. . . . The surgeon ordered the heads of several to be shaven, and I made woolen caps for them."*

"Lady, come here," beckoned the sick, some near delirious with fever and pain. "I want a woman to take care of me when I'm sick." Some men were so diseased and preyed upon by body pests that Dada noticed they were "quite reduced to skeletons." An impression, for certain, engraved into Nurse Dada's memory.

SIXTH OCCUPATION: JUNE 18 - JULY 14, 1863
THE GETTYSBURG CAMPAIGN

It was an ominous omen. From their signal station atop Maryland Heights, the Federals spied them coming. Tens of thousands of Rebels, their marches outlined by miles of clouds of rising dust, were heading north. Was Harpers Ferry their target?

No. General Lee had learned his lesson the previous fall - a stall that resulted in his loss at Antietam. His goal was Pennsylvania, so he flanked the Ferry, crossing the Potomac upstream en route to the Mason-Dixon Line. But the Yankees did not know Lee's intentions, and nearly 10,500 Northerners prepared for Confederate investment.

"The place must be held," came orders from the Union high command. "If you are besieged, you will soon be relieved."

"I am sending everybody over to Maryland Heights," responded the post commander. Thus began another "great skedaddle" — "a motley crew of fugitives of every shade of color" evacuating Harpers Ferry for the safety of the fortifications on the mountain.

> *"What a frightful waste of property attended the evacuation of this position! Dried apples, hard tack, rice and sugar, all mixed and jumbled together, lay in heaps, from two to three feet deep . . . . Piles of tents, as good as new, save that each has been slit once from top to bottom, and heaps of Springfield muskets, many of them with broken stocks . . . lie scattered about. . . . Everything shows a hurried, and ill considered, and ill planned evacuation."*
>
> William Lincoln, 34th Massachusetts Infantry

Confederate detachments seized the town, and would hold it for nearly three weeks. But as the contending armies moved toward a collision at Gettysburg, orders arrived to abandon Maryland Heights too. In a driving rainstorm, and mostly in darkness, Union soldiers struggled to remove artillery, munitions and supplies down the rugged mountain slopes. "Rain was pouring in sheets and the mountain roads were becoming beds of torrents," recollected a Maryland soldier.

The hasty evacuation produced deadly results. Explosion! While defusing shells, a thunderous roar shook the earth, and in seconds, "fragments of shell, rock, and timber" hailed down upon a Maryland regiment. "And shocking to add, human bodies also . . . limbs without bodies and bodies [falling] at [our] feet."

This 1862 photograph illustrates, as well, Harpers Ferry as it appeared following the Gettysburg Campaign. Before departing the town, the Confederates burned the Union supply base at the old armory once again.

SEVENTH OCCUPATION: JULY 10, 1863 - JULY 4, 1864
NEARLY A YEAR WITHOUT CHANGING FLAGS

The war moved far away after Gettysburg. An occasional Confederate guerrilla attack in the region would send sirens and shivers through the Harpers Ferry garrison; but otherwise, eyes shifted to a Union siege upon Richmond and Petersburg and the strangulation of the shrinking Confederacy.

This respite offered opportunity for some simple enjoyments in life. Thanksgiving Day, as example. "I did not do much of anything but eat," flourished a Massachusetts soldier. He and his brothers-in-arms feasted on "three large turkeys, four or five chickens and pies, cakes, cheese, [and] apples innumerable." A comrade prepared a nice large plum pudding, "I believe as good as I ever eat."

The soldiers even found time for dancing and merriment. The 34th Massachusetts Infantry hosted a "Grand Military Ball" at the Lockwood House on Camp Hill on Thanksgiving evening. No less than three generals attended, along with wives and daughters of officers and "all the prin-cipal ladies in and about the town." As the regiment's brass band serenaded from the outdoor porch, beautiful decorations adorned the interior hall, including a chandelier "made by a circle of bayonets."

> *"Festoons of evergreen were gracefully and fantastically entwined about every pillar and projection of the architecture, while here and there stack of polished muskets intervened, the brilliancy of which in the bright lamp light, formed a beautiful contrast with the dark evergreen background."*
> Charles Moulton, 34th Mass.

Some frolic indeed, but also time for school. School for the *first time ever* for 65 former slaves. A philanthropic New England organization called the American Missionary Association opened day and night schools. W. W. Wheeler and his wife Ellen began using the Bible to teach reading and writing to their spirited and industrious new pupils. "[W]e feel ourselves greatly honored, in being permitted to open a school for those very ones for whom [John Brown] died within a few rods of the [Fort] in which he took refuge."

Another Rebel invasion, however, forced the refugees to flee.

WAR WOUNDS

Charlie Moulton met the war.

Arriving with the first U.S. regiment to enter Harpers Ferry following Gettysburg, the lad from Worcester entered town the third week of July 1863, with the 34th Massachusetts Infantry (a brand new outfit just recruited). As Moulton stepped upon the "sacred soil" of enemy country for the first time, the majesty of Mother Nature impressed him—"splendid landscape scenery for the artist"—but the destruction of man disgusted him.

> "[N]ow all is desolated and utter ruin; war has had its effect and laid every thing waste and barren....[T]he larger portion of the houses all lie in ruins and the entire place is not actually worth $10."

As an excellent scribe with precision penmanship, Moulton soon discovered himself detailed to the provost marshal, where he helped enforce martial law and order within the Harpers Ferry Military District. The provost ruled with an iron hand, and had absolute authority. He determined your rights—no *Bill of Rights* in occupied Harpers Ferry. The provost was your jailor, your prosecutor, your judge, and if necessary, your executioner. His power controlled your existence. He owned you.

From his office on High Street, Corporal Moulton dealt with three types of violators: civilians, deserters and soldiers. His daily work required that he administer loyalty oaths (to the United States, of course); issue passes for travel, transport and even for food; inspect all baggage, possessions and deliveries for prohibited articles (such as whiskey); process Confederate deserters and prisoners of war; and enact punishment upon U.S. soldiers for infractions of military rule (such as sleeping at post). The John Brown Fort became the favorite jail.

As a youthful bachelor, Moulton's favorite "power" was documenting the identification of women seeking passes. "[We] stare at them to ascertain the color of their eyes, hair, and complexion, and ask their heights and if they don't know, why they must be measured. Many a pretty girl blushes through this apparent impudence."

Moulton also had the unpleasant task of assisting with an execution. William Loge, known as "French Bill," was a notorious guerrilla bushwhacker, murderer and assassin who had deserted from the Union army and joined the Confederate cause. His crimes demanded death. On December 2, 1864—five years to the date of John Brown's execution—the con-demned man climbed the scaffold on Bolivar Heights. The rope tightened about the neck; the hatchet dropped; the trap door sprang. As the prisoner dangled, the scaffold broke.

Moulton was mortified. "The poor prisoner in his last struggles of agony, while being brought to the scaffolding a second time, cried that they would only shoot him and put him out of his misery."

Charlie Moulton's nightmares came not on the battlefield, but on the border.

Background: A soldier stands guard on Shenandoah Street and a Provost Marshal's pass from 1863. All comings and goings in Harpers Ferry were closely monitored by military personnel..

EIGHTH OCCUPATION: JULY 5 - 9, 1864
THE LAST CONFEDERATE INVASION

There was no time for celebrations this July 4th. "It was time for the yearly skedaddle."

General Lee, in a daring and risky move, had detached nearly one-third of his army (14,000 men) away from the defenses of the Confederate capital with orders to strike the U. S. capital. The invasion route was via Harpers Ferry.

Watching the Rebels approach, the Union post commander notified Washington authorities of the impending threat and pronounced: "I must leave town, but shall hold Maryland Heights at all hazards." A hurried evacuation of quartermaster, commissary and ordnance supplies emptied the armory depot, and local denizens abandoned the town with the troops. "The people had entertained the fond hope that the war was nearly over," recorded town resident Joseph Barry. Instead, "[a]t no time during the war was there as deep a gloom on Harpers Ferry as on that anniversary of the birth of the nation."

As Confederates probed the Maryland Heights fortifications—thwarted each attempt by pinpoint long-range artillery fire—the Union gunners also targeted downtowns Harpers Ferry and Bolivar, "full of rebels." The shelling killed and wounded more civilians than any other event of the war.

Finally, after four days, the Southerners departed, circumventing the defenses and then racing toward Washington. The thundering roar of cannon, and their missiles of death, thankfully ceased.

Saturday, July 9, marked a milestone in Harpers Ferry's Civil War history. The town changed hands for the final time. North and South had swapped possession of the Ferry eight times in three years. Although peace in the country was months away, Harpers Ferry was, according to Barry, "happily exempted from any more of its accustomed calamitous evacuations."

> "The roar of the cannon is continuous, and there is nothing to be done but to endure it and thank God that the balls and shell whiz by high enough to leave [us] unscathed. . . . It is a tedious, irksome, weary time of watching and of dread. When will it cease?"
>
> Annie Marmion, July 1864

Margaret Kelly met the war.

The young lady was living on High Street with her family when the Confederates suddenly seized Harpers Ferry in July 1864. Rebel sharpshooters posted themselves throughout the town, so annoying the Union commander atop Maryland Heights that he "notified citizens to vacate houses, as he would shell the town." But it was too late. With the railroad bridge destroyed, there was no escape. The fireworks of this July 4th were deemed for death; and for two days, the "village of Harpers Ferry had its worst experience of a Bombardment."

An unknown woman was slain on High Street. An African American woman who had ventured forth for water also was killed, her lifeless body stranded on Shenandoah Street all day. A shell penetrated the house of James McGraw on High Street, but passed directly through without harming any one.

Its momentum carried the dastardly intruder through a wall into the next-door Kelly home, sizzling and sputtering, "where it fell on a bed without exploding." Standing astride the bed was Miss Margaret.

Would that bed ever again offer rest?

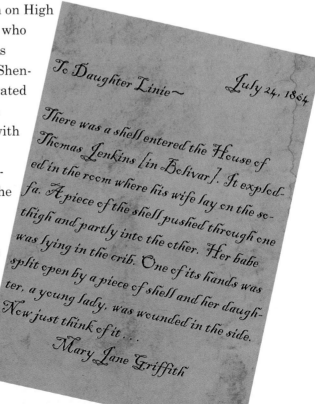

To Daughter Linie~   July 24, 1864

There was a shell entered the House of Thomas Jenkins [in Bolivar]. It exploded in the room where his wife lay on the sofa. A piece of the shell pushed through one thigh and partly into the other. Her babe was lying in the crib. One of its hands was split open by a piece of shell and her daughter, a young lady, was wounded in the side. Now just think of it . . .

Mary Jane Griffith

John Mobberly met the war.

The lad from Loudoun County grew up just opposite the Ferry, across the Shenandoah. His father abandoned him as a child, and young John lived a tough existence. He tried to make ends meet for his destitute mother by driving a wagon team for an African American butcher. Mobberly matured into an expert equestrian, and enlisted in the Confederate cavalry.

But he quickly went rogue. He began roaming the Harpers Ferry region, organizing "a reckless band of cut throats and marauders, robbing every soldier they came across, stealing horses from the citizens and committing all sort of daring depredations."

Mobberly terrorized the region for more than two years. Detested by the Union army, and feared by local citizens, Mobberly would become the focus of a coordinated ambush. The bait, of course, was good horses—irresistible for Mobberly. The trap worked. On April 5, 1865, four days before the surrender at Appomattox, a Federal cavalry detachment assassinated the unsuspecting gangster.

"His body, with the head perforated in three places by bullets, was thrown, like a sack of grain, across [his] horse's back, and conveyed to Harpers Ferry." Upon arrival, he was taken to the military district headquarters (the Master Armorer's House on Shenandoah Street), and "his body exposed to public view."

> *"[Mobberly's] body was almost denuded by relic hunters who, with their jack knives, cut pieces off his clothes as souvenirs of the war."*
> ~Joseph Barry

Charles Moulton recalled the scene. "A large crowd assembled around his body. He was an awful looking sight, covered with blood from head to foot and his hands were completely dyed in blood which were caused to be clutching at his wounds in agony."

Mobberly's death ridded the community "of its greatest terror."

Emblematic, perhaps, of a bigger outcome.

The great terror of the Civil War was ending.

WAR WOUNDS

John Singleton Mosby met the war.

One word brought instant fear to the lips of every United States soldier: *Mosby*.

John Singleton Mosby was the most successful and pervasive rebel guerrilla.

"To my mind, Mosby was the ideal fighting man, from the tip of his plume, to the rowel of his spur," wrote John Munson, a member of Mosby's 43d Virginia Cavalry. "Stories of his wonderful achievements came into Richmond from every direction. Joan of Arc never felt the call to go to battle any stronger than I felt it to join Mosby."

Rumors of Mosby's attacks and escapes created a Mosby mythology and made him a hated nemesis of the Federals.

"No one who has not experienced a night attack from an enemy can form the slightest conception of the feelings of one awakened in the dead of night with the din of shots and yells coming from those thirsting for your blood," exclaimed a Union cavalryman.

U.S. forces made repeated attempts to "bag" Mosby and his men. Almost always they failed.

Images of War

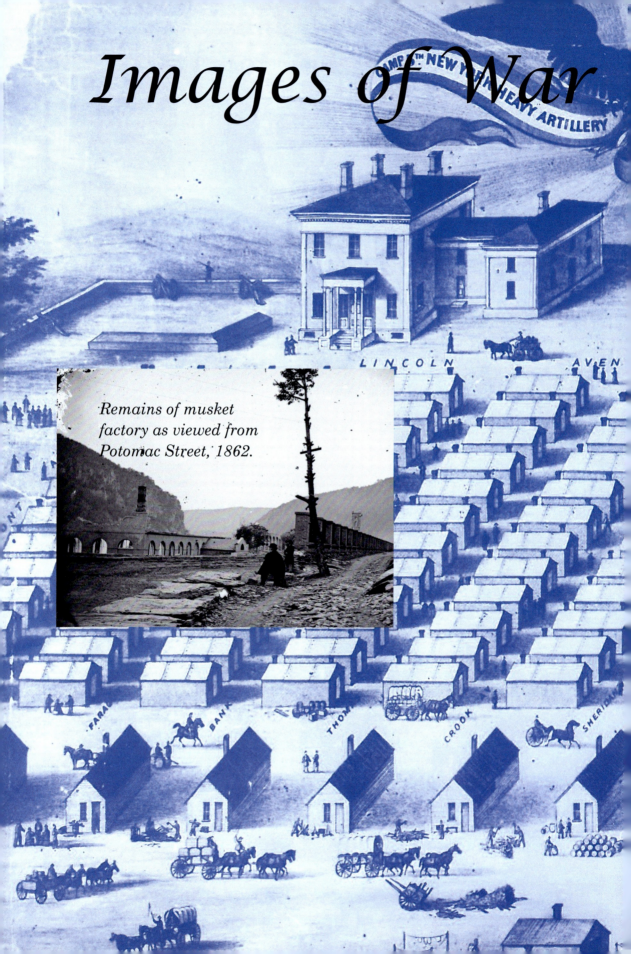

Remains of musket factory as viewed from Potomac Street, 1862.

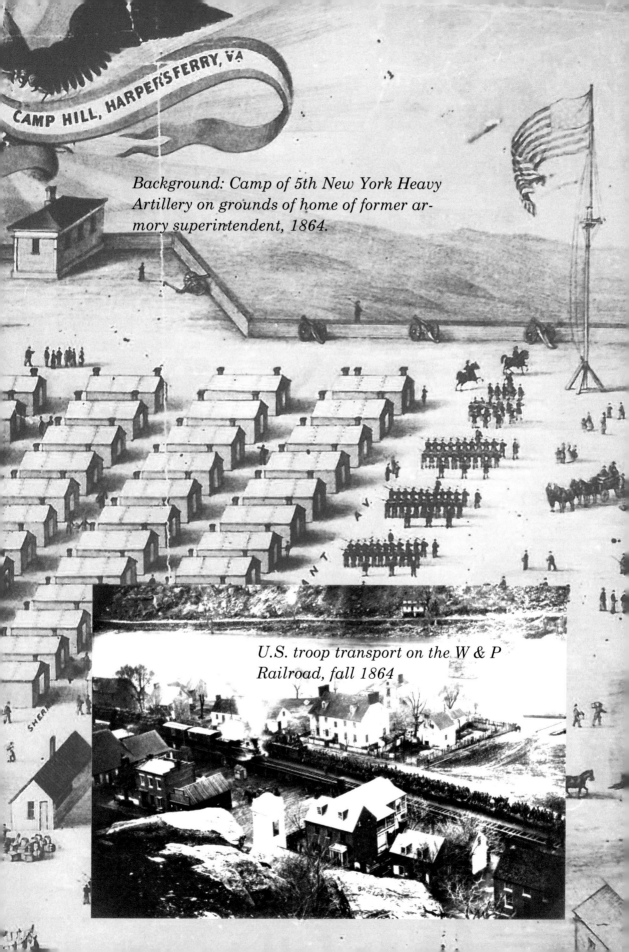

CAMP HILL, HARPER'S FERRY, VA

Background: Camp of 5th New York Heavy Artillery on grounds of home of former armory superintendent, 1864.

U.S. troop transport on the W & P Railroad, fall 1864

NINTH OCCUPATION: JULY 9, 1864 - JUNE 30, 1865
THE WAR ENDS

Tired of Confederate exploitation of the Shenandoah Valley, Federal authorities determined to wipe out Southern resistance there. "Give the enemy no rest," demanded Union commander General U. S. Grant. "Follow him to the death. . . . If the war is to last another year, we want the Shenandoah Valley to remain a barren waste."

Grant's instructions were clear for new Valley commander General Philip Sheridan. He arrived in Harpers Ferry on August 6; promptly established his initial headquarters at the Lockwood House; and plotted the demise of the Shenandoah Southerners. Ten weeks later, he had defeated the Confederates four times in four major battles; captured nearly a third of the Rebels he faced (7,000 prisoners were processed at Harpers Ferry); and he would nearly famish the Valley's population after seizing thousands of sheep, cattle and hogs. Sheridan also burned and destroyed thousands of bushels of wheat and corn and dozens of flour mills. Total war destroyed the Confederacy.

Harpers Ferry supplied Sheridan's 50,000-man army, and the post depot hummed with activity not seen since the antebellum armory days. The rolls showed 289 civilians performing 35 different jobs, including blacksmiths, wheelwrights, carpenters, saddlers, painters, teamsters and laborers. Wages were good—some making $75 a month—five times the pay of a private.

Sheridan's legions proved too much for the Southerners; and by December, most of his men redeployed to the Richmond/Petersburg front. There, too, the noose tightened. General Lee was forced to abandon the Confederate capital. By Palm Sunday, he had surrendered.

During the following eleven weeks at Harpers Ferry, the army dismantled its base of operations, removed the artillery from the forts, and mustered out its men.

> On June 30, 1865, exactly six years after John Brown had arrived in the Harpers Ferry vicinity, the war he started there ended.

Ruins of the Rife Factory along the Shenandoah, a testament to the destruction wrought upon Harpers Ferry throughout the Civil War.

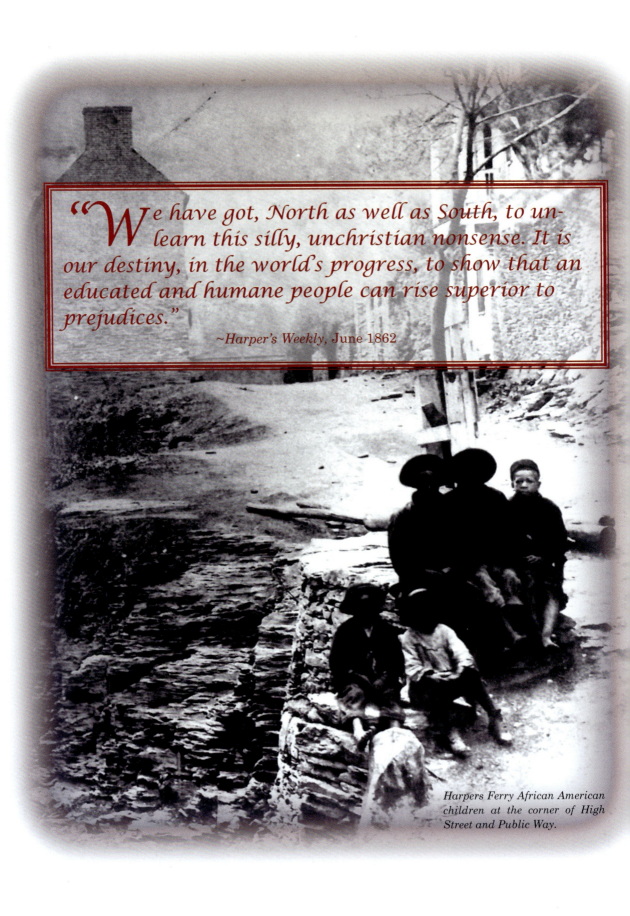

"We have got, North as well as South, to unlearn this silly, unchristian nonsense. It is our destiny, in the world's progress, to show that an educated and humane people can rise superior to prejudices."
~*Harper's Weekly*, June 1862

Harpers Ferry African American children at the corner of High Street and Public Way.

Chapter 7
REDEEMERS, RESISTERS

The Civil War ended American slavery; but it did not exterminate racism.

The Civil War established freedom; but it eluded civil rights.

The Civil War changed America; but most Americans did not change.

Racial tension and strife have been America's longest lasting and most continuous disharmony. Relations between blacks and whites in the United States persistently have defied the cornerstone of the country's Declaration of Independence. Americans love the words, "all men are created equal." Yet as a nation, "We, the people," have failed to practice these five determinant words for most of America's existence. The struggle for equality has been endless.

This epic engagement—this enlightenment for human dignity and human equality—embodies Harpers Ferry's story after the Civil War.

The handshake between Generals Grant and Lee at Appomattox altered America's trajectory, but it did not transform racial attitudes. Almost all white Southerners, and most white Northerners, believed the African American inferior. The Supreme Court underscored this perspective. Blacks were "beings of an inferior order," the Court declared in its infamous 1857 Dred Scott decision, "altogether unfit to associate with the white race, either in social or political relations." The Court concluded that African Americans "were so far inferior, that they had no right which the white man was bound to respect."

Congress overruled this decision in 1868 with the Fourteenth Amendment, affirming basic rights to life, liberty and property for *all* the nation's citizens. Congress could not, however, mandate a change in racial attitudes.

Regardless of region, race relations were tense. In the absence of slavery, white leaders perceived two futures: permanent apartheid, or amalgamation. This latter prospect particularly horrified whites. In the capital of Pennsylvania, as example, a Harrisburg newspaper editor witnessed kids of different colors playing together on street corners. "The juvenile admixture of blacks and whites…may hereafter increase them to such a degree as to disgrace the community and deteriorate the [white] race!…Let it not be forgotten that ours is a Government, of white people, and that all inter-mixture with inferior races degrades our own, producing a motley rabble unfit for self-government."

CONFLUENCE

The Democratic Party, opposed to the abolition of slavery prior to the end of the Civil War, stoked the fears of Northern white laborers who now felt threatened by newly freed blacks.

> "[Let] these negroes remain in the South and earn their living on the plantations where they have been reared....We do not want them here [in the North]...to throw our white laboring population out of employment, to steal from our farmers and to fill our Poor Houses and Prisons. We have as many colored people here as we need." -Harrisburg *Patriot and Union*

Republicans, as well, acknowledged the realities of racism. The Civil War was waged "not so much in the interest of slavery as from the innate horror with which the whites regard the black race," declared President Lincoln's postmaster general. "The white people of the United States will not live side by side with black men as their equals."

The Federal government acknowledged racial rifts, but focused its energies in the conquered South. Between 1865 and 1877, it occupied the former Confederate states with tens of thousands of U.S. soldiers during the Reconstruction Era, partly to protect the liberated and to enforce provisions of the three post-war amendments that guaranteed freedom, life, liberty, property and suffrage. The Congress also created the Freedmen's Bureau to assist ex-slaves' transition from bondsmen to citizens.

Harpers Ferry was designated as a Freedmen's Bureau office soon after the war ended. The move made sense. The Ferry had been a magnet for those seeking freedom since the outset of the Civil War; the government still retained the valuable property of

Right: This editorial from a local newspaper defines the culture that permeated postwar Harpers Ferry.

Opposite: African American refugees, referred to as "contraband" during the war, camped on the former armory grounds very near John Brown's Fort.

Spirit of Jefferson
December 5, 1865

"Our exchanges from various directions contain no very favorable accounts as to the present or prospective condition of the Freedmen.

In many cases they are represented as unwilling to work, and live alone upon pillage. In other instances they are congregating together in the cities and large towns in such numbers as to engender disease which, from filth, exposure and want of proper medical nursing, is carrying them off by the hundreds....

Some of the most philanthropic of our statesmen, North and South, are beginning to reason logically, as to the future extermination of the race. We hope for better things, but are frank to say that neither history, observation or experiences, give much encouragement.

If freedom shall prove to them that boon which their pretended friends have assumed, none will rejoice more than the Southern heart, whose real sympathy and kindness has always been on the side of the 'poor, down-trodden African....'

As their acknowledged STATUS, however, has been now fixed, whether for weal or woe, and we are to be common occupants of the same community, we hope nothing of strife or discord many arise in the future[.] [A]nd whilst the action of the one class is marked by charity and kindness, that of the other will be uniform and respectful as to all proper submission."

REDEEMERS, RESISTERS

the defunct armory; and the U.S. military occupation of the post had established the government's disciplined authority.

A large native-born black presence mattered as well. Nearly thirty percent of for-mer slaves in the new state of West Virginia (established July 20, 1863) resided in the two counties nearest Harpers Ferry. Almost three-tenths of Jefferson County's antebel-lum population were enslaved. When combined with neighboring Berkeley County, the number of chattels just before the Civil War reached 5,610 people.

Black refugees at Harpers Ferry faced horrific conditions following the Civil War. "We have a colored population…huddled together with almost no where to live and nothing to live on," despaired a relief missionary. As the number of congregated Freedmen fluc-tuated between 500-700 people—more than double the town's pre-war African American population—they encountered limited housing, exorbitant rents, makeshift shelters, a paucity of food and clothing, and omnipresent pestilence, resulting in infant mortality.

"There is something very touching in seeing these poor people coming into camp—giving up all the little ties that cluster about home, such as it is in slavery, and trustfully throwing themselves on the mercy of the Yankees, in the hope of getting permission to own themselves and keep their children from the auction-block."

Alfred Waud, newspaper illustrator, 1864

A government inspector general, following a visit to the Ferry, discovered blacks living "in a state of filth, disorder and wretchedness." His discoveries defied existence. "The colored people live in filthy overcrowded tenements, destitute of every conv[en]ience. Insufficiently clad, often without food and idle, they are necessarily exposed to frequent attacks of disease." A Freedmen's Bureau officer labeled the Ferry a "nest of paupers," and concluded that "nothing but a revolution or something similar will change this state of affairs."

A revolution—through education—was forthcoming.

Nathan Cook Brackett arrived at Harpers Ferry with a mission.

The 28-year old preacher from Maine, and a Dartmouth graduate, had been serving in the Shenandoah Valley with the U.S. Christian Commission during the final year of the war. He returned to his native state to resume preaching following peace. But Brackett had earned a "tireless energy" reputation. "It was impossible to give him too much to do." His penchant for labor and challenge, and his passion for the Freedmen, garnered the attention of the Freewill Baptist Home Mission Society and the American Missionary Association.

They had a job for Brackett: return to the South and establish schools for the freed African Americans.

"I found a colored population poor and helpless, surrounded by white people desperately hostile to their improvement," reported Brackett, following his arrival at the Ferry on October 28, 1865. The New England missionary connected promptly with his Freedmen's Bureau partners, and the bureau commissioned him superintendent of Freedmen's schools for Jeffer-

---

LAW OF VIRGINIA!

ALL MEETINGS of free Negroes or mulattoes at any school house, church, meeting house, or other place for teaching them reading or writing, either in the day or the night shall be considered an unlawful assembly. Warrants shall direct any sworn officer to enter and disperse such Negroes and inflict corporal punishment on the offenders at the discretion of the justice, not exceeding **twenty lashes.**

ANY WHITE PERSON assembling to instruct free Negroes to read or write shall be fined not over **$50.00**, also be imprisoned not exceeding **two months.**

It is further enacted, that if any white person **FOR PAY** shall assemble with any slaves for the purpose of teaching them to read or write, he shall for each offense be fined, at the discretion of the justice, **$10.00-$100.00.**

Laws like this 1831 edition of the Virginia Code, Ch. 39, had governed Harpers Ferry life for generations. The notion of educating Freedmen was revolutionary.

"Education must be the stepping stone to intelligence and a better life.

Lt. Augustus Ferzard Higgs
Harpers Ferry Freedmen's Bureau
September 30, 1866

Nathan Brackett

son and Berkeley counties. Additionally, Brackett was given responsibility for establishing schools throughout the Shenandoah Valley, where nearly 30,000 Freedmen now resided.

The government assigned Brackett the Lockwood House at Harpers Ferry for his local school and quarters. Situated on the eastern edge of Camp Hill, and overlooking the Harper Cemetery, the house boasted marvelous views, but its condition was decrepit. Used throughout the war as a headquarters, a hospital, a prison and a barracks, the building had been "wantonly abused...mostly by our own [U.S.] troops." It also had been shelled. Holes in the walls and an opening in the roof "told where a shell had unceremoniously entered."

Despite its condition, Brackett gratefully accepted the mansion for students' study, religious meetings, and for his home. After some quick patchwork repairs, word circulated rapidly that he had opened a school for the Freedmen. Within one month of Brackett's arrival, as many as eighty eager students were attending day classes, while the night school attracted nearly half as many.

"The capacity of the colored people for education is rather a stale subject," observed Brackett, noting that two and a half centuries of racial subjugation had deemed African Americans incapable learners. "I will simply say that my experience tends to prove that they are every way human, subject to the same passions and incited by the same motives as other men."

> *"The large rooms are convenient for schools and meetings and we consider it an excellent location for our school."*
>
> Anne Dudley
> Missionary Teacher
> at Lockwood House
> December 1865

Southern neighbors disagreed.

"Certain is this," wrote a local newspaper editor, "in the association of the Northern Puritan and the Southern darkey, the darkey will be the sufferer, both in religion and character." The journalist continued, '[W]hile we have ever regarded the freeing of the negro as the worst calamity that could have befallen him, it will be heaping livid coals of cruelty upon him if he is to be educated by the Puritans of the North."

Brackett and his missionary associates knew they were reaching into a rattlesnake den. Jefferson County and the Shenandoah Valley had been a bastion of the Confederacy during the war. The local county, including Harpers Ferry, had recruited ten companies of infantry, cavalry and artillery for the Southern cause—1,600 Confederate soldiers. Hundreds of men had served in Robert E. Lee's army. A majority fought with Stonewall Jackson in his famous Stonewall Brigade. Others rode with cavalry icon Jeb Stuart and the Laurel Brigade. Many matriculated with Mosby, the most remarkable of all Confederate guerilla commanders, prowling behind Union lines and protecting their homeland neighborhoods. Dozens of these fathers, sons, brothers and nephews became corpses for the Confederacy. Many families lost two generations of manhood, wiped out by the war. They acknowledged their losses. They accepted that they lost. But they refused to purge their pride.

Missionaries from Maine constituted yet another Yankee invasion. For local former Confederates, the war continued, not with shells, but for the salvation of the Southern soul. The abolitionist doctrine of the Maine missionaries, and their passion for the Freedmen, epitomized everything the locals hated about the North.

For the natives, every missionary represented another John Brown.

"We have no room and no sympathy for any who[m] grieve over the old murderer, John Brown," quipped an area newspaper. "We saw him swing and only mourn because many another of his kind failed to meet their deserts at the same time."

"[We] must confess ourselves so utterly hardened and set in our ways as to prefer the continuance of the 'night of barbarism' [slave society]…to the enlightenment of our northern neighbors."

> "[The teachers] should remember that rebel eyes are constantly upon them seeking some occasion to injure them and retain or prevent our work of mercy among the Freedmen."
>
> Rev. Silas Curtis
> Freewill Baptist Home Mission
> February 8, 1866

Such pronounced prejudice forewarned the Maine missionaries to step carefully and slowly. They understood they were entering a minefield, dialed for detonation. They encountered, however, too many trip wires in a Southern culture with strict rules of behavior between whites and blacks.

A simple stroll, as example, spiraled into scandal.

Miss Sarah Jane Foster, one of four young missionary women who followed Brackett to Harpers Ferry as a teacher for the Freedmen, discovered early in her tenure that an unmarried white woman, escorted from school to her home by a black man, violated Southern social codes. The indignation was immediate and threatening. "[T]he roughs are terribly exasperated," Miss Foster shared in her diary. She was forced to abandon her white boarder's home "for fear they might be mobbed." She and her school in Martinsburg (about 15 miles from the Ferry) were so endangered by violence and vandalism that the Freedmen's Bureau rushed troops to the town to ensure order.

"I am in trouble…I have been slandered by the mob…it cuts me deeply," trembled

Foster. Taunted, tormented and tested, Missionary Foster turned to her faith. "God is at work here," she deemed. "Oh Father let me stay. I cannot give it up now."

Missionary teacher Anne Dudley suffered a similar experience in Charles Town, eight miles from the Ferry. Escorted into town by federal soldiers, white boardinghouse operators refused her quarters, and her presence brought repeated sneers, jeers and threats.

The thirty-two-year-old, unmarried Dudley felt compelled to keep "a good axe and six-shooter at the head of my bed at night, resolved to sell my life as dearly as possible—if need be." She established her first school in a log cabin with a stone fireplace, moved in some rough board benches, and closed the shutters "to hinder the chance to shoot at us at night, for we had night school, and strongly barred the doors." As Miss Dudley so surmised: "The spirit that hung John Brown still lives."

"We did not and will not open our arms and our houses to any Yankees from Maine or any other State," thundered a local newspaper, "who come down to affiliate with the negroes and go arm in arm with them, visit at their houses and eat at their tables."

Perhaps no village in the Shenandoah Valley resented the Maine missionaries more than Charles Town. Its people felt personally violated by the invasion of John Brown. Its court house, its jail and its gallows site offered daily reminders of the origins of the calamitous Civil War. Its residents had contributed considerably to the Confederate cause, offering its manhood for the battlefields. Repeated U.S. invasions and occupations had scarred the court house and stained its streets with blood. The violence and vandalism had wrecked much of the town. Fresh graves and Southern defeat hurt these people. The continued presence of Yankees—not as soldiers, but as teachers—inflamed these people.

"The n—r teachers have the permission of the people of the South to remain in their own land….But the meddlesome disposition of New England Yankeeism will not permit them to do this," wrote a local newspaper editor. "They must quit their own self-righteous and idolatrous clime, and in the character of missionaries force themselves where their presence is neither agreeable nor useful."

> "It is unusual to go to the post office without being hooted at, and twice I have been stoned on the streets at noonday."
>
> Kate Anthony
> Missionary Teacher
> 1866

Background: John Brown's Fort. The specter of the Northern abolitionist warrior continued to haunt—and enrage—the minds of townspeople.

> March 13, 1866
>
> "I never was in a work that so thoroughly aroused my whole being, and gave life such a zest."
>
> Sarah Jane Foster
> Missionary Teacher

CONFLUENCE

In Harpers Ferry, too, Brackett's school and students encountered threats and violence. "We are having serious trouble just now—or our pupils are," reported Brackett, three months following his arrival. "The blood hounds are all loose. They have attacked our evening scholars several times lately." This was occurring at the district headquarters of the Freedmen's Bureau, with federal troops posted about. "Last night four of the men fought their way through quite a crowd," wrote Brackett. "They are threatening to burn our house."

Further complicating the missionaries' presence was a local conviction of stolen identity. West Virginia had been established as a Union state, by Union separatists, with enforcement by the Union army. When veteran Confederates returned home to Harpers Ferry and Charles Town following the war, they ventured not into their native Virginia, but into a foreign state named West Virginia. This resulted in a pervasive reminder of the U.S. conquest of the South, and generated daily animus toward anything Yankee.

"Hang me! If I say West Virginia," commented a humorist on a visit to Charles Town. "No, I will not call it West Virginia....Maps may say what they please, but I say this is Virginia."

Amendment XV

The right of citizens of the United States to vote shall not be denied or abridged by the United States or by any state on account of race, color, or previous condition of servitude.

The Fifteenth Amendment to the U.S. Constitution, ratified in 1870, extended voting rights to African American men as a matter of law. Making this a practical reality, however, was another fight—one that would endure for generations.

Voting rights for African American men also exploded against the missionaries' mission. White Southerners considered the franchise a sacred right, impossible to share with former slaves. The very notion that a black man could cast a vote with the same singular power as a white man's vote was incomprehensible. For Southerners, this represented a tyranny of Yankee overreach in the aftermath of the Civil War. It leaned too much toward equality.

"[L]et every [white] man opposed to negro suffrage, and consequent negro equality, come manfully forward and put his shoulders to the wheel," exclaimed a Harpers Ferry writer identified as "X."

K. K. K.
All those interested in the organization of a Society of the Ku Klux Klan, are requested to meet at the U. M. S., to-morrow (Wednesday) morning, at 9 o'clock, where the object of the organization will be fully explained. By order of the Eminent
March 31—1t.* KUI KHO KHAN.

As reform swept through the South, groups such as the KKK rose in response. This invitation to potential members appeared in the Spirit of Jefferson in 1868, while the nation was debating the 14th Amendment—a law that would eventually be used to further civil rights for Blacks.

REDEEMERS, RESISTERS

"Do not be deluded with the assurance that negro suffrage is not the issue in the State," continued "X," the anonymous agitator. "Union men of Jefferson County, will you stand supinely by and see this giant wrong perpetuated?...Arouse then to the importance of the issues—gird on your armor, and roll back the flood of fanaticism threatening soon to engulf us."

Fueling this combustion, also, was the fact that ex-Confederates were prohibited from voting or holding any elected office, unless they passed a loyalty test administered by their arch enemies, Radical Republicans. This, in effect, disenfranchised thousands of white males throughout West Virginia, who ruptured in wrath against the Radical Republicans who supported black suffrage and prevented their political participation. Though the Maine missionaries did not come into the South with political intent, the locals viewed them as blunt instruments of the hated Radical Republicans, exacerbating their welcome.

> *"The late rebels here manifest a purpose to oppress the colored people all they can....[T]he disloyal element rent all their spite upon the heads of the poor Blacks, and I am sorry to say that I have Observed many loyal persons as strongly prejudiced against the Freedmen as the disloyal."*
>
> Capt. H. Stover How
> Freedmen's Bureau
> January 31, 1866

Undaunted by animosity, families like the Lovetts—Free Blacks turned wartime refugees—seized the opportunities offered by Brackett's school. Several Lovett children graduated, and went on to help create a strong African American community despite a rigidly segregated society.

Nativism and rabid racism, however, failed to deter or dissuade the Maine missionaries, nor their African American students. More than 1,000 eager learners were attending day and night classes, ranging in age from eight to seventy-seven, with one walking up to six miles to school. Teachers were paid $15 per month ($2 more than a private in the Union army during the war), but were expected to donate back one third of their salary to the Freewill Baptist mission effort. Soliciting donations of books, bibles and newspapers from New England supporters was a principal motivator as each female mentor taught elementary reading, writing and arithmetic.

"The black race will not again be enslaved," beamed Sarah Jane Foster. "Just now education is their aim, and nothing is suffered to hinder them in its pursuit." In a letter to the Freewill Baptist newspaper, circulated to thousands in New England, Foster acknowledged success. "As I look back I am astonished at the progress that some of my scholars have made. True, some need driving to learn. Others need strict discipline,

118

CONFLUENCE

which is difficult in a crowded room, but yet I see progress, and mean, God helping me, to persevere till Providence shall close the door now open for me here."

It soon became evident to Brackett that the African American demand for education surpassed his supply of teachers. He then realized his next vision: *establish a school to train the ex-slaves as the teachers.*

ANNUAL REPORT 1867
FREEWILL BAPTIST HOME MISSION SOCIETY

Your Committee appointed to inquire into the expedience of establishing a Normal school among the Freedmen are fully convinced that their wants cannot be met in any other way. If we were able to supply them with teachers from the North it would not be best for them to depend upon us for them. They can never be elevated by our lifting them up; they must be taught to raise themselves, and this can be done in no way so effectually as to qualify young men and women of color to be educators of their own youth. . . .

We must not only have a Normal school, but that Harpers Ferry is the place for its location, and the following are among the reasons:

1. Harpers Ferry is on the line between that part of the country from which the money and fostering care must come, and that part from which the pupils must come, and to which they will go and labor.

2. It is easy of access from both of these sections of country, as five lines of railroad center there.

3. The scenery is wild, grand and beautiful, inspiriting to the student.

4. The climate is healthy and invigorating.

5. It is historic ground, sacred to the Freedmen, and full of interest to all other. . . .

Philanthropist John Storer of Stanford, Maine, became the school's benefactor, offering $10,000 (the equivalent of thirty-three American workers' annual salaries) toward the establishment of an eventual college in the Southern states "at which youth could be educated without distinction of race or color."

John Storer (1796-1867) hinged his donation to the fledgling school on the condition that Brackett turn it into a degree-granting institution, and admit students without regard for race or gender.

The local press was unimpressed:

> "[A] College for the education of colored persons is about being erected at Harpers Ferry. The pupils, we presume, are to be imported, as our home darkies, as yet, do not aspire quite so high."

Storer College officially opened its doors on October 2, 1867. Its first order of business: soliciting more doors.

Since first arriving at Harpers Ferry, Brackett had coveted four empty government mansions crowning Camp Hill. Once the homes of the armory's elite, they had been abandoned and damaged during the Civil War. Now the government was considering their disposal. Brackett already occupied the Paymaster's (Lockwood) House, but he lacked a permanent arrangement there, and the student demand required expansion. Acquisition of the government buildings would establish the nucleus of the new school and create a college campus.

This vision required the endorsement of Congress—a murky and treacherous path, especially for something so myopic.

Enter United States Senator William Pitt Fessenden. A champion abolitionist from Maine, Fessenden adopted the visions of fellow state brothers Storer and Brackett. From his position as chairman of the Congress' "Joint Committee on Reconstruction," he wielded power and influence, muscling through legislation in 1868 that granted Storer College the four buildings as a donation from the government.

Fessenden's machination and maneuvers distressed the local press. "[M]any of the citizens of [Harpers Ferry]…may be deprived of their homes which they purchased from the government with the distinct understanding that the price was to be paid in work in the shops," complained an area journalist. "[T]heir employment having been taken away, they are now to be driven out of house and home while their sheltering roofs are to be sold to endow a negro college!"

Donations of vacant armory buildings and hard-won fundraising campaigns, often featuring the school's choir, for new structures, eventually enabled Storer College to expand across Camp Hill.

> **CONSTITUTION**
>
> of the State of
>
> **WEST VIRGINIA**
>
> ---
>
> Article XII, Sec. 8
>
> *White and colored persons shall not be taught in the same schools.*
>
> Revised by Convention   1872

Displeasure with the school fomented at the state level, too, where the West Virginia legislature was considering Storer College's charter. The college founder insisted that the school be open to all sexes and all races. Hence, the charter placed before the legislature in 1868 included this language: "a college for teaching all classes of persons, without distinction of color." This caused consternation in the state capital, where leadership believed segregation of black and white children should be the law for public schools. Storer, though a private institution, would stand out as an inconsistent exception to this rule.

"The denominational feature [religious association] is not half as obnoxious as the mingling of the races," reported Sen. Joseph T. Hoke, the representative from the Eastern Panhandle and a native of Martinsburg who was a Freewill Baptist himself. "However I think we can pass it."

Indeed, the integrated language in the charter survived by one vote—Hoke's.

This infuriated the local population, who stewed over the charter for a year.

"[G]reat dissatisfaction is felt and expressed among the citizens in regard to the subject," noted Joseph Barry of Harpers Ferry. "The people held a meeting some time ago and petitioned the State Legislature to revoke the charter." In 1870, Hoke, once again, stepped forward on behalf of Storer College, and the annulment attempt failed.

Meanwhile, as Storer College was standing firmly in a tornado of Southern culture, another storm struck. Ex-Confederates had succeeded in obtaining relief from the onerous oath requirements during the last years of the 1860s and were gaining considerable power as Conservative Democrats. Incensed by the war-time West Virginia constitution (written by Republicans), the ascending Democrats demanded a new constitutional convention in 1871. Since African American males had the right to vote, Storer hosted a meeting to discuss options.

A racial volcano exploded. "The Radicals

> TEACHER'S INSTITUTE.—There will be a Teacher's Institute in Jefferson county, commencing Tuesday, August 22d, continuing four days. Competent instructors have been engaged by the State Superintendent, and a Lecture on some educational topic will be given each evening of the Institute. The friends near by will be expected to entertain those from other towns. Where shall it be held?
>
> N. C. BRACKETT,
> County Superintendent.
>
> We received the above notice from Mr. N. C. Brackett, of Harper's Ferry, the County Superintendent of Public Schools, and we would suggest that the Institute be held in this place. We are confident that the Teachers in attendance will find our town a very pleasant place for a few days sojourn.—*Register*.
>
> [The *White* teachers of the county would no doubt find a hearty welcome in Charlestown, but as for Mr. Brackett, his *absence* would be most acceptable to our people.

This June 21, 1870, Spirit of Jefferson *editorial highlights the incessant animosity toward Brackett, the school, and its mission.*

of Berkeley and Jefferson Senatorial district, that is forty n—rs and twenty whites, met in Convention at the n—r 'institoot' at Harpers Ferry," wrote a local editor. "The place of holding the Convention was fitting in the extreme. Where else but within the walls of a n—r college, could the white Radicals sit in conclave with so much propriety?" The editor concluded, "Being deserted by all white men who have any respect for themselves, those who remain are forced to get down on their narrow bones to the n—r."

Particular ire was focused upon Brackett. He had waded into local politics during the latter years of the 1860s and was labeled a Radical Republican. Brackett hosted this interracial meeting, soon dubbed by the press as the "Black and Tan Conference." In response, a local newspaper demanded desperate action. "[W]e . . . call upon every [white male] voter to exercise his privilege and to perform his duty, and now and forever to place a crushing heel upon the head of the serpent whose stings we have so long felt." The paper insisted that after nearly a decade of Radical Republican rule the time had arrived "once for all to thrust out the insolent adventurers that aspire to hold our posts of honor and to make laws for our people."

LOVE FOR THE NEGRO!

Within the past week Mr. J. C. Brackett, one of the carpet-bag nominees for the Legislature from this county, fearing a division in the African vote of the county, has sent a negro messenger to Geo. McKinney, colored independent candidate for the same office, requesting him to withdraw from the field.— This McKinney emphatically refuses to do, and we glory in his spunk. How beautifully Mr. Brackett's love for the negro is displayed in this transaction, the intelligent portion of our colored population may easily discern.— As long as negroes can be made the stepping stone upon which to elevate them to office, these smiling smirking carpet-baggers will fawn and fondle around them as their very brothers; but when one announces himself as a candidate for the suffrages of his colored brethren for the same position, he is politely asked to *stand aside*. He may vote for the carpet-bager, but he must not have the audacity to run for a *paying office*.

Although secret meetings have been held night after night among the negroes by Ames, Brackett, Leisenring & Co., and all the vile slang of New England treachery attempted to be instilled into the minds of our colored people, we have yet confidence enough in the majority of them to believe that they know what these professions are worth, and where their true interests lie. If they do not, we have nothing more to say.

REMEMBER, WE LOST THE STATE LAST YEAR BY STAY-AT-HOME CONSERVATIVES!

Above: As shown in this October 25, 1870, editorial in the Spirit of Jefferson, *race was a major issue in politics. Left: Brackett, third row from top, third from left, with a group of early students and staff.*

CONFLUENCE

Despite all racial obstacles, regardless of all threats, in spite of all the insults, notwithstanding all the jests, Storer College matured and Storer stayed alive.

Ultimately, the school closed in 1955, following the nationwide desegregation of education mandated by the U.S. Supreme Court. Yet for eighty-eight years, the little school on the "hill of hope" persisted in offering a safe space for African American students to socialize, study, explore, and now and again, *resist*.

Top: Storer baseball team, with second college president Henry McDonald top center.

Middle: Storer choir

Bottom: Storer band

Opposite: Storer graduate

The miracle of Storer College is not that it endured almost ninety years, but that it survived its first ten.

[T]he very air of heaven seemed to fan the whole hill sides, and there never was a more lovely place on this earth for one to learn a lesson, for we could see the key to all lessons where nature had designed for a grand school of learning.

Kate Drumgoold
A Slave Girl's Story, *1898*

A MEMORIAL DAY CELEBRATION
"To Pay a Just Debt Long Due"

The most famous African American of the nineteenth century agreed to come to Harpers Ferry—finally.

Twenty-two years after he rejected John Brown's plea to join him on his strike at Harpers Ferry, Frederick Douglass, at last, accepted an invitation from Storer College to offer a commencement speech on John Brown.

As a Storer trustee, Douglass permitted the college and the Freewill Baptists to sell his speech as a fundraiser to endow a "John Brown Professorship."

A large crowd of blacks and whites—including former Confeder-ates and local newspaper editors who had savaged Storer since its in-ception—assembled on the campus on Memorial Day, May 30, 1881. A remarkable sight rocked the senses of history: Aside Mr. Douglass on the speaker's platform was Andrew Hunter, the prosecutor who tried John Brown in Charles Town.

The mountains of Harpers Ferry echoed that day with Douglass' soaring oratory. Here are excerpts from *John Brown: An Address:*

"The negro-worshippers may canonize John Brown as much as they please, but we don't mean to let them forget that the first victim of the old murderer was an inoffensive, industrious and respected colored man, brutally shot down without provocation or excuse. Fred Douglas [sic] neglected to mention it."

Virginia Free Press
June 18, 1881

> "If John Brown did not end the war that ended slavery, he did at least begin the war that ended slavery."

Not everyone concurred with Douglass' assessment of Brown.

I come to pay a just debt long due, to vindicate in some degree a great historical character, of our own time and country, one with whom I was myself well acquainted, and whose friendship and confidence it was my good fortune to share and to give you such recollections, impres-sions and facts, as I can, of a grand, brave and good old man. . . .

It certainly is not a story to please, but to pain. It is not a story to increase our sense of social safety and security, but to fill the imagination with wild and troubled fancies of doubt and danger. It was a sudden and startling surprise to the people of Harpers Ferry, and it is not easy to conceive of a situation more abundant in all the elements of horror and consternation. . . .

The bloody harvest of Harpers Ferry was ripened by the heat and moisture of merciless bondage of more than two hundred years. That startling cry of alarm on the banks of the Potomac was but the answering back of the avenging angel to the midnight invasions of Christian slave-traders on the sleeping hamlets of Africa. . . .

When John Brown proclaimed emancipation to the slaves of Maryland and Virginia he added to his war power the force of a moral earthquake. Virginia felt all her strong-ribbed mountains to shake under the heavy tread of armed insurgents. Of his army of nineteen her conscience made an army of nineteen hundred. . . .

His zeal in the cause of race was far greater than mine—it was as the burning sun to my taper light—mine was bounded by time, his stretched away to the boundless shores of eternity. I could live for the slave, but he could die for him. . . .

To the outward eye of men, John Brown was a criminal, but to their inward eye he was a just man and true. His deeds might be disowned, but the spirit which made those deeds possible was worthy of highest honor. . .

I told him finally that it was impossible for me to join him. I could see Harpers Ferry only as a trap of steel, and ourselves in the wrong side of it. He regretted my decision and we parted. . . .

With the Allegheny Mountains for his pulpit, the country for his church and the whole civilized world for his audience, he was a thousand times more effective as a preacher than as a warrior. . . . Mighty with the sword of steel, he was mightier with the sword of truth, and with this sword, he literally swept the horizon. . . .

"The battle we wage is not for ourselves alone, but for all true Americans"

Equal rights proved near impossible for African Americans to attain in the decades following the Civil War. State legislatures, both North and South, adopted "Black Codes" and "Jim Crow" laws that dictated legal segregation of the races in virtually all aspects of life, including schools, trains, hotels, restaurants and complete communities. The Supreme Court legitimized lawful segregation, and the United States reigned as the largest apartheid nation on earth.

Black scholars and civil rights activists refused acceptance of the "separate but equal" doctrine. In 1905, a passionate group led by Dr. W. E. B. Du Bois—Harvard's first African American doctorate—assembled near Niagara Falls, Canada, to organize resistance and advocate for reform.

A year later, in August 1906, Harpers Ferry was selected as the location for the second Niagara Conference, and the Storer College campus as the host. The four-day meeting included 150 men and women from all segments of the country. They came to conquer racism, and they chose Harpers Ferry to acknowledge the leadership and symbolism of John Brown, including a "pilgrimage" to John Brown's Fort to honor his memory.

The second Niagara Conference culminated with Dr. Du Bois' *Address to the Country*. His impassioned oratory rivaled the speech of Frederick Douglass on John Brown, delivered at Storer 25 years earlier.

Du Bois, fifth from right, at Harpers Ferry Niagara Conference

"[We] turn toward the nation and again ask in the name of ten million the privilege of a hearing. . . .

We will not be satisfied to take one jot or tittle less than our full manhood rights. We claim for ourselves every single right that belongs to a freeborn American, political, civil and social; and until we get these rights we will never cease to protest and assail the ears of America. The battle we wage is not for ourselves alone but all true Americans. It is a fight for ideals, lest this, our common fatherland, false to its founding, become in truth the land of the thief and the home of the Slave. . . .

Stripped of verbiage and subterfuge and in its naked nastiness the new American creed says: Fear to let black men even try to rise lest they become the equals of the white. And this in the land that professes to follow Jesus Christ. The blasphemy of such a course is only matched by cowardice.

In detail our demands are clear and unequivocal.

First, we would vote; with the right to vote goes everything: Freedom, manhood, the honor of your wives, the chastity of your daughters, the right to work, and the chance to rise. . . . We want full manhood suffrage, and we want it now, henceforth and forever.

Second. We want discrimination in public accommodation to cease. Separation in railway and street cars, based simply on race and color, is un-American, undemocratic, and silly. . . .

Third. We claim the right of freemen to walk, talk, and be with them that wish to be with us. No man has a right to choose another man's friends, and to attempt to do so is an impudent interference with the most fundamental human privilege.

Fourth. We want the laws enforced against rich as well as poor; against Capitalist as well as Laborer; against white as well as black. We are not more lawless than the white race, [yet] we are more often arrested, convicted, and mobbed. . . .

Fifth. We want our children educated. . . . And when we call for education we mean real education. We believe in work. We ourselves are workers, but work is not necessarily education. Education is the development of power and ideal. We want our children trained as intelligent human beings should be, and we will fight for all time against any proposal to educate black boys and girls simply as servants and underlings, or simply for the use of other people.

We have a right to know, to think, to aspire. . . ."

CONFLUENCE

TWO MONUMENTS, TWO PERSPECTIVES
CONTROVERSY & CONVERSATION

Two monuments stare at each other along Potomac Street in old town Harpers Ferry. One displays three words; the other over 100. One says little; the other says a lot. But it's not the number, but the meaning of the words that matters.

One sits atop an artificial hill, covering its battlefield. The "John Brown Fort" monument is a simple obelisk of tiered marble, installed by the B & O Railroad in 1895, not as a memorial, but as a reminder of the location of the original Fort.

The other stands fifty yards distant, on the opposite side of Potomac Street. It's a massive boulder of granite, with words sharply engraved, commissioned and installed by the United Daughters of the Confederacy and the Sons of Confederate Veterans in 1931.

The obelisk witnessed no ceremony upon its installation. The Confederate memorial drew a crowd, including Henry McDonald, the white president of Storer College, and the school's African American college singers. The ceremony dedicated the "Faithful Slave Memorial," meant to honor Heyward Shepherd, the black baggage porter killed in John Brown's Raid.

During the unveiling, UDC President Elizabeth Burford Bashinsky, an Alabama native born two years after Appomattox, loftily described a prewar South she herself had never witnessed. "People unfamiliar with the patriarchal relationship between the whites of the South and the Negro do not understand the conditions. For logical reasons the people of the South inherited slavery, but with all the responsibilities that…a Christian conscience could impose." Bashinsky went on to praise the black "mammies" who had raised generations of white Southern children. "How she loved her white 'chillun," Bashinsky mused. "How could anyone get these sons of these black mammies to take up arms against their masters?"

A young lady in the choir objected. "I certainly do not wish to create bitterness," said Storer choir director Pearl Tatten, "but I could not stand there and hear those things without being deeply hurt. I just had to speak out and say what was crying to be said."

W. E. B. Du Bois and the NAACP also had something to say. They proposed a rebuttal plaque for installation on the John Brown Fort, then situated at Storer College. Dr. McDonald refused, considering the wording too controversial.

Passions simmered and stewed. Twenty-two years later, the National Park Service inherited inherited the UDC monument. The Confederate monument was re-moved in 1975 due to a reconstruction project; park management buried it in the maintenance yard, perhaps to be forgotten. Miss Lucille Busch of the local UDC, however, led a spirited effort for years for the monument's return. She succeeded. But the park concealed the monument behind a plywood box, concerned it may be offensive.

The park eventually discovered the lost words of Du Bois. This allowed the Confederate monument to speak for itself, and Du Bois to speak for the John Brown Monument.

Visitors today may decide for themselves which voice of history they prefer.

Words of Rebuttal
by W. E. B. Du Bois

Here

John Brown

Aimed at Human Slavery

A Blow

That woke a guilty nation

With him fought

Seven Slaves and sons of slaves.

Over his crucified corpse

Marched 200,000 black soldiers and 4,000,000 freedmen

Singing

"John Brown's Body lies a mouldering in the grave

But his Soul Goes Marching on!"

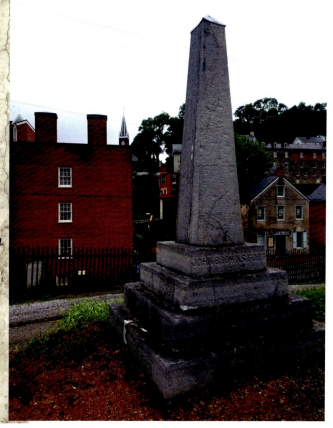

The John Brown obelisk, installed by the B & O Railroad on the original site of the John Brown Fort. In background, left, against the brick building, can be seen the Shepherd Monument.

John Brown's Fort
Mobility, Nobility

As Harpers Ferry struggled to rebuild after the war, the preservation of John Brown's Fort was anything but a priority.

John Brown's Fort departed its original battlefield thirty-two years following Brown's capture there.

In 1891, a group of mid-western investors purchased the building, unceremoniously dismantling it brick by brick, and shipping it to Chicago, where it was rebuilt as a tourist attraction for the 1892-93 World's Fair. The investment scheme failed. "For about ten days the exhibition lived a precarious life," noted the *Chicago Tribune*, "and then it died with a record of eleven paid admissions and an outlay of more than $60,000." The fair ended. The Fort languished, saddened and lonely, 600 miles away from home.

Kate Field rescued it from oblivion. The renowned journalist and philanthropist had earned recognition and protection for John Brown's burial site and his upstate New York farm, and she organized a campaign to return the Fort to Harpers Ferry. Field succeeded in raising the funds, but the challenge was finding a new home. The original battlefield location was buried under 20 feet of rock and debris by the B & O Railroad's new alignment.

Field examined several alternatives, including the Storer College campus, but settled instead on the Alexander and Mary Murphy farm, about two miles from the Fort's original location. The Murphys donated the site (the deed was for $1 in 1895).

REDEEMERS, RESISTERS

John Brown's Fort once again marveled at the mountains of Harpers Ferry from its own mountain-top perch (the southwestern tip of Bolivar Heights).

Kate Field

Fort at the Murphy farm, 1895-1909

Storer College coveted the Fort, desiring to have its presence on campus to inspire its students. It also hoped to attract tourists and attention to the cash-strapped school. In 1909, by the 50th anniversary of John Brown's war to end slavery, Storer had acquired the Fort; and the next year, moved it for its third time, rebuilding it at the nucleus of the Storer campus.

The greatest symbol of freedom and human dignity in Harpers Ferry now inspirited students—grandchildren and great grandchildren of many former slaves—to strive for self-respect, selfless service and successes in life.

"From an ordinary engine house it has been transformed into a new Cradle of Liberty."

Henry McDonald
Storer College President

John Brown's Fort at Storer College, where it was used as a museum. When the college ceased operations in 1955, the fort's fate would rest in the hands of the National Park Service.

132

Destruction along Shenandoah Street, flood of 1942.

"Heaven, in its anger at the folly and ingratitude of man, had marked the place for total destruction."

~Joseph Barry

Chapter 8
RENAISSANCE REPELLED

The Civil War destroyed Harpers Ferry.
The unanswered question: could it recover?

Eyes focused upon the U.S. government. Would the federal armory return?

As the last Union troops pulled out of the Ferry's fortifications almost three months after Appomattox, the war-ravaged town appeared desolate, destitute and deceased.

"Where is the hotel?" inquired John Trowbridge, arriving soon after the declaration of peace. The journalist was embarking on an expedition into post-war Rebel country, recording his impressions for a forthcoming book. For the first time, the New York-born Yankee was stepping into the former Southern Confederacy.

"That is it…the only hotel at Harpers Ferry now," chirped the response.

Trowbridge ventured to the remnants of the once flourishing Wager House Hotel— where now stood only a new, cheaply constructed, unpainted four-story wooden building that "looked more like a soldiers' barracks than a hotel." In the Shenandoah House (that overlooked the Potomac), "there was not a window-blind or shutter to be seen," wrote the dismayed traveler. His hospice was "an illustration of the mushroom style of building that springs up in the track of desolation, to fill temporarily the place of the old that has been swept away."

Trowbridge's experience worsened. His room displayed itself as a "mere bin to stow guests in…There was no paper on the walls, no carpet on the rough board floor, and not so much as a nail to hang a hat on." Trowbridge grew even more distressed as he tired and prepared for a night's rest. His mattress "had the appearance of being stuffed with shingles," and his sheets were

Shenandoah Street was the very definition of a ghost town.

"The town itself [lies] half in ruins... Of the extensive buildings which comprised the armory, rolling-mills, foundry, and machine shops, you see but little more than the burnt-out, empty shells....And all about the town are rubbish, filth, and stench."

Harpers Ferry, 1865, as witnessed by journalist John Trowbridge. The Shenandoah House is located at the right end of the bridge.

CONFLUENCE

dirty and too short. He had no pillow, so he made his shawl suffice; the next morning, for some privacy, it doubled as his window curtain.

Redemption arrived with sunrise, however, when Trowbridge witnessed the majestic mountains towering over the confluence. "It was hard to believe that those [natural] beauties had been lying latent around me during the long, wearisome night."

As happens to many travelers upon their first glance at Harpers Ferry, Trowbridge then transformed into philosopher:

"The dull life we live, close and dark and narrow as it seems . . . is surrounded by invisible realities, waiting only for the rays of a spiritual dawn."

But Harpers Ferry's beauty could not suppress its ugliness. "War has changed all," observed Trowbridge. "

Amongst the desolation and despair, Trowbridge noticed something peculiar. *John Brown's Fort.*

"Almost alone of the government buildings...[it] has escaped destruction," marveled the traveler. "It has come out of the ordeal of war terribly bruised and battered, it is true; its windows blackened and patched like the eyes of a pugilist.

"[B]ut there it still stands, with its brown brick walls and little wooden belfry, like a monument which no Rebel hands were permitted to demolish."

Turning back toward the town, Trowbridge pontificated. "Harpers Ferry affords a striking illustration of the folly of secession."

RENAISSANCE REPELLED

But Trowbridge gleaned hope. "[W]ith the grandeur of its scenery, the tremendous water-power afforded by its two rushing rivers, and the natural advantage it enjoys as the key to the fertile Shenandoah Valley, Harpers Ferry—redeemed from slavery—and opened to Northern enterprise, should become a beautiful and busy town."

A promising prediction spawned from unpromising condition.

It seemed far-fetched that the United States government would reestablish its presence at Harpers Ferry. From its perspective, the place was a nest of traitors. Here, after all, was the first target of Virginia. Here disloyalty destroyed the armory and arsenal. Here occurred repeated Confederate invasions and occupations. Here happened the worst surrender of the U. S. Army during the Civil War.

Harpers Ferry was damaged goods. The war, in many respects, offered the opportunity for the War Department to dump this troublesome burden. From its earliest days, the armory had been plagued. It had suffered decades of inept civilian management; political conniving and corruption; ongoing labor strife; and production—both in quality and quantity—persistently deficient compared to its sister in Springfield.

Above, John Brown's Fort became a significant tourist attraction in the postwar era. At right, its great machines incapacitated at the very start of the war, the former weapons factory spent much of the conflict as a mere storehouse, supplying thousands of troops. What now?

And then there was the ubiquitous problem with water—either too much or neither enough.

Weeks, sometimes several months would pass, when production ceased due to drought. The rivers' flow would reduce so dramatically that not enough water could be impounded or directed to power machinery. *Energy crises* threatened each summer and fall, making reliable production impossible.

Floods presented another hazard. The entire armory and arsenal sat within the flood plain. Wedged between two rivers, vertical cliffs, and in essence on a narrow sand bar—and located at the mouth of the Shenandoah and its 160-mile drainage—it was inevitable that Harpers Ferry would inundate.

"We are in the midst of a great flood," reported an alarmed superintendent in October, 1847. "The lower floors of all shops...were all under water...some of the old shops including the tilt hammer shop to the depth of 8 feet." Two months later, heavy rains caused the Shenandoah to sweep down Shenandoah Street, filling cellars, "where many families were compelled to leave their dwellings and seek shelter elsewhere."

These unwelcome intrusions not only played havoc in the armory, but also at the arsenal.

The lock, stock and barrel of a military firearm, comprised of metal and wood, did not mix well with water. "The flood at its greatest height was nearly 3/4 inch deep on the floor of the Arsenal where we had about 14,700 muskets," reported a dismayed superintendent in 1843. "[M]ost of them fortunately resting on the points of the bayonets."

Nine years later, in 1852, the situation was less fortunate. "[O]ver 20,000 stands of Arms all of which were entirely covered with water and mud, and must be at once stripped and cleaned."

Nothing compared to the great flood of 1852. "Our country has been visited by an awful calamity," cried a local newspaper. "The destruction of property is beyond all description."

The armory superintendent indicated his mortification and helplessness in his April 23rd report to the War Department. "[W]hat was supposed to be in places of security some 3 feet above any flood ever known at this place were overflowed by the rise of water during the night." He reported the water ten-feet deep throughout the length of the Potomac Musket Factory. "All the men I could employ have been engaged...to clean up the buildings, machinery, damaged parts, tools, etc." The superintendent begged for emergency funding, indicating he would require a large force to return operations to normal. Meanwhile, "the manufacture of Arms is suspended for a time, and this Armory will not be able to turn out [its quota] during the fiscal year."

Not only were armory and arsenal inundated. "Every house on Shenandoah and Potomac streets was almost entirely submerged—the water being six feet higher than at any other period within the recollection of man." The aftermath of mud and muck left the cellars and streets "in a miserable and filthy condition" and a cesspool for sickness and disease, "unless the cellars and streets be cleaned and limed at an early day." Since the armory had the biggest payroll in the factory town, local officials appealed to the U.S. government for aid. Otherwise the armorers' "lives and the lives of their families will be greatly endangered and the government operations seriously impeded."

Even three months after the flood, the superintendent reported he still had a large force employed in "polishing [weapons] parts and putting them together." One light did shine out of this natural debacle. "[M]uskets have been stripped and completely dismantled, their parts being thrown into large heaps. Upon reassembling the arms every part fitted regardless of which arm it had been taken from."

Ironic, indeed, that it required a destructive flood to prove the wonders of interchangeability—Harpers Ferry's great technological gift to the world.

Incidents like the 1852 flood left long and sour memories in Washington. Coupled with the myriad of other terminal problems at Harpers Ferry, along with its wartime destruction and bolstered by a desire to establish a new armory west of the Mississippi, officials in the War Department deemed disposal of the armory its best solution. "Harpers Ferry cannot, in my opinion, be ever again used to advantage for the manufacture of arms," claimed the government's Chief of Ordnance in 1866. "[T]he retention of the property of the United States at that place is not necessary or advantageous to the public interest."

Death blow? *Not if the politicians could resuscitate.*

First an effort occurred in Congress to cede the federal holdings to the nascent State of West Virginia, ensuring local control and destiny. That failed. Then legislators considered retention of the facility, but the cost for rebuilding and replacement topped two million (astronomical in an economy where the average laborer worked for one dollar a day). Then the Senate and House could not agree on a future for the property, with the Senate voting repeatedly to rid the place; but the House tenaciously trying to retain it. Complicating matters, lawyers became involved in a quagmire debating whether the government actually owned water-power rights in the rivers.

Finally, in 1869, after four years of tortured testaments and pathetic progress, the government reached a conclusion: sell.

"The proposed sale...has infused new life and hope in the people of that place," effused a local county newspaper, "and the dawning of a brighter day is in anticipation."

> "Harpers Ferry cannot, in my opinion, be ever again used to advantage for the manufacture of arms."

Background: The inner workings of the water-powered federal armory lay bare to the elements for years after the war.

CONFLUENCE

The announcement attracted national attention, and outside editorials also portended prosperity. "[P]robably no position in the whole country commands superior advantages for manufacturing purposes," boasted the Alexandria *Gazette*. "[O]ne of the largest manufacturing centers in America may yet spring up, if capital and enterprise are employed," opined the *Baltimore Sun*. "Harpers Ferry may become a second Lowell."

Speculators predicted success. Property values in Harpers Ferry skyrocketed. Since the government still owned almost 1,700 acres and 25 dwellings, in addition to the ruins of the armory workshops and its dams and canals, it appeared the public auction would reap benefits for the U.S. Treasury.

The power of the rivers powered this high-stakes speculation. The Potomac (boasting a fall of 25 feet) and the Shenandoah (14-foot fall) had pile-driven through solid rock over the last 11 million years, carving their way through the Blue Ridge at the confluence. Both rivers possessed the greatest energy source of its day to power man's machinery.

This stamp was used to mark barrels leaving the Child and McCreight mill.

The rebirth of water-powered industry at the Ferry did not await the government. The private sector, instead, spurred new development with the 1869 opening of the "Harpers Ferry Mill Company" on Virginius Island. Locating their enterprise in a former cotton mill—most recently used as a Civil War hospital, and later as a prisoner-of-war pen for captured Confederates—two Springfield, Ohio entrepreneurs named Jonathan Child and John McCreight gambled on Harpers Ferry's revival. They hired a workforce that labored for fifteen months preparing the building and its machinery, adopting the latest in flour-milling technology. Their mill became "a marvel of ingenuity."

"This immense establishment, one of the finest perhaps in the United States, so far as perfection of machinery and completeness of arrangement," initiated production at 400 barrels of flour each day (equal to 18 railroad carloads of grain). "Everything about this superb mill is arranged to work by machinery," observed the local newspaper. "[T]he only hand labor performed in the production of a barrel of flour [is] the heading of the barrel after the flour is packed."

Both the process and the product earned accolades. "[T]he bread from it was good enough to grace the tables of the aristocratic," wrote the local news editor. "[M]y better half—and she knows—says it works like a charm, making up smoothly, and [rises] gratifyingly. We judge it as we see it on the table, and know that it is rich,

The four-story flour mill as viewed from Jefferson Rock; note photographer and camera in left front.

Harpers Ferry as viewed from Maryland Heights, 1882-1891. This photo shows the eager postwar resurgence of Harpers Ferry as a transportation gateway, even as roofless armory buildings pose potent reminders that the town's defining industry was gone forever.

white and sweet."

Other local businesses arrived and began to thrive. Spurred by the B & O Railroad and the C & O Canal—both finally able to operate without disruption after four years of persistent interruption during the Civil War—retailers commenced receiving merchandise, wares and supplies commensurate to a booming economy.

Every storefront on Shenandoah and High Streets filled, supplying every convenience for modern living.

Rosenberg's "Clothing and Gents Furnishing Store" flourished. McGraw's coal, lumber and housing materials business bellowed, along with his offer of the "best quality safely cured 50,000 herring and 2,000 shad." George Leisenring's locale featured variety, selling a range of products including clothing, glassware, saddles, coffee, fish, sugars, perfume, whiskeys, cigars and horseshoe nails (and more! in a dizzying assortment). John Kern's restaurant supplied "oysters in every style. Cool ale & choice cigars on hand."

Even the once decrepit Shenandoah House enjoyed a makeover. "We learn that it is undergoing thorough repair, and is to be reopened as a first class Hotel," reported an area newspaper.

Shenandoah Street commercial district, late nineteenth century.

Further fueling this economic enterprise was a grand, gorgeous B & O Railroad bridge. After tumbling nine times into the Potomac during four years of Civil War, stability reigned for the new bridge. The iconic structure spanned nearly 860 feet, employing a web of cast iron tension members that dizzied the eyes in a pallet of painted patterns.

This engineering model, first utilized at the Ferry before the Civil War and named after B & O designer Wendel Bollman, ushered in the era of iron bridges as a sub-stitute for traditional wood. For decades to come, the Harpers Ferry Bollman bridge greeted travelers, displaying a human design of grace and beauty compatible with Mother Nature's creation at the confluence.

But all was not well for the B & O. At the government sale of the armory property—concluded ironically on December 2, 1869, ten years to the day after John Brown's execution—the railroad was outdueled in a bidding war for the Potomac River frontage comprising the old Musket Factory. Captain Francis C. Adams won the contest, paying $1,000 more than the railroad's final offer of $175,000. This cheap decision proved a gar-

The Bollman bridge over the Potomac at Harpers Ferry.

gantuan mistake for the railroad. Unbeknownst to the B & O, Adams and his company were conniving to rid the railroad of its right-of-way, declaring the B & O had no legal access through the lands they now owned. The railroad, of course, expected extortion; and off to the courts raced the combatants. Progress along the Potomac settled into a sedi-mentary stall.

Adams, though, ostensibly promised. He pledged. He promoted. He prophesied. His enterprise, the "Harpers Ferry Waterpower and Manufacturing Company," comprised wealthy "Capitalists" from Washington, New York and Boston. They had mettle and the money to muscle the old factory town back to life. He promised jobs, envisioning woolen and cotton factories paralleling the Potomac, bolstered by a paper mill along the Shenan-doah at the former Rifle Factory site.

Harpers Ferry residents leaped with joy when the government auction ended. They were ecstatic with the entrepreneurs' engagement. Convinced they had discovered their savior, "cheer after cheer rent the air—the assembled residents seeming to read in the dim future a glorious record for Harpers Ferry."

They did not know what awaited them.

REPUTATION AND REFUTATION
THE SALE OF U.S. GOVERNMENT PROPERTY

After more than four years of haggling within the Congress, legislation adopted on December 15, 1868, authorized the Secretary of War "to sell at public auction the United States lands, buildings, surplus machinery, and water power privileges at Harpers Ferry." Prior to the sale, S. Howell Brown, a surveyor and native of Jefferson County who had served as a cartographer for Stonewall Jackson, platted the armory property into lots. The government purchased ads in newspapers announcing the sale, proclaiming the "value of this property for manufacturing purposes is too well known to render it necessary to describe."

Almost one more year would pass before the War Department finally consummated the auction. The sale lasted three days, from November 30 to December 2, 1869. Terms of sale were easy, with credit extended to the highest bidder and up to two years' time to pay.

"Of the point of Harpers Ferry I may say that it has been next to dead ever since John Brown invaded it," wrote journalist George Alfred Townsend in the CHICAGO TRIBUNE *several weeks before the sale. "[I]t is now a village of paupers, who hang upon the approaching sale . . . as their last and vital chance for existence."*

"A tissue of lies," snapped back the editor of the *Spirit of Jefferson*, a local newspaper. "[A] gross slander upon many of our citizens . . . [by] this carpet-bagging vagabond."

Particularly infuriating was Townsend's characterization of "a village of paupers." The sale refuted this reputation.

With the exception of the factory complexes and the water rights, most of the residential lots and government-owned buildings were purchased by the people of Harpers Ferry. As example, local merchant James McGraw paid $6,000 for a Shenandoah Street block (the equivalent of 20 years annual pay for an average American). Residents also acquired most of the new 30-foot lots facing Shenandoah Street in the former Arsenal Square, opening enormous opportunity for commercial enterprises in the heart of the town.

All totaled, the government sold 248 lots for $297,793.50. The *Spirit of Jefferson* proudly proclaimed these pecuniary successes, labeling Townsend as "the recognized libeler of all men better than himself."

Spirit of Jefferson

December 2, 1869

"It is the purpose of the young gentlemen of Harpers Ferry & vicinity to give a grand ball at the Shenandoah House on Friday evening New Year's Eve. The most extensive and complete preparations are in progress & the gentlemanly proprietor of the house, the genial Kirwan, is determined that nothing shall be wanting on his part to make it one of the grandest successes that has ever attended a ball at Harpers Ferry—which is saying a great deal. The arrangements for the whole affair we are assured are such as to leave no doubt that it will be an entertainment of the most superb character."

This ad represents an air of celebration, exactly ten years after Brown's execution.

Armory, ca. 1865

Nearly twenty years would pass after the end of the Civil War before the U.S. government *finally* disposed of its armory grounds along the Potomac River. Private sector fraud and court battles delayed the sale, resulting in extreme deterioration of the Musket Factory complex.

Armory ca. 1890

CONFLUENCE

> "[O]ur town was just beginning to recover itself when this fresh calamity came upon it."
>
> Appeal from the Citizens of Harpers Ferry
> October 2, 1870

The year 1870 started with great joy.

It ended with a murderous flood.

It started innocently, as it always does, with rain. Precipitation commenced falling in the upper reaches of the Shenandoah Valley the last week of September, 1870. An odd occurrence, as the fall season often predicted a dry spell, unless a visitation from the heavens introduced a hurricane or tropical storm or "Nor'easter"—a weather anomaly that hugged the eastern coast. History did not record the type of the 1870 storm; but a pregnant cloud stalled over the Shenandoah Valley that last week of September, dumping prodigious buckets of rain into its coffers.

Friday night, September 30, arrived at the Ferry with few concerns. The rain fell steadily, but not alarmingly. The Shenandoah was rising, but not much surprising. Then all changed. In the depth of darkness, as most were asleep, a strange sound awakened residents. A sudden roar, followed by a rattling of windows, a shaking of walls...an *explosion of water*.

As if a dam had burst, the angry Shenandoah rampaged violently. Trees were ripped from their roots and transformed into surging spears. The current, swift and powerful, dared anything to stand against its rage. And the dismal darkness, with no light to see and no illumination to guide, exacerbated the fear. Horror consumed Harpers Ferry.

The river rose six feet in four minutes, according to some reports. Residents on Virginius Island and adjoining upstream islands were cut off and trapped by the "impetuous torrent." During the darkened hours of Friday night and Saturday morning, helpless people "remained in their awful prisons, with the billows surging around them, no chance of escape, and naught but death staring them in the face." One observer recalled how "the spectral light of a young moon wading through heavy masses of cloud gave a weird coloring to the frightful picture."

1870 flood, illustrated.

147

RENAISSANCE REPELLED

Four houses crashed in less than five minutes. "Poor women and children were on the streets who had just escaped a watery grave," recalled one witness. "[E]very few minutes a low rumble would be heard, the startling signal that one of their once happy homes had sunk beneath the waters…perhaps containing loved kindred and friends, whose dying wails could be heard on the midnight air."

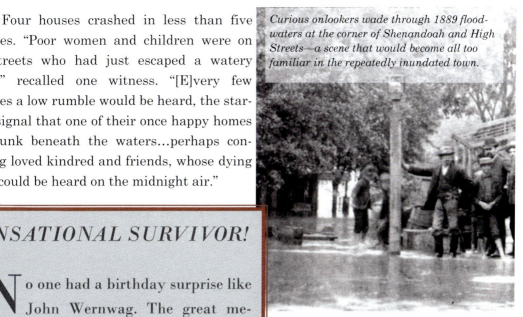

Curious onlookers wade through 1889 floodwaters at the corner of Shenandoah and High Streets—a scene that would become all too familiar in the repeatedly inundated town.

SENSATIONAL SURVIVOR!

No one had a birthday surprise like John Wernwag. The great mechanical genius, happiest as a hermit, resided alone at his machine shop on Virginius Island, "surrounded by strange tools and devices of his own planning and construction." The 1870 Flood demolished his building in Saturday's morning light.

Before horrified witnesses at Jefferson Rock, Mr. Wernwag disappeared beneath his dislodged roof, soon smashed to pieces when it collided with a tree. He popped like a cork into the swirling Shenandoah, and latched onto his house debris as a last-effort life jacket. Wernwag "rose to the surface between two joists, upon which he seated himself, and shortly afterwards securing a floating window sash, he placed it upon the joists and continued his voyage down the river." Six miles down the Potomac, he was pulled ashore. By evening, he had returned to the Ferry via a B & O passenger train.

A remarkable day on his 76th birthday.

Rescuers threw baskets, tied to ropes, in heroic attempts to save souls. But when the water receded, the drowning deaths were shocking—forty-two killed. More than half the dead were African American; the large Bateman family was wiped out, losing eighteen men, women and children. Many of the flood victims' bodies were never recovered.

"We hope that our people will respond at once in money, clothes and provisions," read the appeal to the citizens of Jefferson County. "Let our hearts and purses be opened without stint….The distress is great and we beg our people not to be behind when such a deserving call is made upon them for charity."

Losses were staggering. Every building on the islands from Shenandoah City to the old Rifle Works site was gone. Along the Shenandoah shore, from the Rifle Works downstream to the confluence, few houses remained standing. Estimates ranged up to fifty buildings destroyed.

"All hope of rescue was cut off from us"

Emily Child moved to Virginius Island from Springfield, Ohio, when husband Jonathan invested in a flour mill business adjoining the Shenandoah in 1867. She did not expect to fight the river for her life three years later.

She relayed her terrifying account to her mother and sister in Vermont:

We [had] no idea of the danger until it was too late to escape from the island. Last Friday [September 30] towards evening the water commenced rising rapidly. Before two hours every way of escape and all hope of rescue was cut off from us. So we were compelled to stay within the crumbling walls which sheltered us from the terrible water which seethed and dashed around us. There were two bridges connecting the Island with the mainland . . . so violent was the water that these were torn to fragments and carried away.

As soon as we saw there was danger of the water coming into the house we commenced to tear up carpets and moving furniture upstairs but so hurried were we that we were compelled to leave some . . . we lost many indispensable and some valuable articles. . . .

Twelve buildings on the Island (some of them heavy stone and brick walls) are leveled to the ground. Our house is considered the strongest residence on the Island . . . our back kitchen and all our outhouses and many trees are entirely gone so completely that we can scarcely realize they stood there. . . .

Three families took refuge with us. . . . None of [their] houses are entirely destroyed. . . . Doors and blinds are wrenched from their hinges, partition walls torn down, staircases shattered and floor torn up In two of them the entire front walls fell out. . . .

We have all worked very hard since we [first arrived] here in order to save what we could until [the] business got started and had just begun to breathe easier when this disaster came. . . . Our school house was swept away and all the children's books with it. They seem, [daughter] Anna especially, to mourn over them more than anything else. . . .

Opposite, flooding at High and Shenandoah Streets in 1924.

Flood Neurosis

The Civil War altered a watershed. So much of the Shenandoah Valley's forests and wood lots had been denuded during the war, with barren lands blighting the landscape where green lushness once reigned. Soldiers from both armies roamed the Valley for four years—in essence mobile cit-ies of tens of thousands of men. They consumed tens of thousands of acres of wood for their campfires, cooking and warming fires, and their scorching fires—a U. S. policy of total war to burn anything of value that sus-tained the enemy Confederacy. The result of these war-rior combinations would prove fatal for Harpers Ferry only five years after the war's close.

Water, of course, travels downhill, and Harpers Ferry is at the very bottom of the Shenandoah Valley. The Valley's watershed includes almost two million acres and over 1,400 miles of rivers and streams. With exception of that absorbed into the ground, every drop of every inch of rain pours into Harpers Ferry.

A further dubious dynamic that afflicts Harpers Ferry is the funnel effect. As the river flows north, it creeps closer and closer to the edge of the Blue Ridge, constricting its flow into a narrow and elongated gorge, like the spout of a funnel. Pressure and speed increases as the water races through the funnel. At the expulsion end of the funnel: Harpers Ferry.

The Potomac River, typically, floods at the same time as the Shenandoah, unless a storm is highly con-centrated (as was the case in 1870, with the Shenandoah Valley as ground zero). Since the Potomac is a wider and stronger river than the Shenandoah, when it floods, it forms a "dam" comprised of water; i.e., it blocks the flow of the Shenandoah as it attempts to exit the funnel. This impedes the Shenandoah, clogging it up into the mouth of the funnel. This results in a "lake effect"—a rise in the river's depth that sinks Harpers Ferry underwater.

CONFLUENCE

Economic boom and catastrophic bust afflicted Harpers Ferry for 25 years after the Civil War.

A pattern of prosperity, followed by poverty, repeated itself as the two rivers determined to wage war with progress.

The town recovered from the killer 1870 flood. Proud residents constructed new buildings, attracted new businesses, and encouraged new residents. Unfortunately, the flood of 1877 knocked it back down.

The cycle repeated. The survivors of Harpers Ferry stood up, washed the mud and destruction from their streets, and determined to break the seeming curse wrought by the Potomac and Shenandoah rivers. Iron-willed perseverance restored homes, businesses, and hope. Then, the flood of 1889 buried the town.

The 1889 flood ("Johnstown Flood") was the highest in recorded history during the nineteenth century. Three photographs capture the trauma. Above, John Brown's Fort in the flood. Below, west end of Shenandoah Street. Above right, the swollen rivers during the "Johnstown Flood."

But the residents proved resilient. Yet again they rebuilt. Once again, the community recovered. This time, however, there was respite. For two generations, the people of the Ferry and Mother Nature coexisted in peace. Thirty-five years would pass before the confluence transformed once again into Lake Harpers Ferry in 1924.

1924 flood, east end of Shenandoah Street.

The danger of floods was not just the amount of water, but the foul soup of jagged, rotting, and in some cases, deceased debris that invaded the town. The 1924 flood, shown here, carried massive quantities of wooden missiles down from the Virginius Island pulp mill, smashing into homes and businesses. Reaching 27.6 feet, the 1924 flood swept away three sections of the Bollman bridge over the Potomac, and closed the C & O Canal for good.

> In addition to battling restive rivers, on the industrial development front, Harpers Ferry was "sacrificed to the greed of a set of heartless speculators."

The same waterpower that drowned the town also represented wealth for those who could harness that power. Great anticipation arose when the federal government sold its waterpower rights (along with its armory holdings in 1869). But that energy source remained unutilized.

The fraud of F. A. Adams and the Harpers Ferry Waterpower and Manufacturing Company—to extort a legal right-of-way from the B & O Railroad—set back industrial development for a decade and a half. "All this time the people of Harpers Ferry were suffering from hope deferred and truly sick were their hearts."

This debacle ended when the government regained title to its land (Adams and his conspirators had defaulted for years). In 1886, the U.S. finally sold the land to New Jersey entrepreneur and manufacturer Thomas Savery, who revived water-powered manufacturing after a 25-year hiatus. Savery subsequently built a paper pulp mill on each river, improving or rebuilding dams, opening clogged canals, and constructing his factories utilizing foundations and old stone from the armory ruins. Savery's operations

RENAISSANCE REPELLED

employed several dozen locals, but it never matched the hundreds employed by the armory and past manufactures. Savery's renaissance of water power did, however, bring a revolution to the community. His hydro power brought "light" into the world at Harpers Ferry with the generation of electricity.

Sale of the old armory grounds to Savery wrought the biggest landscape change in Harpers Ferry since the establishment of the armory itself.

The B & O Railroad—long anxious to overcome its engineering obstacles at Harpers Ferry—obtained from Savery an improved right-of-way through the heart of the old Musket Factory tract. The railroad promptly proceeded to realign its tracks to eliminate the sharp-angled turns across the Potomac bridge designed some sixty years earlier. In 1894, a twenty-foot embankment buried half the armory grounds under tons of rock and earth, serving the railroad's utilitarian needs, but destroying a century-long historic setting along the Potomac River. At the same time as this dramatic alteration, the railroad also built a new bridge, and it tunneled through Maryland Heights to facilitate passage through the water gap. It constructed, as well, a Victorian-style passenger station at a strategic point overlooking Shenandoah Street.

But the railroad's planned improvements caused a casualty: John Brown's Fort. The venerable building was in the way of the new railroad alignment. Savery understood this misfortune. He subsequently sold the Fort to some speculators, who dismantled and shipped it to Chicago, where it was reassembled as a tourist attraction for the 1893 World's Fair.

"[E]verybody at the [Ferry] wishes them well and hopes that they realize a good price for this interesting relic," remarked a local resident, "but many regret that they did not retain it, as age but added to its value . . . for many a tourist has tarried a day at the place expressly to get a good sight of it."

Harpers Ferry's most famous building was no longer in sight.

John Brown's battleground now was buried under an artificial hill.

Lower opposite: Savery's pulp mill factory on the Potomac. The canal was the original armory power canal.

Right: Civil War markers astride the John Brown Fort Monument, located on the 1894 B & O Railroad embankment.

CONFLUENCE

Growing a Tourist Destination

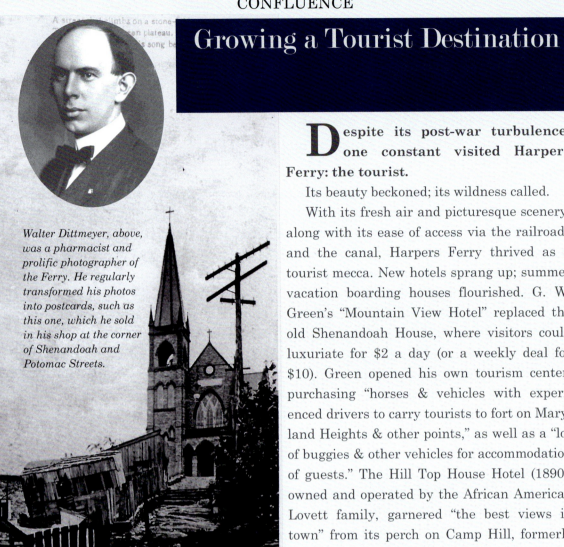

Walter Dittmeyer, above, was a pharmacist and prolific photographer of the Ferry. He regularly transformed his photos into postcards, such as this one, which he sold in his shop at the corner of Shenandoah and Potomac Streets.

Despite its post-war turbulence, one constant visited Harpers Ferry: the tourist.

Its beauty beckoned; its wildness called.

With its fresh air and picturesque scenery, along with its ease of access via the railroads and the canal, Harpers Ferry thrived as a tourist mecca. New hotels sprang up; summer vacation boarding houses flourished. G. W. Green's "Mountain View Hotel" replaced the old Shenandoah House, where visitors could luxuriate for $2 a day (or a weekly deal for $10). Green opened his own tourism center, purchasing "horses & vehicles with experienced drivers to carry tourists to fort on Maryland Heights & other points," as well as a "lot of buggies & other vehicles for accommodation of guests." The Hill Top House Hotel (1890), owned and operated by the African American Lovett family, garnered "the best views in town" from its perch on Camp Hill, formerly the site of the armory magazine.

The Bollman bridge became a popular place for weddings. The main railroad attraction, however, was the B & O's Island Park,

RENAISSANCE REPELLED

which opened in 1874. This elongated land mass, located about a half-mile up the Potomac from the confluence, stretched nearly 500 yards parallel to the Potomac's southern shore. It became a destination for local and regional picnics, organization and company gatherings, veterans' reunions and church outings. Associations for farmers, firemen and the Free Masons frolicked there regularly, as the B & O installed a dancing pavilion, dining hall, and ornamental music stand that became a centerpiece for concerts.

Hotel Connor welcomed travelers arriving at the nearby B & O Railroad station.

"Pen and pencil would fail to convey an adequate idea of its awe inspiring grandeur . . . to be fully appreciated, [it must] be seen not with a cold calculating eye, but with an enthusiasm of a lover."

Georgetown Courier, 1871

Dittmeyer postcard 1907, from Maryland Heights

CONFLUENCE

Families enjoyed swings and seesaws, and the railroad even installed a "steam-powered merry-go-round" in 1890. One former mayor referred to it as Harpers Ferry's own "Coney Island."

Island Park became a stage for events. Attractions included hot-air balloon ascensions, tight rope performances, gymnastic feats, tournaments and annual July 4th celebrations. The railroad averaged three train excursions a week by the 1880s, with weekends bringing in 4,000-6,000 visitors. The B & O held the largest activity, hosting annually up to 10,000 company employees and their families on the island. G. W. Green's hotel dining room benefitted handsomely, serving 4,000 chicken dinners in just the summer months during America's Centennial year celebrations.

Summer boarding by Washington and Baltimore elites turned handsome profits as well, especially for Storer College. The school converted three of the former armory mansions on Camp Hill—Lockwood House, Brackett House and Morrell House—into inns that provided a major source of revenues and offered students summer employment. This venture became so successful that Storer added a third story and Mansard Roof to the Lockwood House, taking advantage of the grand view of the confluence overlooking the hallowed Harper Cemetery.

Lockwood House interior as boarding house

> "Visitors came, and were charmed by the surrounding, pleased with the bearing of the [Storer] students, who waited on them, and sent for their friends. From year to year other buildings were fitted up and opened, till Camp Hill, which had previously been quite like a graveyard in the summer, has become the center of life in the town, having all available rooms filled to overflowing with an excellent class of summer boarders. Several hundred guests come annually, and the number increases every year. This gives business to the town, and employment to a considerable number of the students, while the guests are sure of having intelligent, honest and faithful attendants."
>
> Kate Anthony, *Historical Sketch of Storer College, 1891*

Above, Harpers Ferry's most famous hotel, the Hill Top House, 1913.

At left, a tightrope walker appears to hover in midair on Island Park. Also visible is the gazebo, the only structure from the island still standing. It now resides on the mainland in a Harpers Ferry town park.

"If ever there was an area richly endowed with natural beauty; if ever there was an area rich in historical lore; if there was ever an area characterized by what could be called 'gracious living,' this is it."

Senator Jennings Randolph (WV)

Chapter 9
HISTORY'S HARNESS

March 20, 1936, promised to be an historic day in a town of historic events.

A citizens group from Harpers Ferry had chosen spring's inaugural to breathe life into a vision to transform Harpers Ferry into a National Park Service historic site. Preparations were made. The meeting was set. Invitations were sent. An illustrated letter predicted a bright future.

But no meeting occurred; no plans were presented. Disaster nearly washed away the promise.

Just days before the March 20th meeting, torrential rains and melting snow transformed the Potomac and Shenandoah rivers into raging monsters. Lower Town Harpers Ferry sank beneath thirty-six feet of water—the highest flood in recorded history. Both highway bridges into town collapsed. Buildings were demolished. Debris piled high in the once busy streets.

The Potomac nearly reaches the railroad bridge in the 1936 flood.

A violent current batters one of the Potomac bridge spans. Railroad cars were moved onto the bridge in hopes of keeping it from sweeping away.

"I witnessed one of the most awe-inspiring, terrifying cataclysms of nature that may ever fall my lot to behold.

I was awakened by the sound of angry, turbulent waters rushing and gushing down-stream as if a thousand demons were chasing them. I looked out upon the muddy waves leaping higher at every turn, as if dancing for joy at release. . . .

I hurried down to the water-side and found that the waters had gotten a good start. They had covered a few smaller buildings and were gradually reaching the second floors of the taller ones. People were staying in their houses until it was impossible to remain. Those with three-story buildings simply moved up, loath to leave their cherished possessions humble though they might be.

Some were walking around with saddened brows, gazing with stricken eyes at the two seemingly great giants, the Potomac and the Shenandoah. Yet, those two selfish beasts were becoming more and more enraged because three weak creations of man—bridges—were hindering their tumultuous journey. They lashed and constantly beat these barriers like mad. . . .

I saw houses floating upon their waves like mere match boxes tossed in a tub of water. Huge logs and all sorts of objects were riding in those whirling, tumbling waters. . . . [O]ur generally little-noticed town was crowded with hundreds of people walking to and fro viewing this wonderful though gloomy sight."

Elsie Shelton
Storer College student

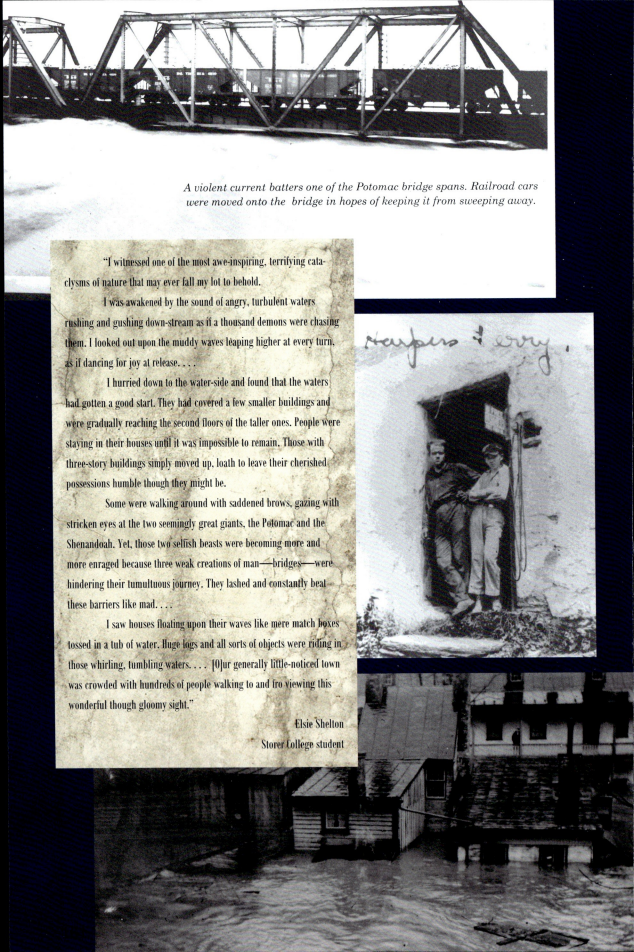

This page and opposite: images of the 1936 flood and its cleanup.

CONFLUENCE

Several days after the savage waters had subsided, United States Congressman Jennings Randolph, of West Virginia's 2nd District, and Henry McDonald, President of Harpers Ferry's Storer College, walked slowly through Harpers Ferry's muddy and flood-torn district. As the two men marveled at nature's destruction, both recalled the town's rich and varied history.

Then a challenge became evident: Harpers Ferry must be saved; its history must be preserved; it must become a national historic site.

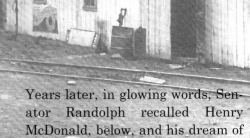

"We walked down near the river's edge on ground that had but a few days before been covered by the flood waters. The mud was up to our ankle tops. And as we walked—waded would be a better word—through that slush, I recall . . . the words of Dr. McDonald: 'We ought to have a national park here.' If you should ask me when the project that culminated in the Harpers Ferry National Monument was born I would answer you by saying that it was on that day in March of 1936 in the mud of the rivers down below. I relate this incident . . . for the purpose of giving you insight into the sort of man Henry T. McDonald was.

The mud was up to his ankle tops—but he was looking at the stars.

You might say that was his life: no matter how deep the mud, he always kept his eyes on the stars."

Years later, in glowing words, Senator Randolph recalled Henry McDonald, below, and his dream of a national park.

HISTORY'S HARNESS

The challenge presented, Randolph and McDonald eagerly accepted. For the next fif-teen years both men labored together to make "the project" a reality. Initially, "the pro-ject" envisioned Harpers Ferry as a link in a proposed Lincoln Memorial Highway. With its beginning in Washington, this historic and scenic drive would parallel the Potomac River to Harpers Ferry, then venture north to Antietam and Gettysburg before looping back to Washington. Another proposal contemplated continuing the Skyline Drive along the crest of the Blue Ridge from Front Royal to Harpers Ferry.

McDonald confidently predicted that "thousands of tourists annually...will mean a continuous golden wave of wealth to this whole general section." Tourist dollars depend-ed, however, on National Park Service approval of Harpers Ferry as an historic site.

Consequently, at the suggestion of Congressman Randolph, the Park Service in 1937 conducted an extensive inquiry and survey of the proposed Harpers Ferry site. This analysis—which included not only the lower town between the rivers, but also Maryland Heights in Maryland, Loudoun Heights in Virginia and West Virginia, and Bolivar Heights in West Virginia—convinced the Park Service of the "desirability of inclusion of the area" into the National Park System.

Young men explore the Stone Fort on top of Maryland Heights. Scenic vistas and Civil War ruins on the mountain had been been calling to curious visitors for years. The inclusion of Harpers Ferry's history-laden, tallest mountain in the new national park seemed obvious to preservationists.

With Park Service backing guaranteed, Randolph and McDonald progressed to phase two of their campaign: encouraging the public to persuade the United States Con-gress to authorize Harpers Ferry as a National Historic Monument. At an enthusiastic public meeting on February 17, 1938, over 200 participants witnessed legislators from Maryland, Virginia, and West Virginia pledge support for the project. A "Committee of

CONFLUENCE

Committees" was established (with McDonald as chairman) to coordinate the states' efforts on a local and national level and to "raise the funds necessary to buy the tracts desired." "This is not a selfish or merely local project," proclaimed McDonald. "It is a three-state project. It is more than that; it will be one of the GREAT national projects." The *Martinsburg Journal,* a local newspaper, agreed: "The project has merit. It seems logical to develop it…It would seem a duty, therefore, to see that it is done."

Optimists Randolph and McDonald, seemingly driven by the *Journal's* challenge of duty, began waging a determined campaign. In the political arena, Randolph proved tireless. He introduced legislation; garnered support from fellow congressmen; received assurances from the governor of West Virginia; aligned the West Virginia Conservation Commission behind the proposal; and he received pledges from Panhandle legislators. At the grassroots level, Henry McDonald energetically established county-wide committees to sponsor and support the movement. McDonald initiated title searches on properties within the boundary of the site. Hundreds of letters were written requesting financial and political support for the project. Time was spent courting the press.

Then an interruption: World War II.

Momentum stalled. The epic international conflict threatened world order and millions of lives. Establishment of a national park seemed trivial. But both Randolph and McDonald remained tenacious. They continued to build public interest. They orchestrated persistent pressure on national and state and local politicians. They refused to yield despite prolonged economic depression and deadly war. They were impassioned by mission.

"Home-land and foreign travelers for nearly two hundred years, in papers, books, periodicals, and by sketches, have emphasized the grip and meaning of Harpers Ferry," preached McDonald. There existed "a zeal for the establishment in due time of a park or monument."

Due time arrived, finally, on June 30, 1944. After eight arduous years of determined effort, President Franklin Roosevelt signed the Congressional bill establishing Harpers Ferry National Monument. Three weeks after D-Day, as America fought for its future, it honored its past.

The monument now was authorized to accept 1,500 acres of *donated* land which commemorated "historical events in or near Harpers Ferry." Elated by final success, Congressman Randolph praised "the comradeship of men who believed a job could be done" and summarized the Harpers Ferry project as a "long one of many dreams."

But major obstacles remained. The Monument existed as a legislative reality—on paper only. Congress appropriated no funds to purchase lands. West Virginia and Maryland would have to buy all properties. "Congressman Randolph has done an excellent job in getting the legislation through," commented Conrad Wirth, then Chief of Lands for the National Park Service. "The second step, to get the land, is yours."

QUEEN OF THE MOUNTAIN
Mary Vernon Mish & the Fight for Maryland Heights

On Independence Day 1946, Mary Vernon Mish gathered with other dignitaries atop South Mountain near Boonsboro, Maryland, to rededicate the country's first monument to George Washington. She was president of the Washington County Historical Society, and had invited former Harpers Ferry mayor and Storer College president Henry McDonald to speak to the crowd.

Mary had not met McDonald before. She listened as he spoke passionately about the Washington Monument and the role of the community in preserving the past. "People without memorials of their heroes and great events are barbarous," he said, perhaps recalling his own longstanding battle to create a national monument at Harpers Ferry. "American history may be short in time [but] it is long in the record of enduring worth."

McDonald was speaking Mish's language. After the ceremony, he explained that a Harpers Ferry National Monument had been authorized in 1944, but no land had been obtained for it. McDonald asked Mish if the historical society would help him with land acquisition for Harpers Ferry. Mish accepted the challenge wholeheartedly.

Within months, Mish had persuaded her society to ratify a resolution of support for the Harpers Ferry National Monument. She then began lobbying Maryland's governor, as well as state and federal legislators. Although her efforts were stymied by political shifts and the outbreak of the Korean War, she persisted.

She drew on personal connections whenever possible—and they often were, given her Washingtonian upbringing.

Once, when faced with a personality that McDonald feared was opposed to their project, Mish calmly replied: "His wife is my oldest sister-in-law's best friend of many years standing." Mish indeed had the situation under control. A Maryland state senator introduced legislation for Harpers Ferry—a bill that had the support of powerful players in the Maryland legislature—who happened to be Mish's "staunch friends and members of [the] Historical Society Board."

Another element of Mish's strategy was marketing.

The monument had faced adamant opposition. Some people feared the site would focus only on the glorification of John Brown. Joseph Kaylor, Maryland's Director of Forests and Parks, fully embraced this view, and repeatedly spoke against the project. Undaunted, Mish launched a campaign to broaden the scope of the park in the public's mind. She befriended newspaper editors and journalists and penned a number of articles herself. She argued to the press and politicians that anyone calling Harpers Ferry "the John Brown park," rather than the Harpers Ferry National Monument, was "inaccurate and biased."

After McDonald's death in 1951, Mish continued the crusade. Maryland approved appropriations for the project as early as 1952, with a token transfer of property in 1954. Frustration continued for Mish, however, as she faced the legal technicalities of clearing deeds to "unimproved acreage" on Maryland Heights. She would persist for another decade, pushing the deeds through until their completion.

Mary passed away on June 1, 1968. Throughout her life, she used her wits and privilege to ensure a key part of Harpers Ferry would be preserved for the public.

Today, as hundreds of thousands of park visitors admire the Maryland Heights view, Mrs. Mish smiles upon them.

And so the campaign continued. As chairman of the Harpers Ferry National Monument Association, Henry McDonald spent the next seven years soliciting purchasing funds from the West Virginia Legislature. Efforts in Maryland continued as well, but most of the work in the Old Line State fell upon Mary Vernon Mish and the Washington County Historical Society.

These delays in land acquisition further impoverished Lower Town Harpers Ferry. As one traveler observed in 1948, "whole sections of store fronts have been boarded up. It's sure a sorry sight compared with the Harpers Ferry I used to know." Yet McDonald maintained faith in the Monument project. Even without land, the now-retired president of Storer College began collecting books and articles for the Monument's library. One prized addition was a set of the Baltimore and Ohio Railroad's *Book of the Royal Blue,* a yearly magazine that featured numerous articles on the Harpers Ferry area.

> *"[T]he small amount of money necessary to develop the area is inconsequential compared to the increase in the real value to the country."*
>
> Conrad Wirth
> National Park Service

Finally, on March 12, 1951—with the strong backing of West Virginia Governor Okey L. Patteson and continued support from Congressman Harley O. Staggers—the state legislature unanimously appropriated $350,000 to acquire 514 acres for the Monument. Harpers Ferry's Lower Town, the north face of Loudoun Heights, and large segments of Bolivar Heights soon would be transferred to the National Park Service.

The news warranted celebration. "Not since George Washington succeeded in having Congress establish the national arsenal here," reported the *Washington Star,* "has Harpers Ferry been so hopeful of the future." "Surely," McDonald exclaimed, "the Harpers Ferry National Monument will, at no distant day, be moving toward reality." McDonald never witnessed that reality, however. He died in November 1951, three years before the National Park Service actually began to administer the site.

"I think I have seen more and great changes here than any other may hope to experience," recorded McDonald just days after Congress authorized the Monument. "We came when the old was here. We have lived to see the end of one era and the establishment and continuance of another, and better one."

HISTORY'S HARNESS

Eventually, NPS would bear the burden of examining several ruins and determining which might be preserved. At right, the Episcopal church, which had watched over the Harpers Ferry gap for generations. Although it survived the Civil War, the structure was afterward abandoned and nature took its course.

Below: Shenandoah Street as witnessed before park restoration.

Background, Senator Randolph, second from left, ever optimistic for Harpers Ferry's future.

Fortunately, Gilbert Perry, Mayor of Harpers Ferry and ardent supporter of the Monument project, immediately filled the leadership void created by McDonald's death. Mayor Perry pressed West Virginia forward with its title searches and property acquisition. Finally, on January 16, 1953, Governor Okey Patteson donated a deed for 400 acres to the National Park Service. "Citizens of the Eastern Panhandle can red-circle this date," proclaimed Patteson, "as an epoch in the modern history of this section."

Indeed, a new era had begun.

When John T. Willett walked into Harpers Ferry as the first "permanent park commissioner" in September 1954, he faced a monumental adventure. Decaying, dilapidated buildings were everywhere. Garbage and filth saturated the environment. Hogs roamed unchallenged through the streets. A foul odor permeated the air.

> "I felt as if I had come upon a ghost town. Buildings stood deserted, deteriorating. Gray walls of heavy fieldstone gaped with empty window openings. Through them I glimpsed fallen rafters, creeping vegetation, and tattered bits of open sky. It seemed ages, not just years, since people could have lived and worked here."
>
> ~Volkmar Wentzel,
> *National Geographic* March 1957

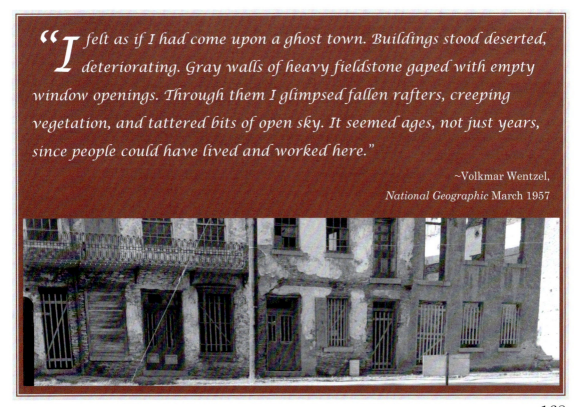

CONFLUENCE

Above, archaeology underway at the former arsenal site.

Below, restoration of Harper House in 1961.

Opposite, park visitors on pilgrimage to Jefferson Rock. 1952.

Yet a growing optimism soon prevailed. Unsafe buildings were stabilized, fallen roofs removed. Dirt and rubble disappeared. Streets and sidewalks were cleared and swept. A team of architects soon arrived, armed with pencils and tape measures. They crawled all over the Monument's buildings, analyzing the lumber, scraping the paint, examining the woodwork, and studying the techniques of old. Historians soon followed to search through documents and deeds, and archeological excavations unveiled tantalizing information. The puzzles of the past slowly fell into place.

As the data collected, the Park Service developed plans to restore the town to its 1859-1865 appearance: from the time of John Brown's Raid through the end of the Civil War. Restoration began in earnest in 1956 with the Harper House, the town's oldest building. A pleased local community quickly backed the project, and the garden club promised to furnish the interior with nineteenth-century furnishings. The Monument also razed non-historic structures; installed new water and drainage systems; increased parking facilities; opened a John Brown Museum; excavated the old arsenals; and installed maps, signs, and self-guiding trails.

HISTORY'S HARNESS

Favorable publicity, including a full-page illustrated article in *The New York Times* and a *National Geographic* special bulletin, greatly increased visitation to Harpers Ferry. The new Monument became a favorite topic of *The Washington Post*. A *Parade Magazine* article in 1958 circulated to over sixteen million readers.

When Jennings Randolph boldly predicted in 1955 that the monument would someday attract one million visitors annually, disbelievers hooted and howled. Increasing numbers soon befuddled the skeptics. In 1958, for example, visitors from 26 foreign countries and every state except North Dakota spent some time in Harpers Ferry.

But this all was preparatory. The big moment was coming.

The next year, 1959, marked the Centennial of John Brown's war to end slavery.

Harpers Ferry, suddenly and unexpectedly, discovered itself thrust in the midst of a national controversy.

Chapter 10
SPARK STILL SMOLDERS

What do you do with John Brown?

No, not John Brown's body; John Brown's *anniversary*. How do you deal with a body that has stopped moldering, but whose soul is still smoldering?

John Brown stabbed the U.S. government in 1859 over the issue of slavery. One hundred years later—in the midst of the Civil Rights Movement—the memory of Brown continued to prick federal policy and elicit fear within federal agencies. Was it appropriate to formally remember him? Was it safe?

Few individuals in American history have generated as much controversy and scorching debate as the fiery abolitionist. His attack on the Harpers Ferry armory and arsenal lasted but thirty-four hours. Yet the tornado spawned by his subsequent trial and execution for murder, treason and slave insurrection spun upheaval into the consciousness of generations.

Americans do not deliberate John Brown. Instead, we *feel* his enduring legacy. We feel the fear of the Southerner—or the resolve of the Northerner. We feel the anger in Dixieland—or the triumph in New England. We feel the rape of a culture. We feel the freedom of a race. Emotions inevitably dictate the discussion.

Saint or Madman? Murderer or Liberator? Devil or Martyr? Terrorist or Freedom Fighter?

John Brown is not what we think, but what we feel.

This geographic polarization of feeling started almost immediately.

"So hideous—so devilish—so monstrously wicked—and yet so absurd did the whole story seem," editorialized a Southern newspaper. Former President John Tyler, himself a Virginia slave holder, summed up the South's response: "But one sentiment pervades the country: security to the Union, or separation."

Compare that to volcanic voices in the North. Ralph Waldo Emerson declared Brown "the saint" whose death made "the gallows glorious like the cross." Abolitionist reformer Wendell Phillips compared Brown's effort to the Revolution of 1776, declaring: "Harpers Ferry is the Lexington of today." Henry David Thoreau reserved nothing and proclaimed Brown: "the best news America has ever heard."

Division of minds. Division of hearts. Division into parts.

Brown forced America into a defining debate. How could legal enslavement—lawful owning of human beings as property—coexist with the lofty sentiment of the Dec-

CONFLUENCE

Visitors consider the John Brown question at an early national park exhibit.

laration of Independence, that "all men are created equal?"

"Is it not possible than an individual may be right and a government wrong?" postulated Thoreau. "Are laws to be enforced simply because they were made?"

John Brown hurled the country into conundrum. He convulsed the nation into dangerous delirium. He ensured "that North and South [were] standing in battle array."

"If John Brown did not end the war that ended slavery," proclaimed Frederick Douglass, "he did at least begin the war that ended slavery."

One hundred years later, Americans could not remember the Civil War themselves, but wanted remembrance for it. For the centennial, people predicted pageantry, parades and politicians celebrating the reunion of the country. The warriors and the war would be honored, the battlefields hallowed and the graveyards decorated.

But when would this centennial commence?

A simple question, it seemed, with no simple answer. John Brown's enduring specter again catapulted into the conscience of Americans, a people still divided—now not by disunion, but by disharmony.

"The people of the South would be unanimous in opposition to any celebration of the John Brown Raid," explained Karl S. Betts, executive director of the Civil War Centennial Commission, *"and most conservative people in the North would be strongly opposed to it."*

Betts concluded in an interview in September 1958, that "7/8ths of the people of the United States would look with serious concern upon such a celebration."

And the one-eighth who would not? The African American population.

Centennial celebrants in Civil War attire. A parade of gowns, guns, and glowing odes to military sacrifice and gallantry was anticipated as the war's anniversary drew near. Whether or not John Brown would be included in the affair, however, was a point of sharp divide.

Opposite: Peace was a misnomer. Protesting enduring resistance to integrated schools, over 25,000 high school and college students marched on Washington, D.C., on April 18, 1959—exactly six months prior to John Brown's 100th anniversary.

Although the Civil War had bestowed freedom for the slave, equality had not been realized. Thirty-one years after the Civil War, the Supreme Court affirmed the longstanding practice of exclusive "whites only" spaces and "separate but equal" facilities. Nine decades after Appomattox, Jim Crow still pervaded race relations in the South and the North. After the Supreme Court reversed sanctioned school segregation in 1954, the Civil Rights Movement agitated for integration. But the doctrine of separate but equal remained entrenched. Battles waged at school doors. Blood spilled on the streets. Police dogs ripped flesh. Fire hos-es doused demonstrations.

The John Brown Raid "came at a bad time in 1859," Betts proclaimed, "and conditions today are such that it would be a bad time to celebrate it in 1959."

The Civil War Centennial Commission was created by Congress in 1957 to foster public interest in the war's history, and to encourage states to establish their own agencies to promote local commemorative events. Gen. Ulysses S. Grant III chaired the commission, and Karl S. Betts served as his day-to-day deputy. "Grant and Betts were conservatives with abundant empathy for Southern whites," discovered Robert Cook, author of *Troubled Commemoration: The American Civil War Centennial*. "Neither they, nor the Southern state commissions, were interested in fostering public awareness of the role that Blacks had played in the Civil War."

Nor were they interested in John Brown. Nor slavery. Nor Brown's war against slavery.

Any mention of slavery, in fact, must be avoided. Any observance of John Brown's war "might have the effect of antagonizing the entire South to the great damage of the proposed Civil War Centennial observances," contended Betts. He specifically demanded that NPS "soft-pedal recognition of the event in 1959."

> *"My grandpappy was a Confederate, and we're not going to talk about John Brown."*

The controversy of John Brown swiftly embroiled NPS officials in internal strife.

NPS had shepherded the creation of the Civil War Centennial Commission, and Betts's doomsday tone made leaders in Washington nervous. "Civil War Centennial Commission officials…recognize the controversial nature of the John Brown episode and the desirability of avoiding a glorification of the Raid," acknowledged NPS Assistant Director Jackson E. Price in October 1958, adding, "We share their apprehension." He then further informed the regional director who held bureaucratic control over the Harpers Ferry park that "the John Brown episode may be a disturbing element in engendering a bipartisan feeling."

Feelings at Harpers Ferry already were partisan. The park's first superintendent, Edwin M. "Mac" Dale, arrived in 1956 with a fervent desire to ignore John Brown. "My grandpappy was a Confederate," Dale boasted to one NPS historian, "and we're not going to talk about John Brown." Superintendent Dale's opinion ran counter to official government prospectuses dating back to 1943. "The best known event in the history of the town was John Brown's Raid," reported Interior Secretary Harold Ickes during deliberations to establish the site as a national monument. "Brown's raid created violent resentment in the South and intensified sectional animosity."

Animosity boiled over in the summer of 1957 when Superintendent Dale encountered an up-and-coming, thirty-seven-year-old research historian named Charles W. Snell. Snell, who had been raised in Schenectady, N.Y., and held history degrees from Union College and Columbia University, represented the academic antithesis of the desk-pounding, ranger-intimidating, brow-bashing superintendent.

"I said to him that the national significance of the park appeared to be mainly on the John Brown Raid because this touched off the Civil War," recalled Snell, who had been hand-selected by the regional director to "study the problems" at Harpers Ferry. Dale reacted violently, hammering his fists on a table and screaming views that reflected a still-segregated Harpers Ferry and West Virginia, where "people around here believed John Brown was a devil."

Snell was the person "that was selected to argue with him."

> "I explained to Mac Dale," Snell remembered, "and later when we talked to the townspeople, that we were not making a monument to John Brown. We were going to tell the story and it would be factual. We wouldn't say he was great or bad—that's your opinion—form your own opinion."

Snell departed from Dale and preceded to the highest sanctuaries of the NPS, where he advocated his plan to restore Harpers Ferry to its John Brown/Civil War-era appearance in preparation for the John Brown Centennial. The NPS leadership boldly adopted Snell's recommendations, and by September 1957—the same month the Civil War Centennial Commission was established by Congress—Snell was assigned to Harpers Ferry as the supervisory historian.

The Park Service had determined its direction regarding John Brown. Dale and conservatism were out; Snell and progressivism were in. And to ensure no interference with the Snell agenda, the NPS replaced Dale with a ranger who had spent most of his career in the wilds of Yellowstone, far removed from the schisms of segregation. Frank Anderson arrived as the new Harpers Ferry superintendent, and Snell relished that he was "a gentleman who did not hate John Brown."

Historian Charles Snell and family (in costume) at the Brown Centennial.

SPARK STILL SMOLDERS

For the next year, under the tutelage of Anderson and Snell, Harpers Ferry hummed toward the centennial. Backed by a NPS endorsement that "without John Brown (controversial though this figure may be), Harpers Ferry would probably not have meaning to the average American today," extensive research commenced, post-Civil War buildings were demolished and the town revamped to a mid-nineteenth-century appearance.

With momentum building toward the Brown Centennial, Park Service officials became giddy with excitement. "This will be our first observance of a Centennial anniversary associated with the Civil War," exclaimed Regional Director Daniel J. Tobin in an August 1958 letter to the NPS director. Buoyed by anticipation, the Park Service commenced negotiations to acquire the John Brown Fort. The NPS coveted the former fire engine house—the only surviving building from the U.S. Armory—where Brown had been captured. But it had been moved more than once and now stood on the grounds of the defunct Storer College, atop a hill more than half a mile from its original site. NPS planners dreamed of returning the fort to its home, and doing it prior to the John Brown Centennial. Time was short. Only one year remained. Action must occur now.

First step: contact the Baltimore & Ohio Railroad, which owned the original site. Surely the railroad would cooperate in this mission of national import.

Subsequently, the Park Service director sent a letter to the president of the B & O Railroad. This letter, an innocent request to obtain the actual historic site of the John Brown Fort, ignited a firestorm that engulfed the Park Service in the flaming passions of segregation.

The first B & O response looked promising. "This railroad was very much involved in activities during the raid," effused B&O president Harold Simpson. "[The B&O] has a deep interest in Harpers Ferry as a great national monument." Simpson even offered the Park Service contacts with the railroad real estate office. But behind the scenes, B&O executives were troubled. Attached to the September 17 letter were NPS plans for the Brown Centennial, under the title "Celebration." That word—and its meaning—set off a spiral of controversy that convulsed the Civil War Centennial Commission and ensnared the National Park Service and Harpers Ferry in the social, cultural and political web of segregation.

Concerned the NPS was "celebrating" John Brown, the railroad brass shared its reservations with Civil War Centennial Commission members. No longer in its infancy, and now an established voice of the federal government, the commission promptly expressed alarm that the Park Service would embrace Brown.

This prompted a telephone call to the NPS Chief Historian's office from Karl Betts, Centennial Commission executive director. In this October 6, 1958, conversation, Betts expressed "serious misgivings" over the proposed John Brown observance, stating the Commission "strongly opposed" any celebration as presented in the NPS letter to the railroad. Shaken by Betts's demonstrative declaration, the acting chief historian immediately fired off a memorandum to the NPS director. He strongly suggested that officials make it clear exactly how far the Park Service intended to go in observing the Brown Centennial—"if we still plan on having an observance now that the feelings of the Commission are known."

The Park Service reacted in astonishing time. One week after Betts's phone call, in a classic bureaucratic maneuver designed to mollify the segregationists and avoid the contentious clamor of the Civil Rights Movement, the agency dumped responsibility for the John Brown Centennial into the hands of the local community. Citing an obscure passage from a doctrine entitled "Policy Statement on Pageants and Reenactments," the NPS hierarchy informed Harpers Ferry Superintendent Anderson that any commemoration of John Brown "should not be Service-sponsored but rather presented by interested groups with Service cooperation." The NPS effectively had abandoned its role, abdicated its responsibility and divorced itself from the controversial Brown.

What was the Harpers Ferry superintendent to do?

Fortunately for history, a little group of local residents rescued John Brown and the National Park Service from the strangling noose of the Civil War Centennial Commission. With the abdication of NPS leadership, the Harpers Ferry Area Foundation galloped into the void.

Led by Chairwoman June Newcomer, the indefatigable and indefectible granddaughter-in-law of the founder of Storer College, the Foundation planned, organized and staged a three-day "dignified observance" over the anniversary weekend in 1959. Inspired by community rather than conviction, the foundation's John Brown activities ranged from a serious panel discussion to a reenactment of his capture to the presentation of an original three-act play .

"John Brown" stands outside the makeshift two-dimensional fort constructed for the commemoration weekend on the former Storer College campus.

SPARK STILL SMOLDERS

While John Brown was the main attraction, none of these events promoted his methods, message or memory. Although foundation planners adored Brown's notoriety, they shunned his controversy. Although history showed slavery as a cause of the war, no one admitted it. Although the region boasted a considerable African American population, few blacks participated in planning, and almost none attended activities. Although John Brown made Harpers Ferry famous, Brown's fame was now harnessed as an economic benefit for Harpers Ferry.

During the Brown Centennial, re-enactors with the Sharpsburg Rifles stand guard outside the real John Brown's Fort—then located on the Storer College Campus.

"The project contemplated for Harpers Ferry," predicted a local editor, "will 'sell' Harpers Ferry as no other single event has since the initial one that transpired there one hundred years ago."

Sell it did! To the horror of the Civil War Centennial Commission, the John Brown "observance" attracted 65,000 visitors to Harpers Ferry during three stellar October days.

"Not since John Brown's historic raid has there been so much activity in Harpers Ferry," admired one newspaper journalist. "Oddly enough, the man who descended upon the community…is the same person responsible for all the hustle and bustle going on today."

Even worse for the Commission's efforts to derail notoriety toward John Brown, the national media embraced the story, spreading the Brown Centennial to millions. Inspired by the David (the town foundation) versus Goliath (the Commission) struggle—and imbued with John Brown's influence on segregation and the Civil Rights Movement—leading newspapers splashed coverage across the country. "John Brown Raids Again" proclaimed the *New York Times*. "The Wrathful Vintage" declared the *Washington Post* and "Harpers Ferry Readies for New Invasion" predicted the *Baltimore Sunday American*.

The undesirable publicity and the Commission's covert segregationist policies exposed it to national ridicule. "The observance is being arranged by the local citizenry without aid or recognition by the Civil War Centennial Commission," wrote the *New York Times*. "The Commission has decided that the official calendar of centennial events would not start before January, 1961." The *Washington Post* joined in the critique. "Just as John Brown jumped the gun on the Civil War with his abortive stroke against slavery, Harpers Ferry got off to a head start on the Civil War Centennial." And to add an exclamation point on where the Civil War commenced, the *Washington Post* declared: "The first shots of the Civil War Centennial were fired here today as Harpers Ferry was raided again."

Perhaps the biggest blow to the Commission's desire to "soft pedal" John Brown occurred when *Newsweek*—in conjunction with the anniversary weekend—featured Brown on its cover. With a pen and ink sketch of Brown's portrait dramatically superimposed over a gallows, and a headline etched in bright bold red, *Newsweek* announced: "John Brown's Raid: The Spark Still Smolders."

"John Brown's death was not an end; it was a beginning," declared the *Newsweek* writer. "It fired sparks that even today smolder on the American scene." The five-page article, featured in the center of the magazine, addressed the legend, the man, the raid and the consequences, with the bulk of the article focusing upon consequences in 1859 *and* 1959.

"This week, the nation is observing the anniversary of John Brown's Raid on Harpers Ferry," *Newsweek* proclaimed.

The nation. Not Harpers Ferry alone. Not the National Park Service. Not the Civil War Centennial Commission. Not the North. Not the South.

In 2009, Harpers Ferry National Historical Park marked John Brown's 150th anniversary.

John Brown belonged to the nation for the ages.

"[W]e cannot dedicate, we cannot consecrate—we cannot hallow—this ground. The brave men, living and dead, who struggled here, have consecrated it far above our poor power to add or detract. The world will little note, nor long remember what we say here, but it can never forget what they did here."

Abraham Lincoln
Gettysburg Address
November 19, 1863

John Brown's Fort in the mid-1970s.

Chapter 11
MEANING'S MASTER

John Brown's Fort stands as the most famous building in Harpers Ferry's pageant of history—but it stands in the wrong location.

Three times dismantled, moved and reconstructed in the two decades at the turn of the twentieth century, the most iconic monument in Harpers Ferry was not a part of Harpers Ferry National Monument. Obtaining the historic structure became priority number one for the nascent national park.

It rankled NPS officials that the fort—the center of attention for the supremely successful John Brown Centennial—was not owned by the people of the United States. It stood, lonely most of the time, amongst the empty buildings of the defunct Storer College campus on Camp Hill. Located about half a mile from its original site within the armory, the park service had a solution: buy it and return it to its proper place.

But there were two problems. First, the building must be secured. This obviated in 1960 when Congress, led by the relentless Senator Jennings Randolph, approved legislation for the government to acquire the Storer campus. This produced an ironic turn. The government had deeded away these old armory properties to the school; ninety years later, they would now be handed back to the government. This time, however, the mansions and landscapes would not be possessions of the War Department, but of the Department of the Interior.

The second problem proved more dogmatic. The B & O Railroad owned the previous armory grounds. Complicating matters, a twenty-foot stone rubble embankment covered the original fort site, buried now for nearly seven decades. The good news was the railroad had shifted its alignment, tendering the embankment as disposal property. The bad news was the railroad's bureaucracy nearly matched that of the federal government. No resolution would come quickly, or easily.

NPS officials first suggested a symbiotic solution—a property exchange. B & O executives coveted land near Cumberland, Maryland, formerly utilized by its old rival, the C & O Canal. It so happened, as a happy coincidence, that the park service now owned that property. A mutual trade of historic acreage—the armory for the canal—would serve the interests of both parties.

Senator Randolph wasted no time codifying this exchange. Quick to seize a good idea, he included it as a provision in the same Storer College legislation that authorized acquisition of John Brown's Fort. Randolph's bill represented a confluence of private and public sector initiatives, all spurred by the national acclaim Harpers Ferry had gained by the John Brown Centennial. Randolph recognized and seized opportunity.

But that was the last of rapid action. More than forty years—*four decades*—would pass before consummation of the swap.

NPS bureaucrats became obstructive obstacles. Concerned the land exchange would complicate the establishment of a new national historical park for the C & O Canal, park service officials applied brakes to the trade. Former Superintendent Edwin "Mac" Dale, still stinging from his abrupt replacement at the Ferry due to his recalcitrance to the John Brown Centennial, now revelled as administrator of the canal. Flexing his power over the situation, he objected to C & O property being "raided" to benefit Harpers Ferry.

The railroad also obstructed action. Though the government was offering seventy-three acres at Cumberland in exchange for just three acres at Harpers Ferry, the railroad refused. B & O brass insisted that the values of the tracts were unequal and demanded additional monetary payment—or, if that could not be arranged, concessions: a new embankment that would replace the troublesome trestle of the old W & P rail line paralleling the Shenandoah through the old town. Since NPS was committed to restoring the historic scene to the John Brown/Civil War era, this embankment intrusion was a deal-breaker.

Despite persistent efforts by a succession of Harpers Ferry superintendents, no breakthrough occurred. Frustrated and foiled, park officials determined on a bold action: *move the Fort within sight of the armory site.*

A curious spectacle entranced Harpers Ferry residents in March, 1968. A crane lifted up the John Brown Fort from its Storer College home of nearly 60 years; hoisted it onto the flatbed of a tractor trailer; and thence began a two-mile trek down Union Street and onto Shenandoah Street. Venturing down the vertical slope of Camp Hill was particularly hazardous for the operation, as was the steep grade at the juncture of Shenandoah Street and U.S. 340. Any jolt could topple the building from its precarious ride on the flatbed. Gingerly, gradually, almost giddily, the building progressed to its new home as if afloat in a parade.

The NPS moves Joh Brown's Fort from Storer College campus to the corner of Shenandoah and Potomac Streets, March 1968.

MEANING'S MASTER

Much to the relief of NPS historic architect Archie Franzen, who orchestrated the move, the multi-ton brick structure arrived with its walls intact. For the first time in nearly seventy years, it was back in old town Harpers Ferry. But the Fort frowned as it peered at its original home, 150' to the west, despoiled by an abandoned railroad embankment.

But how could its role be understood if John Brown's battlefield remained buried?

John Brown's Fort spurred its own revolution in Harpers Ferry.

As with its namesake, controversy exploded about the structure, altering the course of Harpers Ferry's destiny.

Seven years after the Fort's move into the old town, the NPS became engaged in a demolition and reconstruction program along Shenandoah Street, in the block opposite the Fort. Committed to restoring the town to its John Brown-era appearance, a wrecking ball destroyed three post-Civil War structures at the corner of Shenandoah and High Streets. The century-old debris was hauled to the dump. Steel girders supplanted wood beams; welders replaced mortise and tendon carpenters; and new brick arrived daily by tractor-trailer loads. The goal was to replicate the exterior of these buildings based upon antebellum historic evidence. Interiors were built out as modern office and exhibits spaces, with no conformity to historic arrangements.

According to legend, this brick fell out of the fort during its move and was recovered by one of the workers involved. It was later decorated as a memento and passed down as a private treasure.

Below: The corner of High and Shenandoah Streets prior to restoration.

The mess and commotion became so distracting, rangers sarcastically relabeled Shenandoah Street as "Harpers Ferry National Construction Park."

But NPS architects from Denver, who arrived and superseded the twenty-year wis-dom of resident architect Archie Franzen, in-sisted the multimillion dollar reconstruction abided by planning dictates surmised and re-inforced in the 1950s-60s.

Indeed, the original NPS vision for Harpers Ferry adhered to "the Williamsburg Model" of replicating a specific period in time.

184

Never mind that much had changed in Harpers Ferry since John Brown's day. Buildings added after the Civil War must be eliminated; structures altered must be "restored;" the period landscape reshaped to represent the original. This policy dictated removal of eighty percent of the Storer College structures, as well as post-Civil War buildings on the arsenal square and throughout the old town. This "time-freeze," planners believed, best represented the most significant period in Harpers Ferry's epoch.

But the decade of the 1970s brought a shift in thinking. Spurred by the 1966 National Historic Preservation Act, progressive preservationists began challenging the Williamsburg Model, insisting in the intrinsic value of *evolving history* rather than frozen history. The corporation of Harpers Ferry, itself, adopted the "history-as-ever-changing" philosophy, documenting its myriad of generational buildings as part of the National Register of Historic Places. Two Teutonic plates in preservation theory were about to collide. The earthquake occurred at the John Brown Fort.

The park's demolition and reconstruction program brought an outcry from local citizens, many of whom were new Harpers Ferry residents, dedicated to restoring their own recently-purchased dilapidated properties. Sensitive to history, no matter what time period, they questioned the park service's seemingly insensitive disregard for century-old buildings because they were not old enough.

At a public meeting, local residents excoriated NPS architect Bill Barlow for advocating the wrecking ball. Brash and belligerent, Barlow argued the validity of national significance and belittled lesser histories.

Then an audience member pointed out to Barlow that the John Brown Fort was inaccurate, not just in location but appearance. When rebuilt on the Storer campus in 1909, a glass negative was used for the reconstruction, and as a result, the exterior façade was backwards—a mirror image. In other words, the double doors of the fire engine house appeared on the right of the Storer rebuild, when historical accuracy required they should be on the left side. The NPS had not corrected this anomaly.

So, asked the inquirer, how would Mr. Barlow deal with this matter? The Fort, in its current form, obviously represented an inconsistency.

"I'd tear it down and rebuild it," barked Barlow. The horrified crowd made known their disapproval. Barlow's exit soon became permanent.

Barlow's blunder inaugurated a new era of preservation policy for Harpers Ferry Park. An updated plan "broadens the time period to include the entire nineteenth century," proclaimed the NPS regional director overseeing Harpers Ferry in 1979. Concerned the John Brown/Civil War-era time-freeze "severely limited[ed] the scope and interest of the interpretive programs," the revised concept ensured "the whole sequence of events, including the development of manufacturing and transportation facilities associated with the socioeconomic background of the town and region, will be preserved and interpreted."

MEANING'S MASTER

One of the few college buildings to survive the razing was Anthony Hall. NPS transformed the antebellum mansion into the Stephen T. Mather Training Center—one of only two national training centers specifically for NPS employees. Opposite: bricks litter the Street during reconstruction.

No more would structures within the town be destroyed. No longer would period-looking reconstructions be permitted. No longer was the Williamsburg Model acceptable. The new policy, instead, advocated for restoration of the exterior of existing buildings; but permitted the "rehabilitation" of interiors for "adaptive use." Fancy terms for modern comforts. After twenty-five years of NPS presence, most buildings still lacked necessities such as electricity, light, heat, air conditioning and plumbing. Even visitor enhancements, such as exhibits and restrooms, were minimal after a quarter century of park service administration.

The reason was not negligence, but money. Restoration and rehabilitation of historic structures were worthy, but expensive. The NPS recognized its bank vault was empty, and the situation becoming dire. "For many years the physical resources [of the park] have been deteriorating," warned the regional director. But what would bring attention to the emergency?

Mother Nature.

If ever there was a fortuitous moment for a flood, this was it.

In 1972, for the first time during NPS ownership of the town, a true deluge swept down Shenandoah Street. Tropical Storm Agnes stalled over the mid-Atlantic in late June, dumping buckets of rain along the Appalachians. The Potomac and Shenandoah swelled, cresting almost twenty-eight feet above normal—the highest flood in three decades—swamping every building on Shenandoah Street. For the first time in history, television covered the event, bringing helicopter-theater onto national news broadcasts, beamed into living rooms across the nation. Millions watched Harpers Ferry drown.

The 1972 flood as viewed from Maryland Heights, left, and resulting damage to ranger station, above.

186

CONFLUENCE

The show produced results. In Congress, Senator Robert C. Byrd (WV) had ascended into power, and soon appropriations were levied for downtrodden and damaged Harpers Ferry Park. It represented the beginning of thirty-five years of annual support from Senator Byrd, generating millions for park improvements. Byrd's personal interest and the tax dollars he directed toward Harpers Ferry catapulted the park from its doldrums into a world-class twentieth century destination.

It also prepared the park for the probability of future floods. Improvements in buildings within the floodplain became a priority, all designed to mitigate the devastation of water, mud, muck and mold. Sump pumps were installed in basements. Floor boards were separated to prevent warping. Plaster and paint were made resistant. Heating and air conditioning units moved to upper floors. Electrical wiring encased. Exhibits designed for rapid moves. Artifacts prioritized for evacuation.

A most popular attraction within the park became a flood exhibit. Installed on the exterior of a prominent structure near the Shenandoah River, visitors marveled. Stretching their necks upwards, and straining their eyes, they expressed disbelief at the many markers, revealing flood levels over the decades—several three stories above their heads.

"Why doesn't the park service stop the floods?" they would ask the rangers.

NPS staff work to keep floodwaters at bay in 1985.

MEANING'S MASTER

Restored buildings, by themselves, do not tell history.

Structures must have stories; they require meanings. They cannot be patrons of the past unless they convey perception to the present.

Breathing life into buildings became a Harpers Ferry Park mission. Commencing in 1973, the year after the devastation of the Agnes flood, the park inaugurated an initiative labeled "living history." It soon catapulted into the largest living history program in any national park in the country.

First popularized by Colonial Williamsburg, living history sought to recreate scenes of past living, stimulating visitors' imagination, and immersing them into earlier times. The park service desired to transform Harpers Ferry into its own version of Colonial Williamsburg.

Rangers adorned not in the traditional NPS gray and green uniform, but instead in nineteenth-century garb, began roaming Harpers Ferry's streets. Demonstrations of daily chores from the antebellum and Civil War periods began to stimulate the senses.

Horses started hauling freight wagons up and down the streets, serving as the new trash hauler, while at the same time depositing fresh biscuits of natural waste.

Coal smoke from the blacksmith shop settled over the town, and the clanging of molten metal on the anvil echoed for blocks. Cooking breakfast and dinners on the kitchen wood stove of the Harper House tantalized taste buds as visitors climbed up the historic Stone Steps. Baking in Mr. Roeder's original confectionary—and sharing free samples of bread and biscuits and pies with hungry visitors—captivated audiences. Apple butter, soap-making and clothes-washing demonstrations attracted large crowds. And favorite of all were the rifle and musket demonstrations. The sounds of the armory returned, with the pungent smell of black powder and the repeated echoing of shots off the mountain, forging memories for thousands.

Living history through the years at Harpers Ferry, from top living history staff in period attire, 1984; ice cream making on Independence Day, 2015; "Art of the Forge" blacksmithing workshop, 2017; "Civil War Showcase," 1961.

Harpers Ferry's living history program become so popular and nationally recognized, it became a model for dozens of other historic parks. The demand for authentic period clothing became so intense, in fact, that the park established its own tailor and dress-making shop, producing garments for living history programs across the nation.

Park managers, museum directors and educators traveled from afar to learn about living history based upon the Harpers Ferry model.

From top: a living history gun crew on Bolivar Heights; parking chaos on Shenandoah Street, 1965.

The park's nineteenth-century renaissance produced a cost, however: *too much popularity*. Hundreds of thousands of visitors crammed into the tiny triangle between the rivers, and their disquieting vehicles overwhelmed the very historic environment they came to experience.

Endless lines of traffic choked the three old town streets. Limited parking along the Shenandoah banks filled to capacity at early hours. Auto engines drowned out the sounds of historic demonstrations; emissions polluted the smells of baking and wood stoves; and the relentless roar of motorcycles killed any sense of history. On the Fourth of July, 1976—during a reading of the Declaration of Independence by Civil War-dressed living history rangers on the nation's 200th birthday—a cycle group stopped in the midst of several thousand people on Shenandoah Street, their exhaust pipes blasting, destroying that commemorative moment.

Why this juxtaposition of vehicular insanity into the historic scene?

Unlike at Williamsburg, NPS did not control the streets. Closures required approval of the Harpers Ferry town council, and traffic congestion in the historic setting was not considered a cause for closure. As a result, the incessant and insidious presence of the automobile frustrated generations of NPS administrators. If the car could not be controlled, perhaps it could be mollified.

Branding the historic town a "continuation of inadequate parking, congestion and conflict between pedestrians and automobiles," the regional director overseeing Harpers Ferry endorsed a solution: Purchase land outside the town limits for expanded parking; establish a new park entrance away from Shenandoah Street; and shuttle visitors to and from the historic town. "This will eliminate hazard to pedestrians caused by excessive traffic in the historic area," reasoned the director, "and greatly enhance the interpretive program by removing twentieth-century auto traffic congestion from a nineteenth-century scene."

Change commenced. Senators Byrd and Randolph shepherded the legislation for the land expansion and Byrd garnered the funds for the new parking and transportation solution. A 1,000-vehicle parking lot—triple the parking capacity along the Shenandoah—opened in 1990, complimented by a new entrance and access road leading to the old town, traveled by a bus shuttle equipped to transport thousands of visitors. "This project improves visitor enjoyment at the park by eliminating many modern distractions from the historic scene," commented Superintendent Donald W. Campbell on opening day in the presence of an admiring Senator Byrd.

Though a singular improvement, vehicular intrusion remained. Despite the park service's aspiration, the town allowed unfettered access to its streets, signaling its local independence from federal authority. The Williamsburg living history experience—and immersion into an historic environment free from modern intrusion—represented, ultimately, a park failure. Despite fifty years of NPS effort and tens of millions of dollars, the car reigned supreme. Americans' affair with their vehicles proved too much to overcome.

"We shall overcome" sang as the clarion cry of the civil rights movement. The perpetual struggle for civil rights transformed the emphasis of Harpers Ferry Park as it entered its fourth decade of existence.

Long renowned for its association with John Brown, the role of Harpers Ferry in erstwhile significant African American history largely went unnoticed by NPS. Even with the addition of the former Storer College campus in 1960, the presentation and interpretation of the site's black heritage remained subdued at best, and ignored at worst.

Two events, and three associations, altered this trajectory.

"This Special People's program, *Heritage Days: The Black Perspective*," announced the official program guide, "is part of the American Nation's Bicentennial."

Julian Bond, a keynote speaker at the Heritage Days event, soon was announced as U.S. Ambassador to the United Nations.

190

CONFLUENCE

As the country prepared to celebrate the 200th anniversary of Independence Day in 1976, most attention focused upon Philadelphia and the seat of revolution. But the nation's most illustrious civil rights leaders were converging elsewhere: Harpers Ferry.

Three weeks before July 4, Harpers Ferry hosted its most significant gathering of African American icons since the Niagara Movement seventy years earlier. Luminaries included the first black congresswoman; the president of the national NAACP; the vice president of the U.S. Conference of Mayors; the president of the Southern Poverty Law Center; and the president of the Martin Luther King Foundation and soon-to-be U.S. Ambassador to the United Nations. This star-studded cast ventured to Harpers Ferry to recognize "America's debt to African and Afro-American culture, patterns, habits and traditions...and to call attention to the courageous Black Americans who used Harpers Ferry as a base for a 'do or die' stand for liberty and freedom."

Shirley Chisholm, the first African American Congresswoman, was just one of the notable participants in the Heritage Days *program, hosted at Harpers Ferry National Historical Park in 1976.*

The three-day weekend event—co-sponsored by the NPS, the Storer College Alumni Association, and the Association for the Study of Afro-American Life and History—featured lectures, performances and demonstrations that promised "intellectual stimulation." It also assured "your pride of African and Afro-American heritage will be buttressed."

"This conference is an excellent tribute during our Bicentennial celebration to our Black heritage," commented Senator Randolph in written remarks in the program welcome, acknowledging the Storer College campus as an ideal host. "America today is a strong nation that continues to build on the strength of its heritage." Then Randolph soared to statesman. "Our great country has only one authority, 'we the people.' This is not only our opportunity; it must be our crusade."

Heritage Days: The Black Perspective drew national and international attention to Harpers Ferry. It also compelled the highest levels of NPS leadership to ask this question: are na-tional park sites giving appropriate awareness to African American history?

No...according to the findings of a Howard University analysis, commissioned by the NPS in 1978. "Since racial prejudice and exploitation is a theme that many find unpalatable," reasoned the report, "it obviously must be handled with great sensitiveness in any park service presentation." The investigation, in general, discovered a common practice among the parks: avoidance of controversy was preferable to facilitating sensitive discussion.

The Howard study examined thirty-one national parks "possessing aspects of Black interest and involvement." Five parks, including Harpers Ferry, incorporated on-site inspections. The study deemed all deficient in their understanding and presentation of African American stories. "When American history is perceived and celebrated in terms of the lives and activities of ordinary people," argued the report, "rather than those of political and social elites, then the black presence partakes of the character of that of the American people in general and should be appreciated as such."

> *"[Black History] is a story that must be told; and fortunately, the tools [are] necessary to tell the story."*

Harpers Ferry received particular notice.

> "Of all of the National Park Service landmarks, Harpers Ferry NHP is perhaps best suited to become a center for the study and presentation of black history."

The Howard report enumerated Harpers Ferry's preponderance of African American history. It also revealed its glaring absence in NPS presentation.

John Brown, of course, was represented. But what of his Black participants? What about the interactions of the Free Black and slave populations in the antebellum period? What can we learn from the employment and displacement of Black refugees during the Civil War? What does the Freedmen's Bureau and life during Reconstruction, Jim Crow and segregation teach us? Why was the Ferry associated with the early Civil Rights Movement and the rise of the NAACP? And, not least, what was the influence of Storer College? "The history of the rise and fall of segregated education is essentially the story of the evolution and transformation of American race relations," argued the report.

"[Black History] is a story that must be told; and fortunately, the tools [are] necessary to tell the story."

The story, unfortunately, remained untold after two decades of NPS administration. But that soon changed.

After release of the Howard study, NPS elevated Storer College and African American history as a theme equal to John Brown and the Civil War. This occurred at the same time that the park service expanded Harpers Ferry's historic period to the entire nineteenth century—the same expansion that salvaged post-Civil War structures.

Superintendent Martin R. Conway, left, dedicates a plaque to Blacks in American history, 1976.

Then the park followed up on many of the Howard recommendations. It created a Storer College exhibit first, working in conjunction with Storer Col-

CONFLUENCE

lege alumni. Soon appeared a Black history exhibit that focused upon slavery, emancipation, education and segregation as life encounters in the town. Outdoor exhibits emerged on the Storer College campus and on Camp Hill, sharing the stories of the school's origins, its struggles and its victories. Black History Month became an annual highlight. Ranger tours incorporated African American stories.

From top: Redman Jazz Heritage Awards and Concert; fanfare of the Storer College sesquicentennial; Ranger and longtime Storer Alumni Association Liaison Guinevere Roper, who spent decades helping bring the African American stories of Harpers Ferry to light; participants in the "Lives in Limbo" living history program, sharing the African American experience of Civil War-era Harpers Ferry.

A new "Allies for Freedom" exhibition featured Black participants in John Brown's war. Commemorations of Niagara's centennial (2006), Brown's sesquicentennial (2009), and Storer's sesquicentennial (2017) attracted national audiences and academic scholars. The inception of the annual Don Redman Jazz Heritage Awards and Concert, held each year in June on the Storer College campus, ensured Storer's culture would not be forgotten. The Harpers Ferry Park Association published a commemorative history of Storer that enshrined its myriad of contributions.

Three associations, in particular, shepherded the Black history revelation at Harpers Ferry. The Storer College Alumni Association worked persistently and tirelessly to promote and preserve the memories of its alma mater. A NPS ethnographic study, along with numerous oral history interviews, infused a new life into the college environment. The local chapter of the NAACP, along with the statewide West Virginia chapter, politicked for finances, obtaining hundreds of thousands of dollars to support exhibits and commemorations over three decades. A goal of the Howard study—to strengthen connections with the African American community—was achieved at Harpers Ferry.

Integration of the African American theme into Harpers Ferry's story proved a resounding integration success. Expansion of Harpers Ferry's stories beyond the original John Brown/Civil War era, whether the African American journey, the industrial saga, or the transportation theme, diversified and strengthened Harpers Ferry as a destination. These "expansion" triumphs proved a theorem: a park could evolve.

MEANING'S MASTER

But on another front, expansion exploded into war. Harpers Ferry had once sat on the border between the Union and Confederacy.

Now the battle line was drawn between preservationists and developers.

All expected the Niagara Centennial of 2006 to shine as a sacred moment in Harpers Ferry Park's history. The commemoration of civil rights and its early stalwart leaders finally would receive the national recognition they deserved. Anticipation heightened as the park prepared to welcome scholars, performers and visitors from across the nation to celebrate the civil rights cornerstone laid at Harpers Ferry.

Then the Ku Klux Klan announced its intention to crash the party.

This clash of morality generated an army of U.S. Park Police that became an occupation force on the Storer campus. A surreal mixture of blue-helmets and riot gear jumbled with soaring orations and gospel vocals as the Klansmen (and women)—arrayed not in their customary white hoods and robes, but as civilians—roamed about the lectures and exhibits. The tension thermometer singed, but did not blow, and the event escaped confrontation.

Not the case two miles distant, where arrests were imminent.

Bulldozers and trench excavators were altering the earth on the School House Ridge battlefield at the same time the KKK was stalking the Niagara event. Local developers had selected Niagara weekend as the ideal moment for their surprise attack. They secretly had mobilized on government property on a Friday night, and boldly commenced excavation at dawn on Saturday, surmising there was no way that the NPS could react.

Wrong.

The park's chief ranger responded to the emergency, racing to the battlefield with siren blaring and lights flashing. Three local attorneys greeted her that Saturday morning. They waved a paper right-of-way deed in her face, and dared her to stop them. Not intimidated, the chief ranger informed the violators they had no permit and no permission to dig up federal property. She ordered her rangers to seize all equipment and arrest all trespassers. Everything halted.

Then arrived a lawyer from Washington.

To the dismay of the chief ranger, he began negotiating with the developers' legal gurus. On scene as a First Amendment specialist (attending Niagara to ensure all rights respected)—and with little knowledge of land laws—he superseded the chief ranger, claiming only a federal judge could issue an injunction to halt the work.

The patricians' parlay ended; and the desecration recommenced. All day and night on Saturday, under the glare of mobile stadium lights, churned the earth-moving monsters, abetted by cranes that lifted and placed hundreds of feet of massive piping. By Monday

"The viewshed from numerous places in [the park] will be ruined forever."

Scot Faulkner
Friends of Harpers Ferry NHP
2006

194

CONFLUENCE

Developers literally bulldozing history. Background: School House Ridge North today. The Civil War Trust purchased almost 400 acres of Civil War battlefield on School House Ridge, Bolivar Heights and the Allstadt Farm over two decades, thwarting developers in persistent fights, and proving the value of private sector partners in preservation.

morning, they were gone. Water and sewer lines, buried under hundreds of tons of topsoil, stabbed the heart of the School House Ridge battlefield.

What was happening?

Harpers Ferry had become a favorite playground for developers. Jefferson County had morphed into a magnet for suburbanites commuting into Washington and its environs. So many outsiders were moving in, the county earned distinction as the fastest population growth area in the state by the mid-1980s. Threats began bombarding Harpers Ferry Park.

Jefferson County recognized growth controls were necessary, and in 1988 it became the first county in the state to implement zoning. This matched well with NPS plans a decade earlier, which purposely had limited park expansion and land acquisition. "Scenic and historic protection areas will not require purchase of any property rights if local jurisdictions provide this protection," presumed the NPS regional director overseeing Harpers Ferry Park.

Bad assumption. The park service view was based upon intrinsic value in preserving views. County leaders adopted the developers' dogma of land as wealth. Subsequently, when Harpers Ferry Park recommended agricultural zoning for adjacent lands (reflecting their current usage as farms), the county ignored this suggestion, instead "up-zoning" the parcels for use as high-density residential, commercial and industrial development. Permitted uses included: apartment buildings, condominiums, mobile home parks, nursing homes, supermarkets, malls and oil refineries.

"The national historical park and its surrounding landscape are at a crossroads," lamented the NPS. "Difficult decisions about the park's future lie ahead."

An understatement. Not a square inch of the School House Ridge battlefield was protected. The Murphy Farm—temporary home of the John Brown Fort, site of the Niagara pilgrimage, and locale of significant Civil War tactical maneuvers—was wholly unsecured. Hundreds of acres on Bolivar Heights remained vulnerable. Mr. Jefferson's famous view deferred despoliation, but for how long? By 1989, the park had identified nearly 2,000 acres of history-rich land that confronted hazards.

This was double the size of the existing boundary.

Titanic forces collided. Preservationists dueled with developers. National organizations combated local interests. Public rights wrestled with property rights. Open space opposed living space. The universal and unanswered question: would greed supplant the public need?

This battle raged for seventeen years. It involved different properties, different people and different politicians. But three fixed points remained stern and steady: Superintendent Donald W. Campbell; Senator Robert C. Byrd; and a coalition of fiercely passionate preservationists.

Superintendent Campbell never wavered in his determination to preserve Harpers

MEANING'S MASTER

Ferry's history. His fortitude, his guidance, and most important, his vision, ensured the preservationists a great captain. Senator Byrd displayed patience and prudence, prescient that debate and time would bring public favor.

The preservationists applied constant pressure, never permitting the debate to settle without prudence. Five organizations in particular combined their muscle and their memberships to lead the charge. The National Parks Conservation Association, championed by regional director Joy Oakes, rallied thousands across the nation for the cause. The National Trust for Historic Preservation brought Harpers Ferry to the forefront as a site in crises. The Civil War Trust labeled the park as one of its most endangered battlefields, and stepped forward to acquire hundreds of acres of threatened soil. The Friends of Harpers Ferry NHP, spirited by Scot Faulkner, challenged local adverse zoning decisions in court. And Paul Rosa of the Harpers Ferry Conservancy submitted dozens of pages of technical testimony supporting preservation.

View from the Murphy Farm. The Trust for Public Lands and the National Parks Conservation Association teamed at the turn of the twenty-first century to prevent it from becoming a 188-unit housing development.

One other factor tilted the wave toward preservation. After the county commissioners stood upon School House Ridge with the park historian and informed him, "Nothing happened here, boy!" the park launched an aggressive school curriculum program to educate the county's youth. It worked. In 1989, the first commissioners' vote on park expansion was unanimous: five to zero *against*. A decade and a half later, after thousands of students had experienced the battlefield first-hand under the direction of park rangers, another commissioners' vote was five to zero *in favor* of preserving the battlefield. The power of education.

Senator Byrd shepherded through legislation in 2004 that nearly doubled the park to 4,000 acres; but even that landmark success failed to assure its protection.

Remember the saga of the water and sewer lines? Turns out it was part of a larger scheme to build over two-million square feet of commercial property (the equivalent of sixteen Super Walmarts) at the south end of Bolivar Heights. War erupted yet again over Harpers Ferry's destiny. The Great Recession of 2008 terminated this fight, bankrupting the developers. Ironically, the savior of this portion of the battlefield was a "sensitive" developer who had grown up on School House Ridge.

Few national parks have faced decades of development pressures like those posed at Harpers Ferry. For preservationists, Harpers Ferry is a case study in the power of patience, persistence and perseverance.

In an effort to preserve for future generations the view that so stirred Thomas Jefferson, the Nature Conservancy orchestrated the acquisition of 345 Virginia acres in 1980. This included Short Hill, the center mountain just downstream in this photo.

Partners in Preservation

In 1963, Jennings Randolph shepherded legislation through Congress to authorize a formal name change of the national park site at Harpers Ferry to Harpers Ferry National Historical Park. Above, Senator Randolph, center, welcomes 200 diplomat families from D.C. to Harpers Ferry in 1965.

Like Randolph, Robert Byrd proved a powerfully committed ally for Harpers Ferry in Congress. Above, Debbie Piscitelli of the Harpers Ferry Historical Association (now the Harpers Ferry Park Asso-ciation) presents Senator Byrd with a cake on the opening of the Byrd Visitor Center Complex in 1982.

At right, Harpers Ferry Mayor Bradley Nash prepares to light the lamps for the start of the first an-nual Old Tyme Christmas celebration. A passionate and political 40-year park defender, Nash donated to the park and the American people his 24-acre farm on the north-ern edge of Bolivar Heights in 1991.

The Fine Art of Building—and Keeping—a National Park

Senator and Mrs. Byrd listen as Superintendent Donald W. Campbell, right, explains restoration completed at Harpers Ferry, 1982. Superintendent Campbell steered Harpers Ferry National Historical Park for 29 years. The park's history and its landscape is largely preserved today thanks to his decades of unyielding vision and fortitude.

The completion of a pedestrian bridge across the Potomac in 1985 enabled the rerouting of the Appalachian Trail through historic downtown Harpers Ferry. Outdoor adventurers may cherish the park today as much as historians.

Why preserve a national park?

What is the value of history?

What is the meaning of John Brown? What do we learn from the Civil War? What does the struggle for civil rights teach? What is the proper balance between new technologies and workers' jobs? What is our solution for racial tension?

Harpers Ferry offers us a place to discuss our differences; debate our opinions; and express our thoughts and voices. It epitomizes our American democracy. It characterizes our American evolution. Yet for each of us, this question endures:

What constitutes transformative moments and places? Where our nation's trajectory changed so dramatically it identifies who we *are* rather than who we *were*.

People at Harpers Ferry transformed us. People at Harpers Ferry preserved it for us. People in our future will determine Harpers Ferry's destiny or demise.

But this is certain:
 Harpers Ferry is the *power of place*. Here your soles . . . connect with their souls . . . and touch your soul within.
Few places possess such power.

EPILOGUE

Dr. Thomas Featherstonhaugh was on a mission. Where were Brown's men buried at Harpers Ferry?

He knew seven (maybe eight) bodies were crammed into two "store boxes" and carried across the Shenandoah River, but the exact location of the remote grave seemed lost almost forty years later. He inquired on numerous visits to the Ferry, always without result. Finally he met an old man named James Foreman, who witnessed the internment and led him to the grave site along the Shenandoah shore.

They secured some shovels from Foreman and began digging. Featherstonhaugh then tells this story.

"Some three feet below the surface we came upon the cover of the box which was partially decayed and was sunken in, but was still in a very fair state of preservation. We finally uncovered the whole top of the box and I raised the cover, to which the whole backbone of a man was adherent. . . .

This coffin contained the remains of four of the invaders. Portions of the clothing were still to be distinguished. . . . The bodies were evidently buried in the blankets, for there were great masses of woolen tissue surrounding each one of the dead men. These blankets or shawls were worn by the men as overcoats . . . .

One of the skulls that I picked out from the ooze was all in pieces as if it had been shattered, and this may have been the skull of Newby, who, it will be remembered, was shot through the head and neck by a great spike.

After becoming fully satisfied that we had the remains of the raiders before us, we replaced the cover of the box and refilled the grave. We brought from the river's brink two large flat stones which we placed as headstones to mark the spot. The other grave, in which three of the bodies were placed . . . we did not disturb."

Featherstonhaugh later returned, leading an expedition to have the bodies reburied alongside John Brown (1899) at his farm in North Elba, New York.

Perhaps their spirits still linger at Harpers Ferry.

The long-forgotten burial site of John Brown's killed men rediscovered along the Shenandoah River.

MAJOR U.S. EVENTS	MAJOR HARPERS FERRY EVENTS
1607 Jamestown, Virginia established by English settlers	
1619 African enslaved first imported to Jamestown	1733 First ferry operation established at "The Hole" by Peter Stephens
1754-1763 French and Indian War and British colonial victory	1747 Robert Harper arrives and settles at the confluence
1754 George Washington defeated by the French at Fort Necessity, Pennsylvania	1754 George Washington first navigates the Potomac rapids about Harpers Ferry
1775–1781 American Revolutionary War	
1776 Declaration of Independence	
1780 Freewill Baptist denomination established in New England	1782 Harper dies. Harper House, oldest building in town, completed.
1785 Patowmack Company established with George Washington as president	1785 Washington inspects Potomac Company navigation improvements above confluence; Thomas Jefferson records scenery from 1783 visit "worth a voyage across the Atlantic"
1787 Northwest Ordinance opens the Northwest Territory to statehood (eventually forming states between Ohio and Minnesota) and prohibits slavery in all new states north of the Ohio River	
1788 U. S. Constitution adopted	
1789-1797 George Washington is U. S. president	1794 Washington calls for establishment of U. S. armory at Harpers Ferry
1790 Washington, D.C. established as U. S. capital	
1799 Death of George Washington at Mount Vernon	1796 Government acquires armory property from Wager family (Harper's heirs)
1800 (May 9) John Brown born in Torrington, Connecticut	1799-1800 8th and 9th U.S. Infantry regiments stationed atop Camp Hill
1801-1809 Thomas Jefferson is U. S. president	1799-1801 Armory Potomac dam and power canal constructed;
1802 Potomac Company opens thru-navigation from Cumberland, Maryland to Georgetown	1802 Musket production commences at the armory on full scale

1803 Louisiana Purchase	1803 Meriwether Lewis at the armory to obtain supplies and gear for expedition
1804-1806 Lewis and Clark Expedition	1803-1807 Potomac Company constructs locks and canal on Shenandoah above confluence
1811-1818 National Road (first federal highway) constructed between Cumberland, Maryland and Wheeling, [West] Virginia connects with road leading to port city of Baltimore.	
1812-1815 War of 1812 fought against Great Britain	
1820 Congressional compromise prohibits slavery in all new states established from the Louisiana Purchase north of the southern boundary of Missouri.	1819 John H. Hall awarded contract to produce interchangeable rifle at Harpers Ferry
1825 Erie Canal in New York State completed	1825 Lewis Wernwag completed first bridge at Harpers Ferry
1828 Chesapeake & Ohio Canal commenced construction at Georgetown near Washington, D.C.; Baltimore & Ohio Railroad started construction at Baltimore	1829 Armory superintendent assassinated by disgruntled employee
1831 Nat Turner slave rebellion in Southampton County, Virginia	1832 Cholera epidemic
	1833 C & O Canal arrived opposite Harpers Ferry
	1834 B & O Railroad opened to Maryland shore opposite Harpers Ferry
	1836 Winchester & Potomac Railroad opens to Harpers Ferry
	1837 B & O Railroad covered bridge completed across Potomac
	1841-1854 U.S. military officers command armory rather than civilian superintendents
	1842 "Clock Strike" staged by armorers
1846-1848 Mexican-American War	1843 Two floods in one month submerge armory
	1849 Cotton Mill opened on Virginius Island
1850 Fugitive Slave Law requires capture and return of escaped slaves from Free States. Slave trade abolished in Washington, D.C.; C & O Canal completed and ended at Cumberland, Maryland.	1851-1855 Armory payroll reduced by nearly 50%
	1852 Worst flood of antebellum period
1853 B & O Railroad opened to the Ohio River at Wheeling	
1854 Republican Party established in Wisconsin; Kansas-Nebraska Act allows local residents of these two terri-	

tories to determine whether their states will be free or slave, effectively repealing the Missouri Compromise.

1854-1859 "Bleeding Kansas." Precursor to civil war fought between pro-slavery and anti-slavery forces.

1857   U. S. Supreme Court Dred Scott decision determines slavery legal anywhere within the country, effectively overruling anti-slavery laws in Free States.

1858   Lincoln-Douglas Debates in Illinois in which Abraham Lincoln declares "this government cannot endure, permanently half slave and half free."

Lincoln elected as first Republican president; South Carolina secedes from the Union

1861 In February, Confederate States of America (CSA) established by seven seceded Southern states; in April, **Virginia secedes**

July 21: Battle of First Bull Run (Manassas) first major engagement of the Civil War

1862

March 23-June 9: Stonewall Jackson's Shenandoah Valley Campaign

September 4-20: First invasion of the North by Robert E. Lee's Confederate army
September 14: Battle of South Mountain
September 17: Battle of Antietam
September 22:   Lincoln issues Preliminary Emancipation Proclamation

1863
June 13-July 14: Lee's second invasion of the North
June 20: West Virginia established as 35th state

1858   Armory workforce reaches its largest at 400 employees.

1859 John Brown's attack on Harpers Ferry

1860   Final executions of two of Brown's men in Charles Town

April 18, Arsenal destroyed at outbreak of Civil War
April 19-June 15: 1st Confederate occupation; armory machinery dismantled and shipped south; railroad bridge destroyed and armory burned
July 21-28: 1st U.S. occupation
October 16:   Battle of Bolivar Heights first battle at Harpers Ferry

1862
February 7: U.S. troops torch the Point commercial district
Feb. 24-Sept. 15: 2nd U.S. occupation
May 28-30: Stonewall Jackson threatens during his Shenandoah Valley Campaign

Sept. 13-15:   Battle of Harpers Ferry
Sept. 15-18: 2nd Confederate occupation
Sept. 19-, 1862 - June 30, 1863:   3rd U.S. occupation

Oct. 1-2: President Lincoln visits

1863

June 18-July 14: 3rd Confederate occupation

July 1-3: Battle of Gettysburg

1864
July 3-12: Third invasion of the North
July 9: Battle of Monocacy
July 11-12 Battle of Fort Stevens outside of Washington, D.C.

Aug. 8-Oct. 19 Sheridan's Shenandoah Valley Campaign

1865
March 3: Freedmen's Bureau established
April 9: Lee surrenders to Grant at Appomattox

April 14: President Lincoln assassinated

December 6   13th Amendment abolishes slavery
December 24: Ku Klux Klan established in Pulaski, Tennessee

1865-1866 Black Code Laws adopted in Southern states to limit rights of African-Americans
1865-1877: Reconstruction in the South; U.S. forces occupy former Confederate states

1868 (July 28) 14th Amendment grants citizenship to all persons born or naturalized in the U. S. (including former slaves), and provides "equal protection of the laws."

1870 (February 3) 15th Amendment grants African-American men the right to vote

1872 Yellowstone established as America's first national park; West Virginia constitution required "[w]hite and colored persons shall not be taught in the same school."

July 14, 1863—July 4, 1864: 4th U.S. occupation

1864
July 4-7: U.S. bombardment of Harpers Ferry. More civilians killed than any other time.
July 5-9: Final Confederate occupation
July 9, 1864 —June 30,1865: Final U.S. occupation; serves as supply base for Sheridan's Valley Campaign

1865
April 9: Cannon on Maryland Heights fire 100-gun salute in tribute to Appomattox surrender
September: Freedmen's Bureau opens district office
Oct.-Dec.: Freewill Baptist missionaries arrive and establish schools for former enslaved

November: Lockwood House opened as school to teach African-Americans
1866: Department of War determines armory should be disposed of and property sold
1867: Child-McCreight flour mill opened on Virginius Island; **Storer College established**

1869: Federal government sells armory holdings and water power rights

1870 B & O Railroad completes Bollman Bridge;
Deadliest flood in Harpers Ferry's history September 30-October 1

1877 (November)   Harpers Ferry flooded
1881 (May 30)   Frederick Douglass delivers speech on John Brown at Storer College.

1884: Thomas Savery purchases old Potomac Musket Factory & Shenandoah Rifle Factory sites from federal government.
1888 Savery's Shenandoah Pulp Mill commences operation at former U. S. Rifle Factory site

1889 (May 31) Johnstown Flood

1893   Chicago World's Fair Columbia Exposition

1896 Plessy vs. Ferguson decision upheld racial segregation laws in public facilities, establishing the doctrine of "separate but equal."

1916-1918   America in World War I

1916   National Park Service established by Congress
1920   19th Amendment provides women with the right to vote

1929-1939   Great Depression

1941-1945 America in World War II

1944 (June 6)   D- Day

1950-1953   Korean War

1954   U. S. Supreme Court decision Brown vs. Board of Education prohibits segregation in public schools

1955-1968   Civil Rights Movement, marches, boycotts

1959-1965   Civil War Centennial

1889 (May 30-June2) Second highest flood in all of Harpers Ferry's history
1890   Hill Top House Hotel opened and operated by Thomas Lovett and family

1891 John Brown's Fort sold to investors who dismantle building and ship it to Chicago.

1894   B & O Railroad completes realignment. Includes 20' embankment covering site of the John Brown Fort and portion of the original armory grounds, construction of new Potomac River bridge, tunnel and a new train station.
1895   John Brown Fort returned from Chicago and rebuilt on the Murphy Farm

1906 (August 17-19) W. E. B. Dubois and Second Niagara Movement meeting held at Storer College
1910   John Brown Fort moved to Storer College

1924 (March)   Destructive flood submerges Harpers Ferry and permanently closes C & O Canal

1936 (March)   Dr. Henry McDonald organizes plan to establish national monument; Highest flood in recorded history strikes Harpers Ferry

1944 (June 30)   Harpers Ferry National Monument established

1953   West Virginia completes purchase of old town Harpers Ferry and donates to the National Park Service

1954   First NPS presence in Harpers Ferry
1955   Storer College closes

1959 John Brown Centennial

1962 John Glenn first American to orbit earth	1960 Congress legislates acquisition of former Storer College campus, John Brown Fort, and Potomac Musket Factory site
1963 Martin Luther King March on Washington, "I have a dream" speech; President Kennedy assassinated	
1963-1975 Vietnam War	1963 State of Maryland donates Maryland Heights; Harpers Ferry National Historical Park established
1964 Civil Rights Act ended segregation in public places and banned employment discrimination on the basis of race, color, religion, sex or national origin.	1964 NPS opens national training center at former Storer College
1965 Voting Rights Act outlawed discriminatory voting practices adopted in many Southern states after the Civil War, including literacy tests.	
1968 Martin Luther King, Jr., assassinated	1968 (March) John Brown Fort moved from Storer College into old town
1969 American astronauts first step upon the Moon	
	1970 NPS establishes a nationwide service center for exhibits, films, brochures and museum conservation on the former Storer College campus.
	1972 (June) Tropical Storm Agnes is the 1st flood to strike the national park
	1973 Harpers Ferry inaugurates its Living History program
1974 President Nixon resigns amidst Watergate scandal	
	1975-1980 Block of buildings at northeast end of Shenandoah Street refurbished
1976 U. S. Bicentennial celebration	1976 Black Heritage Days celebrated during the Bicentennial
1979-1980 Iran hostages' confrontation	1979 Donald W. Campbell begins 29-year tenure as park superintendent
1980 Reagan elected president	1980 Short Hill in Virginia added to the park; Howard University deems Harpers Ferry the NPS site "best suited to become a center for the study and presentation of black history."
	1988-1989 Special boundary study conducted to determine threatened resources adjacent to park.
1989 Fall of the Berlin Wall signals end of Cold War	
	1990 New shuttle and expanded parking project completed and opened
1990-1991 Gulf War	
	1994-1997 Block of buildings south of Shenandoah Street refurbished
1998-1999 Clinton Impeachment	

2000 U. S. Supreme Court determines George W. Bush as president in contested election results	
2001 U.S. attacked by Al-Qaeda terrorists	2001: Murphy Farm acquired by the Trust for Public Lands and added to the park.
2003 Invasion of Iraq	2004: Congress expands boundary to include School House Ridge Battlefield
	2006: Developers desecrate section of School House Ridge Battlefield during Niagara Centennial celebration.
2008 Obama elected first black president	2009: Rebecca L. Harriett first woman superintendent; John Brown Sesquicentennial commemoration
	2011-2015 Civil War Sesquicentennial commemoration
2013 U. S. Supreme Court invalidates Voting Rights Act of 1965 requirement that Southern states obtain federal approvals for voting changes	2017 Tyrone Brandyburg first African-American superintendent; Storer College Sesquicentennial commemoration

Has a Harpers Ferry story piqued your curiosity? Want to learn more? Consider these titles as trusted companions for further adventures and discoveries...

Harpers Ferry History (general)

Barry, Joseph. *The Strange Story of Harpers Ferry.*

Gilbert, David. *A Walker's Guide to Harpers Ferry.*

John Brown Story

Douglass, Frederick. *John Brown: An Address by Frederick Douglass at the Fourteenth Anniversary of Storer College, Harpers Ferry, West Virginia, May 30, 1881.*

Horwitz, Tony. *Midnight Rising: John Brown and the Raid that Sparked the Civil War.*

John Brown's Raid, National Park Service History Series.

Oates, Stephen. *To Purge this Land with Blood: A Biography of John Brown.*

Quarles, Benjamin. *Allies for Freedom: Blacks on John Brown.*

Villard, Oswald Garrison. *John Brown: A Biography Fifty Years Later.*

Civil War Story

Frye, Dennis E. *The Battle of Harpers Ferry: History and Battlefield Guide.*

Frye, Dennis E. *Harpers Ferry Under Fire: A Border Town during the Civil War.*

Frye, Dennis E. *Antietam Shadows: Mystery, Myth & Machination.*

Marmion, Annie. *Under Fire.*

Moulton, Charles. *On the Border with Rambling Jour.* Eds. Lee and Karen Drickamer.

African American Story

Baldau, Catherine, ed. *To Emancipate the Mind and Soul: Storer College.*

Blight, David W. *Frederick Douglass: Prophet of Freedom.*

Blight, David W. *Beyond the Battlefield: Race, Memory and the American Civil War.*

Burke, Dawne Raines. *An American Phoenix: A History of Storer College from Slavery to Desegregation, 1865-1955.*

Lewis, David Levering. *W. E. B. Dubois: 1868-1919, Biography of a Race.*

Reilly, Wayne E., ed., *Sarah Jane Foster: Teacher of the Freedmen, a Diary and Letters.*

Industrial Story

Gilbert, David. *Where Industry Failed: Water-Powered Mills at Harpers Ferry, West Virginia.*

Smith, Merritt Roe. *Harpers Ferry Armory and the New Technology: The Challenge of Change.*

Transportation Story

Dilts, James D. *The Great Road: The Building of the Baltimore and Ohio, the Nation's First Railroad, 1828-1853.*

Hahn, Thomas F. *Towpath Guide to the C & O Canal.*

Kapsch, Robert J. *The Potomac Canal: George Washington and the Waterway West.*

Sanderlin, Walter S. *The Great National Project: A History of the Chesapeake and Ohio Canal.*

INDEX

Abolition. Brown, 34; cultural movement, 33.
Adams, Francis C. Amory purchase and, 143-4; B & O extortion, 153-154; manufacturing mecca promised, 144
Adams, John Quincy. C & O groundbreaking, 55; internal improvements to nation, 53.
"Address to the Nation." Du Bois, 128.
Agnes, Tropical Storm. *See floods, 1972.*
Alcott, Louisa May. Worships Brown, 76.
Alleghenies. Obstacle to western travel, 49.
Allstadt, John. Captured, 8; hostage in John Brown's Fort, 46; slaveowner, 8; slaves of, 8, 70; witness in Brown's trial, 70-1
Appalachian Trail. 198, illustrated, 198.
American Missionary Association. Assigns Brackett to Harpers Ferry, 113; establishes first school at Harpers Ferry to educate slaves, 113-4.
Anderson, Frank. Brown centennial endorsement, 175-6; Brown centennial leadership abandoned, 177.
Anderson, Jeremiah. killed, 66; mission, 66.
Anthony, Kate. Describes Storer College boarding houses, 157; threatened, 116.
Appalachians. Brown's stronghold for his plan, 38-9; Hindrance to navigation, 49.
Armory. *See Harpers Ferry Armory and Arsenal.*
Armory fire engine house. *See John Brown's Fort.*
Arsenal. *See Harpers Ferry Armory and Arsenal.*
ASALH. Black Heritage Days co-sponsor, 191.
B & O Railroad. Advantages of, 61; alignment improved, 154; armory and, 25; armory sale and, 143-4; armory tract right of way acquired, 57-8, 154; Bollman bridge and, 143-4; bridge constructed at Harpers Ferry, 57-8, 143-4; Brown attack—militia transported on, 45, passenger train halted during, 10; Brown centennial controversy and, 176; innovation, 56-7, 60-1; Brown's Fort and, 182-3; Brown's Fort Monument and, 129; C & O, battles with, 56; Carroll and cornerstone, 55; com-merce on, 27, 142; Completion to Ohio R., 61; de-scribed, 58, 60; embankment over armory ground, 154; established, 55-6; Harpers Ferry crossing, 57-8; illustrated, 58, 59, 61, 98, 146; locomotive, illus-trated, 59; locomotive destroyed, illustrated, 82; mountain barriers to success, 56; new jobs creat-ed, 59; new vocabulary, 59; outbid in property acquisition, 143-4; passenger service described, 59; Railroad Brigade, 87; slave transport preven-tion, 60; as speculation, 56; steam power develop-ment and, 56-7; underground railroad and, 60; uniform time, 59; rolling stock described, 59; Simpson and, 176; supplies Union Army, 87; train operation described, 59; travel ad, 57; travel time enhanced, 57, 61.
B & O Railroad Bridge. 1894 bridge (new), 154; 1936 flood and, illustrated, 160-2; as Bollman Bridge, 143-4; Constructed first time, 58; destroyed after Battle of Harpers Ferry, 93; destruction described, 82; destruction illustrated, 77, 82; first time destroyed, 81-2; illustrated, 1, 58, 98, 135-6; 143-4, 152; Latrobe and, 58; rebuilt during Civil War, 87, 95.
Baltimore Sunday American. And Brown centennial, 178.
Banks, Nathaniel. Commands at Harpers Ferry, 85.
Barbour, Alfred. Announces and explains Virginia secession, 78; illustrated, 78.
Barlow, Bill. Creates restoration policy controversy over John Brown's Fort, 185-6.
Barry, Joseph. Confederate invasion (last), 101; destruction described, 77, 133; Mobberly scene, 103; Rohr killing described, 88; Storer charter, dissatisfaction reported, 121.
Bashinsky, Elizabeth Burford. Hayward Shepherd Monument and, 129.
Battle of Harpers Ferry. B & O bridge destroyed, 94; Battle map of, 92; Confederate appearance described, 94; Confederates capture slaves seeking freedom, 94; Descriptions of, 92; Jackson's looks described, 94; Miles' orders to de-fend, 91; Jackson captures, 91; supplies captured, 91; Union garrison appearance described, 94; Union surrender, 91; U.S. forces return following Antie-tam, 95.
Beckham, Fontaine. Killed near John Brown's Fort, 43, 46; slave purchase arrangement with Isaac Gilbert, 31, 46; will frees Gilbert's family, 46.
Betts, Karl S. Avoiding antagonizing the South, 173-4; and NPS, 174; expresses misgivings over Brown observance, 174, 176; opposition to Brown centennial, 173.
"Black and Tan Conference." At Storer College, 122; WV constitutional convention and, 122.
Black Codes. And segregation, 127-8.
Boarding Houses. At Storer College, 156; description of, 157.
Bolivar Heights. Battle of Harpers Ferry, 91-2; battlefield preservation, 196; Confederate battery on, illustrated, 81; fortified, 95; living history illustrated on, 189; NPS acquisition of, 167, 196; proposed inclusion in national monument, 164; Stonewall Brigade encamped, 81; view, illustrated, 159.
Bollman, Wendell. Iron bridge construction, 143.
Bollman bridge. 1924 flood and, 153; constructed, 143; destroyed by flood, 160; illustrated, 135-6; 143-4; wedding attraction, 155.
Border ruffians. Illustrated, 35.
Boteler, Alexander. Newby's death described, 43.
Bowen, Eli. B & O Railroad described, 58; C & O Canal described, 58; Harpers Ferry grandeur described, vii; railroad innovation, 60.

Brackett, Nathan Cook. African American education discussed, 114; armory buildings, solicitation of, 120; background of, 113; "Black and Tan" conference and, 122; Fessenden and, 120; Freedmen's schools superintendent, 113; LOCKWOOD HOUSE—at, 114, war damage described, 114; illustrated, 114; with students, 122; recommends establishing school to train teachers, 119; refugees described, 113; Storer establishment and, 120; teachers' institute and, 121; threats to students described,117; threatened, 117; and voting rights, 122.
Brackett House. As boarding house, 157. **Brown, Annie.** Discussion with brother Owen, 43: illustrated, 42; recollects Kennedy Farm, 42.
Brown, Edmund. Harpers Ferry invasion, 87.
Brown, John. Abolition and, 3, 33-4; Annie as sentinel for, 42; armory capture, illustrated, 6; B & O passenger train alters plan, 9-11; Bible of, illustrated, 33; *Declaration of Liberty*, 37; divided nation and, 173; Dred Scott decision and, 36; captured, 65-6; casualties, 43, 46, 62, 65-6; cause, 34; charges filed against, 71, 73; Conductor Phelps, negotiates with, 12; constitutional convention at Chatham, Canada, 37; converses with Daingerfield, 63-4; crimes committed, 71, 73; declares mission to Whelan, 7; Douglass informed of Harpers Ferry plan, 38; Douglass refuses to join, 41; enslaved Gilbert family freed, 28, 45; executed, illustrated, 75; final speech before court, 73; final words, 76; first orders to attack Harpers Ferry, 43; frustration with government, 34; fugitive from justice, 36; God and, 33, 36, 39; guerrilla warfare and, 3, 35; gunpowder used to blow up armory and arsenal, 79; Harpers Ferry as target, 39; Hayward Shepherd first to die during attack, 9-10; hostages as bargaining chip, 46; imprisoned in Charles Town, 68; interrogation, 66-7; jail illustrated, 68; Kansas fighting, 35; Kennedy Farm, 42, 44, illustrated at, 42; League of Gileadites organized, 34; Liberty Guards in Kansas organized, 35; local postwar attitude and, 115-6; meets Fr. Costello in jail, 72; meets Douglass in Chambersburg quarry, 38, 41, illustrated, 38; meets Lewis Washington, 9; meets Shields Green in Chambersburg, 41; men buried by Shenandoah River, 199, illustrated 200; miscalculates railroad importance, 47; Northern response, 69, 71, 75-6; objects to defense counsel, 71; *On Slavery*, 34, 37-8, 67; photo of, 3; plan of operation, 38, 40; pledges to die to end slavery, 34; Pottawatamie, 35; selected as commander in chief at Chatham, 38; sentenced, 71; son Oliver, addresses, 63; Southern response to Brown, 69, 71, 76; Stuart, negotiates with, 64; support in the North, 36; Supreme Court and, 36-7; trapped inside armory fire engine house, 46, 62; trial in Charles Town, 71, 73; underground railroad concept improved 38; war preparations, 42; warning to the people of the South, 67; wife, illustrated with in jail, 71; Washington's artifacts received, 9; Whelan's capture by, illustrated, 6; wounded by Green, 65-6; writes wife that he's content with fate, 72, 75.
Brown, John Jr. And underground railroad, 40-1.
Brown, Mary. Husband expresses contentment with fate, 73; with Brown in jail, illustrated, 72, 75.
Brown, Oliver. Illustrated, 63; mortally wounded, 63; suffering inside John Brown Fort, 63.
Brown, Owen. At Kennedy Farm, 43.
Brown, S. Howell. Plats armory property, 145.
Brown, Watson. At Kennedy Farm, 43.
Browne, Dunn. Wartime description, 95.
Buchanan, James. Orders marines to suppress Brown rebellion, 62.
Burke, John. Defends telegraph office at outbreak of Civil War, 78.
Burton, Eugenia. Learns of Brown attack, 7, 12.
Burton, James Henry. Burton bullet development, 24, illustrated, 24.
Burton bullet. Perfected 24; image of, 24
Busch, Lucille. And Hayward Shepherd Monument, 130.
Butler, John. African American restrictions in court proceedings and, 28-9; veteran of War of 1812, 28.
Byrd, Robert C. Appropriations for park improvements, 187; Harpers Ferry preservation, 194-7; illustrated, 197-8; legislation to double park acreage, 190, 196; opening of parking and shuttle system, 190.
Byrne, Terrence. Captured by Cook, 4-5; converses with Currie, 5; hostage in John Brown's Fort, 46; Leeman escorts, 5; slaveowner, 4.
C & O Canal. 1924 flood closes, 153; cholera and, 28; commerce and, 142; court battles with B & O, 56-7; Erie Canal rival and, 54; established, 54; groundbreaking by J.Q. Adams, 55; Maryland intervention in, 57; illustrated, 56, 58; Mercer's vision for, 54; projected construction expenses, 54; property exchange for John Brown's Fort site 182-3; railroad antiquates, 61; successor to Patowmack Company, 54, 57; travel ad, 56.

Calhoun, John C. And Hall and interchangeability, 20; abolition and, 34; disunion and, 34; slavery and, 34.
Campbell, Donald W. parking facility, 190; illustrated, 198; and preservation, 195-6.
Camp Hill. Civil War encampment at, 89-90, 105-6, illustrated, 89-90, 105-6; Gunpowder brought from to destroy armory and arsenal, 79; School established for Freedmen's education on, 114.
Carroll, Charles of Carrollton. B & O cornerstone and, 55; background of, 55; portrait of, 55.
Catholic Church, St. Peter's. illustrated, viii.
Chambersburg, PA. Brown and Douglass discuss Harpers Ferry plan at quarry, 38, 41; Brown meets Green, 41; underground railroad and, 41; Brown weapons arrive at, 42.
Charles Town (Charlestown). Brown imprisoned at, 68; jail illustrated, 68; Brown execution

at, illustrated, 75; missionaries threatened at, 116; Race relations at, 116; war experience of, 116; warlike appearance of during Brown trial, 68.
Charleston Mercury. No compromise after Brown, 76.
Chatham, Canada. Brown holds constitutional convention at, 37-8; Brown selected as commander in chief, 38; Provisional Constitution adopted, 37.
Chicago Tribune. Townsend article, 145.
Child, Emily. Describes 1870 flood, 149.
Child, Jonathan. Harpers Ferry Mill Company, 141.
Chisholm, Shirley. Illustrated, 191.
Cholera, 28.
Civil Rights Movement. And John Brown centennial, 177-8.
Civil War Centennial Commission. B & O and Brown Centennial controversy and, 176 Derided in national press, 178-179; Established, 174; Harpers Ferry Area Foundation and, 177; opposed to Brown celebration, 174; segregationist policies, 174.
Civil War border town. Civilian casualties, 83; descriptions of, 84, 95-6; fortifications constructed at, 95; illustrated, 88; Lincoln's visit, 95; occupation following Antietam, 95; strategic importance of, 81.
Civil War Trust. Harpers Ferry preservation and, 196.
Clark, James H. Describes Battle of Harpers Ferry, 92.
"Clock strike." And Harpers Ferry armory, 22-3.
Commercial enterprises. Diversity of products, 27, 142, illustrated, 142; number of businesses, 27; Wager family and, 27.
Constitution, Provisional. Brown's preamble to, 37.
Contraband. *see refugee camp.*
Conway, Martin R. illustrated, 192.
Cook, John. Alarmed, 12, 44-5; background, 7; Brown's disciple, 3, 7; Brown's spy, 7; captures Allstadts, 8; captures Byrne, 4-5; captures school house, 2-3, 11-2; captures Washington, 8; discus-sion with Currie, 2-3, 13; illustrated, 4; marriage, 7; ; spyglass of, illustrated, 4; visits Lewis Wash-ington, 7-8; Washington artifacts presented to Brown by, 9;
Coppoc, Edwin. captured, 66; illustrated, 74; letter to uncle prior to execution, 74.
Costello, Father M. A. Administers last rites to Quinn, 72; meets with Brown in jail, 72.
Craig, Henry K. Reduction in armory workforce, 20.
Cross, Albert. Brown's emissary, 10.
Currie, Lind. Captured at school house, 3; discussion with Byrne, 5; discussion with Cook, 3, 13; learns of John Brown's plan, 3; schoolmaster, 2-3, 11.

Curtis, Silas. Warning to missionary teachers, 115.
Dada, Harriet. Condition of patients described, 96; hospital work described, 96; illustrated, 96; nurse at Island Hospital, 96.
Daingerfield, John E. P. Converses with Brown, 63-4; situation within John Brown Fort described, 63.
Dale, Edwin M. Obstructs land exchange for John Brown Fort site, 183; opposes John Brown centennial, 174; Snell and, 175; transferred, 175.
Davis, Jefferson. Threatens disunion after Brown, 76.
Declaration of Liberty, 37.
Delany, Martin. Learns Brown's scheme, 37-8.
Democratic Party. race relations, 111; voting rights, 121-2;West Virginia constitution, 121-122.
Dittmeyer, Walter. Illustrated,155;cards, 155-6.
Donovan, Jeremiah. Defends armory entrance at Civil War outbreak, 78.
Douglass, Frederick. Brown and commencement of Civil War, 125; Brown and end of slavery, 125, 173; Brown's plan of operation and, 38, 40; Brown professorship and, 125; criticized, 125; excerpts from Storer speech on John Brown, 124; meets Brown at Chambersburg quarry, 38, 41; illustrated, 38; Memorial Day lecture at Storer, 125; praises John Brown, 125-6; rejects participation with Brown, 41; Storer trustee, 124; understanding of Brown's original plan, 39; value of slave property and, 39.
Du Bois, W. E. B. *Address to the Country*, 128; illustrated in Niagara photo, 127; objects to Hayward Shepherd Monument, 130; opposes segregation, 127-8; organizes Niagara Movement meeting at Storer, 127; pilgrimage to John Brown Fort, 127; rebuttal to Shepherd Monument, 130.
Dudley, Anne. Lockwood House described, 114; threatened, 116; vows to defend her school, 116.
Drumgoold, Kate. Describes Storer College, 124.
Emerson, Ralph Waldo. Praises Brown, 76, 172.
Episcopal Church. Ruins illustrated, 168.
Erie Canal. C & O Canal and, 54; cost of, 54; described, 54.
Evans, Oliver. And steam power innovation, 57.
Fairfax, Thomas Lord. George Washington and, 48; "Northern Neck" and, 48.
"Faithful Slave Memorial." *See Hayward Shepherd Monument.*
Faulkner, Scot. Harpers Ferry preservation, 194, 196.
Faux, W. Anti-war sentiment of, 23; armory described, 23.
Featherstonhaugh, Thomas. Discovery of burial site of Brown's men, 199-200, illustrated, 200; reburial of Brown's men and, 199.
Fessenden, William Pitt. And Congress' donation to Storer College, 120.

INDEX

Field, Kate. John Brown's Fort and, 131; Murphy farm and, 131-2; illustrated, 132.

Fifteenth Amendment. 117.

Floods. 1847, armory and arsenal damage, 139; **1852,** 139-40; **1870,** cause of, 147, 150; charitable response to, 147-8; death toll, 148; destruction described, 147-9; Emily Child describes, 149; illustrated, 147; rescue attempts, 147-9; **1889,** illustrated, 148, 151-2; **1924,** damage from, 153; illustrated, 150, 152-3; **1936,** described, 161; destruction, 160; highest flood in Harpers Ferry history, 160; illustrated, 160-3; **1942,** illustrated, 133; **1972,** 186-7, illustrated 186; **1985,** illustrated, 187; **Causes** of, 150.

Foreman, James. Burial site of Brown's men and, 199.

Foster, Sarah Jane. Commitment, 116; progress of students, 118-119; threatened, 115-116.

Fourteenth Amendment. Adopted, 110.

Franzen, Archie. NPS restoration policy and, 184; Orchestrates NPS move of John Brown Fort, 184.

Free Blacks Education and, 113; Fontaine Beckham and, 31; Harpers Ferry population and, 30-1; Isaac Gilbert, 31; John Butler and court limitations, 31; mandatory identification, 30; slave ownership by, 31; travel restrictions, 30; white sponsorships, 30.

Freewill Baptists. Criticized for establishment of Storer College, 120; missionaries condemned, 115-6; missionaries threatened and endangered, 115-6; presence established in Shenandoah Valley, 113-4; reasons to establish teachers' college, 119.

Freewill Baptist Schools. Attendance at, 118; established, 113-4; missionaries threatened at, 115-6; teachers at, 118.

Freedmen. Desolate condition, 113-4; education, 113-4, 118; voting rights 117-8; living in Shenandoah Valley, 114; need for teachers' school, 119.

Freedmen's Bureau. Brackett, 114; education and, 114; destitute condition of refugees described, 114; district office at Harpers Ferry, 111; protects Freedmen's schools, 115.

French and Indian War. Washington at Harpers Ferry during, 13, 48.

"French Bill." Executed, 100.

Friends of Harpers Ferry NHP. Harpers Ferry preservation, 196.

Fugitive Slave Law. Brown reacts to, 34.

Garrett, John W. Notifies president of attack on Harpers Ferry, 12.

Garrison, William Lloyd. Defends Brown, 76.

Georgetown Courier. Describes Harpers Ferry grandeur, 156.

Gettysburg Campaign. Harpers Ferry during, 97.

Gilbert, Isaac. Enslaved family freed by Beckham's will, 46; purchases freedom of family, 28, 46.

Goddard, Abba. Harpers Ferry hospital during Battle of Harpers Ferry, 93; hospital matron, 93; resists Confederate seizure of enslaved, 94.

Gondola. On Shenandoah, 52.

Grand Military Ball. 99.

Grant, Ulysses S. Orders Sheridan into Shenandoah Valley, 107; orders destruction of Valley, 107.

Grant, Ulysses S. III. Civil War Centennial Commission and, 174; John Brown centennial and, 174.

Green, G. W. Mountain View Hotel, 155; supplies Island Park, 157.

Green, Israel. Describes Brown's capture, 64-5.

Green, Shields. Captured, 66; captures Washington, 8; "Emperor," 8; Meets Brown in Chambersburg, 41.

Hagerstown, MD. Runaway slaves and, 40.

Hagerstown Herald of Freedom, on abolitionists, 39; racism, 39; runaway slaves and, 39.

Hagerstown Herald and Torch Light. Surprised by Brown's presence, 42.

Hall, John H. American system of manufacturing, 20; boys operating machinery, 20; establishes rifle works, 20; interchangeability and, 20; re-sistance to his innovations, 20.

Harper, Robert. Arrives and settles, 48; heirs as slave owners, 26; heirs negotiate with B & O, 58; Heirs sell land for armory, 16.

Harper House. Illustrated, 169; restoration of, 169.

Harpers Ferry Area Foundation. Stages John Brown Centennial, 177-8.

Harpers Ferry Armory and Arsenal. Advantages of, 15; anti-war criticism of, 25; archeology at, 169; armorers' pay, 17, 21; B & O and, 57-8; B & O Railroad realignment and, 154; Brown's target, 3, 7, 39; Burton bullet and, 24; citizens appeal to after flooding, 139-40; civilian superintendents, 18-9; "clock strike," 22-3; commercial businesses and, 25; corruption, 18; craftsmen's work demeaned, 18; described, 16; donation of buildings to Storer College, 120; economic downturns, 20; fire engine house (John Brown's Fort), 22; floods and, 139-40; guard increased following Brown attack, 67-8; ill-disciplined workforce 16-8; illustrated, 16, 20, 98, 105,108, 112, 135-6, 138-40, 146; inadequacies, 16; inferior workmen at, 18; infrastructure, 16, 21- 2; labor demand, 20; labor discord, 17-23; labor shortage, 16; labor strike, 17; land acquisition, 16-7; Meriwether Lewis and, 26; military superintendents, 18; number of employees, 16, 18, 20; Ordnance Department recommends closure and sale, 138, 140; payroll expansion during war, 20; "Pennsylvania Rifle" influence, 16-7; post-war uncertainty, 138, 140; problems in establishment of, 16; purchased by Francis Adams, 143-4; reduction in workforce, 20; regulations, 17-8; rehabilitation, 23-4; Sheridan's supply depot, 107, illustrated, 107; skilled artisans, 16; slaves and, 21, 27; sold to Savery, 153-4; Springfield Armory compared, 18; Stubblefield, James, Superintendent of, 19; superintendent assassinated, 17-8; target at outbreak of Civil War, 78-80; town population and, 27; Washington recommends establishment of, 15; Washington's commercial interest

214

and, 15; water crises and, 139; weapons damage by floods, 139-40; weapons production and, 25.

Harpers Ferry Conservancy. And Harpers Ferry preservation, 196.

Harpers Ferry Mill Company. Enterprise described, 141; illustrated, 141; metal stamp of, 141; products of, 141.

Harpers Ferry National Historical Park. 1972 flood and, 186-7, illustrated, 186; 1985 flood and, illustrated, 187; Bill Barlow and, 185-6; battlefield expansion and Byrd, 195-6; Black Heritage Days, 190-2; demolition and, 184-5; flood improvements, 187; Howard University African American study and, 192; improvements to, 186-7; interpretation of African American history, 190-2; living history and, 188-9, illustrated 188-9; modeled after Colonial Williamsburg, 188-90; Murphy Farm, threatened, 195-6; name change, 197; new preservation policy, 185-6; plan to address inadequate parking and congestion, 189; power of place, 197-8; preservation and Byrd, 195-6; preservation and Campbell, 195-6; preservation battles, 194-6; preservation partners, 195-6; preservation, threats to, 194-6, illustrated, 195; restoration policy, 184-6; School House Ridge battlefield, 195-6; Storer College elevated as major theme, 192-3; traffic congestion within, 189; Williamsburg model and, 184-6; zoning decisions and, 195.

Harpers Ferry National Monument. archaeology, illustrated, 169; B&O Railroad obstruction and, 182-3; condition of town before national monument established, 167; early monument research and, 169; Mary Vernon Mish and expansion into Maryland, 166; condition of national monument described, 168; favorable publicity on behalf of, 170; illustrated, 168; John Brown era appearance, 176; land acquisition for, 165-6.

Harpers Ferry Town Ordinances. Health, 28; slavery, 27.

Harpers Ferry Park Association, 193.

Harpers Ferry water gap. 1889 flood illustrated, 152; earliest inhabitants, 48; Photo illustrat-ed, 137; "The Hole," 48; transportation portal, 48.

Harpers Ferry Waterpower and Manufacturing Company. Francis Adams and, 144, 153; purchase of armory and, 144; extorts B & O, 153.

Harper's Weekly. Dred Scott, 36; on racism, 109.

Harper's New Monthly Magazine. Anti-war opinion of, 25; armory described, 25.

Harrisburg, PA. Race relations in, 110.

"Harvard Regiment" (2d Mass Infantry). First Union regiment to occupy Harpers Ferry, 85.

Hayward Shepherd Monument. Controversial dedication and, 129; NAACP objection to, 130; NPS response to, 130.

Health. Air pollution, 27; cholera, 28; disease, 27-8; drinking water, 28; sanitation, 28; sewage and, 28.

"Heritage Days: The Black Perspective." Program and activities, 190-2.

Herr, Abraham. Virginius Island and, 25; mill destruction illustrated, 86; property destroyed during Civil War, 86.

Higgins, Patrick. During Brown attack, 10.

Higgs, Augustus. On education, 114.

Hill, A. P. Flanks Union position, 91.

Hill Top House Hotel. Established by Lovett family, 155; illustrated, 158.

Hoke, Joseph T. And Storer charter, 121.

"The Hole": *See Harpers Ferry water gap.*

Hotel Connor. Illustrated, 156.

How, W. Stover. On black oppression, 118.

Howard University. NPS-commissioned study on African Americans in national parks and, 191-3; findings related to Harpers Ferry, 192; NPS response to, 192-3.

Hunter, Andrew. Ad for slave sale and, 29; beside Frederick Douglass, 125.

Hunter, Harry. Describes execution of William Thompson, 44.

Ickes, Harold. Comment on John Brown's raid, 174-5.

Island Hospital. Described, 96.

Island Park. B & O annual company party, 157; established by B & O, 155-6; hosts large gatherings, 156-7; infrastructure upon, 156-7; activities at, 156-7, illustrated, 158.

Jackson, Thomas Jonathan "Stonewall." Assigned command at Harpers Ferry, 81; attack foiled at Harpers Ferry, 87; defeats and captures U.S. garrison, 91-2, battle map of, 92; illustrated, 91; looks described, 94; "Stonewall Brigade" organized, 81; plans to defend Harpers Ferry, 81; removes armory machinery, 81; replaced by Joseph Johnston, 81; service under, 115.

Jefferson County. Bastion of Confederacy, 114-115; permitted land uses, 195; preservation of Harpers Ferry park, 195-6; voting rights challenged, 117-8.

Jefferson, Thomas. Armory production commences, 14; Harpers Ferry described, x-xi; Meriwether Lewis and Harpers Ferry Armory and, 26.

Jefferson Rock. Civil War photo from, 86; illustrated, x, 170.

Jim Crow. Segregation and, 127, 174.

John Brown Centennial. Acquisition of John Brown's Fort and, 176; B & O and NPS controversy and, 176; Civil Rights Movement and, 173-4, march illustrated, 174; Civil War Centennial Commission and, 174; Brown as enigma, 172; NPS concern it is "celebrating" John Brown, 174; emotional response to Brown, 172, 175; illustrated, 173; Harpers Ferry Area Foundation and, 177-8; illustrated, 177-8; media and, 178-9; Newcomer and, 177-8; NPS abdicates leadership role, 176; Newsweek article and, 171, 179; precursor to, 170; publicity on behalf of, 178; racism and, 173-4, 176, 178; Snell and, 175-6; visitors attracted to, 178.

John Brown's Fort. B & O buries original site, 131, 154; B & O obstructs move to original site, 182-3; brick from, illustrated, 184; Brown illustrated within, 64; Brown's defenses, 63; Brown's sons dying, 63; Brown surrounded at, 46; Brown

INDEX

trapped within, 46, 62-5; C & O superintendent obstructs move to original site, 183; Civil War descriptions of, 85; constructed, 24; Illustrated, 108, 115-6, 131, 132, 138, 146, 151, 176, 179-80, 182; hostages in, 46, 63-4, 66; interior, illustrated, 62, 64; in wrong location, 182; jail during Civil War, 100; Kate Field and, 131; marine attack described, 64-6; marine attack illustrated, 65; moved to Chicago for World's Fair, 131, 154; moved to Lower Town, 183-4, illustrated, 183; moved to Storer campus, 132; Murphy family and, 131-2; Niagara Conference and, 127; NPS acquisition, 132, 176, 182; proposed NAACP plaque, 130; rebuilt on Murphy Farm, 131-2; reconstructed as mirror image, 132, 185; speculators and, 131, 154; surrounded by militia, 46.

John Brown Fort monument. 129; B & O and, 129; illustrated, 154.

John Brown Museum. At National Monument, 169, illustrated 173.

John Brown's pikes. at Kennedy farm, 42.

John Brown Sesquicentennial, illustrated, 179-80.

Johnston, Joseph E. Abandons Harpers Ferry, 81.

Johnstown Flood. *See Floods, 1889.*

Jones, Roger. Assigned to Harpers Ferry, 78; preparations to destroy armory and arsenal, 78-9; orders destruction of armory and arsenal, 79.

Kansas. Brown joins civil war within, 35; fighting in, 35; popular sovereignty and, 35;

Kaylor, Joseph. And opposition to "John Brown park" 166.

Kelly, Margaret. Escapes death during bombardment, 102.

Kemper, James L. Response to Brown's attack, 69.

Kennedy Farm. Annie and Owen Brown discuss future at, 43; Brown issues orders to attack Harpers Ferry, 44; Brown's army masses at, 42; Sharps Rifles at, 4, 12, 42; war preparations at, 42; Watson Brown writes wife from, 43.

Kennedy, Virginia. Wife of Cook, 7.

Kern, John. Business at Harpers Ferry, 142.

Ku Klux Klan. Niagara centennial attendance, 194; recruitment ad for, 117.

Latrobe, Benjamin Jr. Background, 58; designs B & O bridge, 58; illustrated, 58.

Lear, Tobias. Negotiation for armory land acquisition and, 17.

Lee, Robert E. Arrives to quash Brown's war, 46; attends Brown's interrogation, 66; capture of Harpers Ferry and, 91; Gettysburg invasion and, 95, 97; last Confederate invasion and, 101; ordered to Harpers Ferry, 63; service under, 115; surrenders, 108.

Leeman, Willie. Background, 5; escorts Byrne to Ferry, 5; on slavery, 5.

Leisenring, George. Business at Harpers Ferry, 142.

Lewis, Meriwether. Collapsible boat and, 26 Harpers Ferry Armory and, 26; illustrated, 26.

Liberty Guards. Brown organizes in Kansas, 35.

Lincoln, Abraham. Gettysburg Address and, 181; visit to Harpers Ferry following Antietam, 95.

Lincoln, William. Describes abandonment of Maryland Heights, 97.

Living history. period clothing 188; Bicentennial celebration interrupted by traffic 189; demonstrations 188-9; model for NPS 189; modeled after Colonial Williamsburg 188;

Lockwood House. Brackett utilizes as school and quarters, 114; boarding house, 157; condition described, 114; Grand Military Ball at, 99; illustrated, 93, 157; school within, 114.

Loge, William. *See "French Bill."*

Logie, James. Sale of Isaac Gilbert family, 31.

Loudoun Heights. Acquired by NPS, 167; Occupied by U.S. Army following Battle of Harpers Ferry, 9; proposed inclusion in national monument, 164

Lovett family. 155; illustrated, 118.

Lowell, MA. Harpers Ferry compared to, 141; Virginius Island compared to,

Mackey, John. Armory paymaster, 17; on labor strife, 17.

Marmion, Annie. Bombardment described, 102; life during Civil War described, 84; illustrated, 84.

Marmion, Nicholas. 84.

Martinsburg Journal. Endorses national monument concept,165.

Maryland. B & O and, 57; Brown plan and, 39-40; C & O Canal and,57; Free Black population, 40; intervention in canal/railroad land dispute, 57; land acquisition for national monument 166-7; prohibits slave transport on railroad, 60; rewards for runaway slaves returned and, 40; slave devaluation, 39; slave escapes and, 39; slave owners' convention, 40; underground railroad and, 40.

Maryland Heights. Abandonment of, 97; Battle of Harpers Ferry and, 91-2; bombardment from, 101-2; Gettysburg invasion and, 97; defense of, 97, 101; first Union occupation of, 85; fortified, 95; Harpers Ferry, illustration looking from, 1, 142, 155-6; Mish and, 166; proposed inclusion in national monument, 164;.Stone Fort on, illustrated, 164.

Mason, James. Questions Brown after capture, 67.

Mather Training Center. 186; illustrated, 186.

Mauzy, George. Boast of vigilantes following Brown's capture, 68; Brown's men described, 67; Comments on outbreak of Civil War, 77-8; 80; letter to daughter on Brown attack, 7, 33; slave deaths during Brown's attack described, 70.

Mauzy, Joseph. Letter to sister on Brown attack, 13.

Mauzy, Mary. Warlike atmosphere following Brown described, 68; letter to daughter on Brown attack, 11, 33, 44.

Mayer, Brantz. Anti-war expression of, 25; armory described, 25.

McClellan, George B. Orders construction of defenses at Harpers Ferry, 95; witnesses advance into

216

CONFLUENCE

Harpers Ferry, 87.
McCreight, John. Harpers Ferry Mill Company, 141.
McDonald, Henry. Comment on monument's establishment, 165, 167; death of, 167; determination against obstacles, 165; fundraising for national monument, 164-5; Hayward Shepherd Monument and, 129; illustrated, 163; John Brown's Fort and, 131-2; monument library and, 167; national monument creation and, 163-5, 167; public support, 164-5, 167; recruits Mish, 166; rejects NAACP rebuttal of Shepherd Monument, 130; tourism and, 164; Washington Monument (MD), 166.
McGraw, James. Businesses at Harpers Ferry, 142.
Mercer, Charles Fenton. Erie Canal as competitor and, 54; establishment of C & O Canal and, 54-5; his vision for C & O Canal, 54-5.
Miles, Dixon Stansbury. Defends Harpers Ferry against Stonewall Jackson, 91-2; surrenders Harpers Ferry, 92.
Militia. Arrival during Brown war, 45-6; at Brown execution, illustrated, 75; seize Ferry at outbreak of Civil War, 79–80; surround Brown, 45.
Mish, Mary Vernon. Deeds for Maryland Heights and, 166; illustrated, 166; Maryland appropriation for land acquisition and, 167; inspired by McDonald, 166.
Missionaries. *See Freewill Baptists.*
Mobberly, John. Background of, 103; corpse displayed and scene described, 103; illustrated, 103; terrorizes Harpers Ferry vicinity during Civil War, 103; trapped and killed, 103.
Morrell House. As boarding house, 157.
Mosby, John Singleton. As guerrilla warrior, 104; illustrated, 104; service under, 115.
Moulton, Charles. Grand Military Ball and, 99; local women, 100; describes Mobberly scene, 103; describes wartime desolation, 100; military execution and, 100; performs Provost duties, 100; writer, 100.
Mount Vernon Compact. 49.
Murphy, Alexander. John Brown's Fort and, 131-2.
Murphy, Mary. John Brown's Fort and, 131-2.
Murphy Farm. John Brown's Fort and, 131-2, illustrated, 132; preservation of, 195-6; view from, illustrated, 196.
NAACP. President of attends Heritage Days, 191; objection to Hayward Shepherd Monument, 130; rebuttal to Shepherd Monument, 130; supports Harpers Ferry commemorations, 193.
Nash, Bradley. Donates farm to park, 197; illustrated, 197.
National Geographic Magazine. Description of national monument, 168; publicity for monument, 170.
National Parks Conservation Association. Harpers Ferry preservation and, 196.
National Park Service Abdicates responsibility for Brown centennial, 176-7; accepts deed for monument, 168; acquisition of John Brown fort, 182-3; Anderson and Brown Centennial, 175-6; B & O and Brown Centennial controversy, 176; Black Heritage Days and, 191-2; Civil War Centennial Commission and, 174, 176; Dale and Brown Centennial, 174-5; Harpers Ferry Area Foundation and, 177-8; Howard University African American study and, 191-3; meeting to establish national park, 160; preservation battles, 194-6; razing structures, 169, 176; restoration and, 169; Snell and Brown Centennial, 175; survey of proposed national monument, 164; tourism and, 170; Willett and, 168; Worth and, 167.
National Trust for Historic Preservation. Harpers Ferry preservation and, 196.
Nature Conservancy. Short Hill preservation, 196.
New York Herald. Reporter questions Brown following his capture, 67.
New York Journal of Commerce. Editorializes against Brown's execution, 72.
New York Militia (22d). Encampment on Camp Hill, illustrated, 89-90.
New York Times. Comments on John Brown Centennial, 178; favorable publicity for monument, 170.
Newby, Dangerfield. Background of, 43; burial, 199; first of Brown's raiders to die, 43, 45; illustrated, 43; receives letter from wife, 43; wound described, 43, 45.
Newby, Harriet. Letter to Dangerfield quoted, 43.
Newcomer, June. Organizes Brown Centennial, 177-8.
Newsweek. Feature article on John Brown Centennial, 171, 179; illustrated, 171.
Niagara Centennial. 194; and the KKK, 194.
Niagara Conference. 127; illustrated, 127.
North Elba, NY. Reburial of Brown's men and, 199.
Notes on the State of Virginia. Harpers Ferry described, x-xi.
Oakes, Joy. Harpers Ferry preservation and, 196.
Ordnance Department. Sale and disposal of armory, 138, 140, 145.
Parade Magazine. Favorable publicity for monument, 170.
Parker, Richard. Presides over Brown's trial, 71; sentences Brown, 71.
Parker, Theodore. Response to Brown, 70.
Piscitelli, Debbie. And Byrd, illustrated, 197.
Patowmack Company. Armory and, 14, 51; boats on, 52; C & O, its successor, 54; George Washington President of, 14, 51; goods and supplies transported by, 51; Harpers Ferry navigation improvements and, 14, 51; limited navigation of, 53; Plans for, 14; Potomac navigation and, 14, 51; problems encountered, 51, 53; Shenandoah navigation improvements, 52.
Patterson, Robert. Occupies Harpers Ferry, 85; orders return of fugitive slaves, 85.
Patteson, Okey L. Appropriation for national monument, 167; Donates deed for national monument, 168.
Pennsylvania. Underground railroad and, 40-1.
Perry, Gilbert. National monument and, 168.

217

INDEX

Phelps, Conductor. Dispatch warning about Brown attack, 12; halts train during John Brown attack, 10; negotiates with Brown, 12; witness in Brown's trial, 71.
Petersburg Express. Editorializes on Brown, 70.
Phillips, Wendell. Defends Brown, 72, 172.
Point, The. Buildings at destroyed, 88; illustrated, 88.
Point of Rocks, MD. As transportation bottleneck, 57.
Potomac Company. *See Patowmack Company.*
Potomac River. Alternative routes west and, 49; Mount Vernon Compact and, 49; navigation of, 48-9; falls, 48; floods illustrated, 150, 160-2; Washington describes falls at Harpers Ferry, 50; Washington first navigates, 48-9; Washington's vision for, 14-5, 48-9.
Potomac Street. Hayward Shepherd Monument and, 129-30.
Pottawatomie Creek. Massacre at, 35.
Presbyterian Church, illustrated, 45; Rev. Charles White preaches at, 45.
Preservation. Earth removal and trenching on School House Ridge and, 194-5; illustrated, 196-7; interference in NPS law enforcement action at School House Ridge and, 195; NPS dependence on local jurisdiction for, 195; permitted land uses and, 195; School House Ridge battle with developers, 194-6; zoning decisions, 195.
Preston, John T. L. Expression at Brown's execution, 75.
Price, Jackson E. NPS on John Brown Centennial and, 174.
Pulp factory. Along Potomac, illustrated, 153.
Quinn, Pvt. Luke. Last rites administered, 72; mortally wounded during Brown assault, 65.
Racism. 36, 39, 109, 111, 113, 114, 115, 116, 117, 118, 120, 121, 122, 127, 173, 174, 176, 178, 191-2.
Railroad Brigade. Harpers Ferry headquarters, 87.
Randolph, Jennings. 1936 flood aftermath described, 163; 1936 flood inspires national monument creation, 163-4; determination against obstacles, 165; Harpers Ferry's uniqueness described, 159; "Heritage Days: The Black Perspective" and, 191; illustrated, 167, 197; legislates name change to National Historical Park, 197; legislation authorizing exchange of property for John Brown's Fort site, 182-183; legislation to acquire John Brown's Fort, 182; legislative coordination, 164-5; NPS survey of proposed national monument and, 164; public support and, 164-5; supports park expansion, 190; vision for national monument, 163-4.
Quint, Alonzo. Describes John Brown's Fort, 8.
Reconstruction. Freedmen's Bureau, 111; military occupation, 111; post-war amendments, 111.
Redman Jazz Concert. 193; illustrated, 193.
Refugee camp. In armory ground, illustrated, 112; as viewed from Magazine Hill, illustrated, 135-6.

Republicans. "Black and Tan" conference and, 122; party created, 33; race relations and, 111; WV constitution and, 121-2.
Richmond Enquirer. Predicts disunion after Brown's final words, 76.
Rifle factory. Brown's men assailed at, 45; illustrated, 108; Rifleworks 20; Shenandoah Canal and, 52.
Roeder, Frederick. First civilian death, 83; his wound described, 83; mortally wounded on Independence Day, 83; predicts demise, 83.
Roeder, Mary Louisa. Father mortally wounded during Civil War, 83; head of household, 83; her home illustrated, 83.
Rohr, George. Ambushed by Confederate snipers, 88; calamity resulting from death, 88.
Roosevelt, Franklin. Signs legislation establishing national monument. 165.
Roper, Guinevere. Illustrated, 193.
Rosa, Paul. Harpers Ferry preservation and, 196.
Ruppert, Pvt. Matthew. Wounded during Brown assault, 65.
Saw Mill Falls. Navigation improvements at, 52.
Savannah Daily Morning News. Editorializes on Brown, 71.
Savery, Thomas. Acquires armory and waterpower rights, 153-4; B & O and, 154; electricity and, 154; establishes manufactories, 153-4.
School House Ridge. Battlefield preservation, 194-6; county commissioners and, 195-6; endangered by zoning decisions, 195; Illustrated, 195-6, ruins on, 197-8; acquisition of, 196.
Segregation. Black Codes and, 127; Du Bois' resistance to, 127-8; Jim Crow, 127; Niagara Movement and, 127; Supreme Court and, 127, 174; WV law, 121.
Sharps Rifles. At Kennedy Farm, 12, 42; stashed at school house, 3, 4, 12.
Sharpsburg Rifles. Re-enactors, illustrated, 178.
Shelton, Elsie. 1936 flood described, 161.
Shenandoah Canal, 52.
Shenandoah City. 1870 flood and, 148.
Shenandoah House. Illustrated, 135-6; New Year's Eve ball at 145; renovations at, 142; replaced by Mountain View Hotel, 155; Trowbridge describes, 134, 137.
Shenandoah River. Burial site of Brown's men, 199-200, illustrated, 200; Hall establishes Rifle Works along, 19; Native American meaning, 48; Navigation boats described, 52; Patowmack Company navigation improvements, 52; private industry and, 25; Washington's vision for, 52.
Shenandoah River Bridge. 1936 flood destroys, illustrated, 162.
Shenandoah Street. As Civil War ghost town, illustrated, 134; illustrated, 100, 112, 134, 142, 184; floods along, 133, 139-40, illustrated, 133, 151-2, 161-2; jail on, illustrated, 1; John Brown's Fort move, 183, illustrated, 183; NPS demolition and reconstruction, 184-5; traffic on, 189-90, illustrated, 189.

CONFLUENCE

Shenandoah Valley. Freedmen and, 114; Freedmen schools established in, 113-4; Harpers Ferry gateway to, 87; invasion by U.S. forces, 87, 107-8; Sheridan defeats Confederates in, 107; Sheridan ordered to destroy, 107; strategic importance, 87, 107; watershed denuded during Civil War, 150.

Shepherd, Hayward. Monument to, 129; mortally wounded during Brown attack, 10; Starry examines, 11.

Sheridan, Philip. Defeats Confederate army in Shenandoah Valley, 107-8; Grant orders to Shenandoah Valley, 107; headquarters at Lockwood House, 107; Shenandoah Valley destruction and, 107; supplied from Harpers Ferry, 107.

Short Hill. Jefferson's view preserved, illustrated, 196.

Simpson, Harold. B & O and Brown centennial, 176.

Slave owners convention. 40.

Slaves. Allstadt enslaved, 8; B & O bans transport of, 60; "Black Tom" purchases freedom, 29; Brown's Provisional Constitution and, 37; census and, 28; Civil War Centennial Commission and, 174; Confederates capture during Battle of Harpers Ferry 93-4; Declaration of Independence and, 172-3; *Declaration of Liberty* and, 37; deeded in will, 28; devaluation, 39; Douglass on Brown and slavery, 173; Dred Scott decision and, 36; educa-tion and, 113; fate of those involved in Harpers Ferry attack, 70; Harpers Ferry Armory and, 21, 27; John Brown Centennial and, 174; legal defini-tion of, 28; prices of, 28, 39; regulations of, 29, 30; occupations of, 29; owners and, 27; owners cap-tured, 8; punishment of, 29-30, 113;   returned into slavery, 85; reward for capture and return of, 40; runaways, 39-40; sales of, 29; seek freedom behind Union lines 85; slave patrols, illustrated, 29-30; trading of, 32; monetary value of, 28, 31-2; slave population at Harpers Ferry, 29, 32; Wagers as owners, 26; Wager enslaved, 28-9; Washington enslaved, 8;

Smith, Isaac. Alias John Brown, 5, 42.

Snell, Charles W. Advocates for centennial, 175-6; assigned to Harpers Ferry, 175; background, 175; conflict with Dale over Brown centennial, 175; illustrated, 175.

Sons of Confederate Veterans. Hayward Shepherd Monument and, 129-30.

Spirit of Jefferson. Anti-Black suffrage editorial, 122; counters Townsend's characterization, 145; freedmen editorial, 111; KKK recruitment ad, 117; New Year's Eve ball, 145; opposition to teachers' institute, 121.

Springfield Armory. Compared to Harpers Ferry armory, 17-8; established, 14; military superintendents at, 18.

Starry, John. Alerts authorities, 11; awakened during Brown attack, 11; examines Shepherd, 11; witness in Brown's trial, 71.

Stone Steps. Illustrated, viii, 155.

Stone Fort, illustrated, 164.

Storer, John. Donation, 119; equality and, 119; illustrated, 119.

Storer College. Acquisition of armory buildings, 120; band, illustrated, 123; banner, illustrated, 193; baseball team, 123; boarding houses, 157; Brown centennial at, 177-8, illustrated, 177-8; campus site hosts "Heritage Days: The Black Perspective", 191-2; choir, illustrated, 123; closure, 123; controversy over charter, 121; exhibits at, 193; graduate, illustrated, 124; Howard University study and, 192-3;   illustrated, 120; John Brown's Fort moved from, 183; John Brown's Fort moved to, 132, 185; Niagara Centennial held at, 194; Niagara Conference and, 127, illustrated, 127; NPS acquisition of John Brown's Fort and, 176, 182; NPS elevates as major theme 192-3; opens, 120; opposition to, 120; Redman concert held at, 193, illustrated, 193; sesquicentennial of, 193-4; significance of John Brown's Fort at, 131-2; as Stephen T. Mather Training Center 186, students illustrated, 122.

Storer College Alumni Association. 193; Heritage Days and, 191.

Strother, David Hunter. Arsenal destruction described, 80, illustrated, 80; B & O bridge destruction described, 82, illustrated, 82.

Stuart, J.E.B. Accompanies Lee to Harpers Ferry, 63; attends Brown's interrogation, 66; negotiates with Brown, 64; service under, 115; signals the attack, 64.

Stubblefield, James. Illustrated, 19; troubled armory superintendent, 19.

Stubblefield, Mary Beckham. Illustrated, 18; influence of, 18.

Taney, Roger Brooke. Defends B & O, 57.

Tatten, Pearl. Objection to Hayward Shepherd Monument, 129-30.

Thanksgiving Day. 1863 Grand Military Ball

Thompson, Dauphin. Killed by Marines, 66.

Thompson, William. Executed by angry mob, 44; illustrated, 44.

Thoreau, Henry David. Defends Brown, 72, 172; on Brown and Puritans, 33; questions law, 172-3.

Tobin, Daniel. John Brown centennial and, 176.

Townsend, George Alfred. "Village of paupers," 145.

Trowbridge, John. Illustrated, 136; hope for Harpers Ferry, 138; John Brown's Fort and, 137-8; natural scenery and, 137; town ruins described, 134-5, 137; visit to postwar Harpers Ferry, 134-8.

Trust for Public Lands. 206.

Turner, Nat. New controls imposed following, 29.

Tyler, John. Armory workers' "clock strike" and, 23; comment on Brown, 172; response to Brown's attack, 69.

Tyndale, Hector. Accosted at Harpers Ferry, 88; background of, 88; destroys commercial district during Civil War, 88; personal escort of Mary

Brown, 88.

Underground railroad. B & O and, 60; Brown suggests improvement upon, 38; in Maryland, 40; infrastructure of, 40-1; slave route of escape, 38-40.

United Daughters of the Confederacy. Hayward Shepherd Monument, 129-30.

U.S. Army Military Police. Model 1805 pistol and, 18.

U.S. Congress. Byrd and, 187; creates Civil War Centennial Commission, 174; disposal of armory, 139, 145; donation of armory buildings to Storer College, 120; establishment of Harpers Ferry Armory, 15; National Historical Park appropriations, 187; Fourteenth Amendment and, 110; Freedmen's Bureau and, 111;

United States Marines. Action described in capture of Brown, 64-5; arrival at Harpers Ferry, 47, 63; attack illustrated, 65; ordered to Harpers Ferry, 62-63; surround Brown, 63.

United States Supreme Court. Dred Scott decision and, 36, 109; segregation and, 127, 174.

Vallandingham, Clement. Interviews Brown, 66-7.

Virginia. Fear of insurrection, 69; militia march to capture armory and arsenal, 78-80; prohibiting Black education, 113; reward for capture and return of slaves, 40; slave trading and, 32.

Virginia Free Press. Ads from, 27, 29, 47, 57; editorializes on Douglass' memorial on Brown, 125.

Virginius Island. Abraham Herr and, 27, 141; compared to Lowell, 25-7; cotton mill, 27, 141; Emily Child describes 1870 flood on, 149; Harpers Ferry Mill Company, 141; Herr's Mill destroyed during Civil War, 86, illustrated, 86; Island Hospital described, 96; John Wernwag and 1870 flood on, 148; private industry, 27, 141; troop transport train on, 106; waterpower, 27, 141.

Voting rights. "Black and Tan" conference and, 122; Challenged in WV, 117, 122; Fifteenth Amendment, 117; Loyalty test required, 118, 121.

Wager family. "Black Tom" and, 29; commercial enterprises and, 27; Harper's heirs, 16; sale of land for armory and, 16; slave owners, 28-9.

Wager House Hotel. William Thompson dragged from, 44.

War Department. *See Ordnance Department.*

War of 1812. Armory empoyees during, 20; John Butler, veteran of, 28.

Washington, George. Address to Congress, 15; armorer strike on his birthday, 16; cites armory's advantages, 15; commercial interest, 15; Falls at Harpers Ferry described, 50; first navigates Potomac Falls at Harpers Ferry, 48-49; first views Harpers Ferry as surveyor, 48; Fort Necessity loss, 48; French and Indian War and, 14; illustrated, 14; Mount Vernon Compact and, 49; nation's defense and, 15; Patowmack Company establishment, 14-5; Patowmack Company president, 14, 51; pistol and sword owned by, 7-8; Potomac navigation, 14-5, 48-9, 51; problems with Patowmack Company and, 51; progress of Patowmack Company and, 51; selects arsenal site, 15; vision for Harpers Ferry, 14-5, 48-49; vision for Shenandoah River navigation, 52.

Washington, Lewis. Artifacts of George, 7-8; captured, 8; Cook visits, 7-8; hostage in John Brown's Fort, 9, 46; illustrated, 8; meets Brown, 9; nephew of George, 8; slaves of, 8, 70; witness in Brown's trial, 70-1.

Washington County Historical Society. Mary Vernon Mish and, 166-7 national monument in MD and, 166-7.

Washington Post. Comments on Brown centennial, 178; favorable publicity for monument, 170.

Washington Star. Hopeful at establishment of national monument, 167.

Waterpower. Energy source, 141; fall of rivers and, 141; manufacturing and, 141; private indus-try and, 27, 141; speculators, 141.

Webster, Daniel. Defends B & O in court battles, 57.

Wentzel, Volmar. Describes national monument's condition, 168.

Wernwag, John. 1870 flood and, 148.

Wernwag, Lewis. B & O bridge and, 58.

West Virginia. Acquires land for national monument, 167-8; established, 117; loyalty test required,121; Radical Republicans and, 118; resistance to, 117; school segregation, 121; Storer College charter and, 121; voting rights within, 117.

Wheeler, Ellen. Opens school to educate slaves, 99.

Wheeler, W. W. Opens school to educate slaves, 99.

Whelan, Daniel. Captured by Brown, 7-8; watchman, 6-7.

White, Charles. Describes route of Brown's soldiers at rifle factory, 45; preaches at Presbyterian Church, 45.

Willett, John. Establishes NPS presence at national monument, 168.

Williamsburg model, 184-6.

Winchester & Potomac Railroad. Ad, 61; arrives at Harpers Ferry, 58; troop transport train on, 106.

Wirth, Conrad. Significance of Harpers Ferry and, 167.

Wise, Henry. Orders militia to Charles Town during Brown's imprisonment and execution, 68

Acknowledgments

Harpers Ferry is an eternal magnet. It attracts fascinating people traveling fantastic journeys. *Confluence* is a testament to all they've contributed, over many decades, to our understanding and appreciation of our beloved Harpers Ferry.

Accolades to Cathy Baldau, executive director of the Harpers Ferry Park Association and editor extraordinaire. Cathy served as an editor of two of Dennis' previous volumes, and was the mastermind publication specialist behind the national award-winner *Harpers Ferry Under Fire*. To Catherine, Cathy has been a tremendous mentor, empowering and encouraging her to take on increasingly bigger challenges. We are grateful for Cathy's vision, her leadership and for her smooth transition into the captain's chair at HFPA.

Debbie Piscitelli deserves special notice. Now retired after 36 years at the helm of HFPA, Debbie built and sustained the organization with dedication and passion. Debbie's years of influence are within *Confluence*.

Curator Michael Hosking opened the doors to the extensive manuscript and object collections at Harpers Ferry NHP, granting our on-going research requests and accommodating our schedules. Many discoveries in *Confluence* occurred due to our access to the material culture that Mike provided. We also appreciate the assistance of longtime Harpers Ferry residents Linda and Ron Rago, who opened their armorer's home to us to explore inspiration from the 19th century.

Our designer, Victor Curran, will be forever in our gratitude for helping bring *Confluence* to life. We benefited, as well, from the efforts of photographers Eric Long and Katlyn Simmons, who ensured every one of their pictures were art. Kudos, too, to Jim Broomall and Jennifer Alarcon at Shepherd University for facilitating our research during the historic and onerous government shutdown.

Thank-yous—and apologies—to Catie and Ashton, Catherine's at-home children, for enduring countless trips to the library, meandering photography walks, and several take-out meals during the final days of this book's production. Also to Caroline, all grown up, whose multiple years as a Youth Conservation Corps member at Harpers Ferry continue to make mom proud, along with all your successive adventures. It is your mother's wish that one day you all will discover a story that moves your soul, and you will feel as if you have found a long-lost friend.

Retired from the National Park Service, Dennis joins wife Sylvia, who retired as the NPS Agency Curator. Sylvia and Dennis literally met over John Brown's family Bible (yes, you read that correctly) - an object Dennis discovered and that she cared for as Registrar at the Harpers Ferry Center's conservation laboratory. Sylvia's background as a proud Texas Aggie in archeology and anthropology privileged her with excavating at The Alamo, and Dennis must genuflect daily to the Lone Star Flag in the "Texas Room" of their Maryland home. Sylvia's experience as chief curator at the Museum of Westward Expansion at the Arch in St. Louis (and the Dred Scott federal courthouse) – as well as her service as Fort Smith National Historic Site's first curator – has sharpened Dennis' understanding of the role of material culture in historic interpretation. It also has ena-bled them to create their own ante-bellum "living museum" within their restored home – General Burnside's post-Antietam headquarters. Surrounded by and supported by Sylvia's passion for history – along with the canine love of Boston Terriers "Mr. Lincoln" and "Bonnie Blue" – provided Dennis constant inspiration for *Confluence*.

A Tribute

From Dennis

I retired in 2018, after nearly nearly 35 years at Harpers Ferry NHP. I was blessed to work with the absolute best park rangers. As interpreters and historians, they were unexcelled. We produced and shared many successes together because we were unafraid of challenge, willing to experiment, and bold enough to risk in a bureaucracy adverse to risk. Because of our vision and efforts, the NPS often extolled us as a model. Most important, the abiding passion of my fellow rangers for Harpers Ferry - and their dedication to its public presentation and its preservation - inspired me every day. I loved coming to work! These fine rangers will forever be within me: Supervisory Park Ranger Todd Bolton. Supervisory Park Ranger John King. Supervisory Park Ranger Catherine Bragaw. Rangers Tom Bates, George Best, Kim Biggs, Jeff Bowers, Autumn Cook, Melinda Day, Chuck Dennis, Scott Devers, David Fox, Lesley Johnson, Elizabeth Kerwin-Nisbet, David Larsen, Jessica Liptak, Mark McGaha, Stan McGee, Kyle McGrogan, John Powell, Gwenny Roper, Eric Sheetz, Paul Smith, Creighton Waters and Samantha Zurbuch. Each of you made me better.

Harpers Ferry NHP research historians Pat Chickering, Mike Jenkins, Stan Bumgardner, Mary Johnson, Deidra Durbin and Kira Ramakrishna literally changed our understanding of Harpers Ferry's history during a five-year investigation of tens of thousands of pages of area newspapers. Many of the discoveries in *Confluence* are a re-sult of their diligent and patient research.

My team at Harpers Ferry NHP could not thrive or survive without support from other special people at the park. I extend my gratitude to Susan Haberkorn, Judy Coleman, Cathy Boyer, Tina Cavalier, Melinda Sease, Rita Mihalik, and Sherry Miller for their hourly administrative, human resources and purchasing assistance, conquering tons of paperwork that would have buried us except for their navigational skills through the minefields. Resource specialists Peter Dessauer (park architect); Steve Lowe (landscape architect); Andrew Lee (historian and archeologist); and John and Cari Ravenhorst (archeologists) employed their exceptional expertise and talents, turning many of my research ideas into projects. Curators Pam West, Trudy Kelly, Michelle Hammer, Richard Raymond, Nancy Hatcher and Hilda Staubs helped me over and again with museum objects and collections. I worked with numerous fellow division chiefs over the decades, and I owe thanks to: Ryan Levins, Sean Isham, Jeff Woods, Jennifer Flynn, and Harvey Sorenson (resource and visitor protection); Richard Trott, Micheal "Cas" Castagnetto, and Tim Fox (maintenance); George McHugh, Gayleen Boyd and Peggy Smallwood (administration); and Bill Hebb and Mia Parsons. Budget officers Norma Rishel and Joanne Beaulieu ensured I stayed out of jail. I am grateful to maintenance leaders who cared about "the look" of our park and were proud of its daily appearance, including: Dennis Ebersole, Larry Moore, Richard Gladden, Merle Miller, and Roger Huffman.

I have been nurtured by, mentored by, and supported by some of the best-known ante-bellum and Civil War historians in the country. I am grateful to the following for their belief in me and for their years of assistance in historical research, writing and publishing: Dr. Mary Abroe. Ted Alexander. Mike Andrus. Dr. James Broomall. Dr. Millard Bushong. Chris Calkins. Dr. Peter Carmichael. Dr. Thomas Clemens. William C. "Jack" Davis. Dr. Kitty Frescoln. Dr. Gary Gallagher. Richard Gillespie. A. Wilson Greene. Dr. Allen Guelzo. Dr. Joseph Harsh. John Hennessy. Dr. James Holland. Dr. Perry Jamieson. Robert K. Krick. Dr. Richard McMurry. Dr. James McPherson. James Murfin. Michael Musick. James Ogden. Frank O'Reilly. Dr. Carol Reardon. Dr. Paula Reed. Dr. James I. "Bud" Robertson. Rev. John Schildt. Dana Shoaf. Dr. Mark Snell. Dr. Richard Sommers, and Dr. John Stealey. Dr. Jerry Thomas, and Dr. Jill Titus.

The best historian in my life has been my father, John C. Frye, the oracle of Washington County, Maryland and the curator of the Western Maryland Room at the Washington County Free Library for the past 50 years. I've never needed an appointment to ask Dad a question pertaining to history. My mother, Janice M. Poffenberger Frye, has roots in the Boonsboro-Sharpsburg area that dates back 250 years. My mother's great-great-great grandfather (Peter Beachley) owned a significant portion of Fox's Gap when the Battle of South Mountain occurred there. Mom is the best teacher I've ever had.

I am thankful for the personal confluence of each person above in my life.

Image Credits

This book would not be possible without the contributions of several artists who have each tried, in their own way, to honor the stories and spirit of Harpers Ferry, and fine institutions which have graciously cataloged their works, preserving them for future generations. A few of these sources are listed directly in the text, but others may be found on the following pages:

B & O Museum, 59.

Dennis E. Frye Collection, Sketch by A. Lumley: 95.

Frank Leslie's Illustrated Newspaper: 93.

From *Harpers Ferry Under Fire* by Annie Marmion: 84.

Harper's Weekly: ii-iii, 3, 81, 82.

Historic Images Collection, Harpers Ferry National Historical Park: ii-iii, xiii, 1, 3, 8, 19, 24, 42, 45, 53-4, 58, 62, 65, 66, 68, 73, 74, 75, 77, 80, 81, 82, 84, 86, 88, 93, 94, 95, 96, 98, 99, 100, 105-6, 107, 108, 109, 112, 114, 115-6, 118, 119, 120, 121, 123, 124, 127, 131, 132, 133, 134, 135-6, 138, 139-40, 141-2, 143-4, 146, 147, 148, 150, 151, 152, 153, 154, 155, 156, 157, 158, 160, 161, 162, 163, 164, 168.

National Archives: 112.

National Geographic Society: 58.

National Park Service/HFCCAC/Hugh Brown, 91; National Park Service/HFCCAC/Keith Rocco, 26; National Park Service/HFCCAC/Steven N. Patricia, 21; National Park Service/HFCCAC/historic engraving hand-colored by artist Richard Schlecht, 29-30, 35; National Park Service/HFCCAC/Richard Schlecht, 6, 17-8, 38, 64, 89-90; National Park Service/HFCCAC/Carol Stuart Watson, 22, 48.

Newsweek Magazine, 171.

NPS Photos: 8, 17, 19, 20, 22, 23, 33, , 173, 174, 175, 176, 177, 179-80, 181-2, 183, 184, 185, 186, 188, 189, 190, 192, 193, 194, 197, 198, 212, 217, 220

Library of Congress: 4, 5, 43, 44, 63, 69, 71, 76, 91, 92, 104, 191, 202

Smithsonian Institution, 213.

From *The Soldier in Our Civil War*, 104.

U.S. Military Academy: 106.

USAMHI: 96.

Washington SPARK, 174

Photo by Dave Gilbert, 187.

Photos by Eric Long, vi, 52, 61, 184.

Photos by Catherine Mägi: xi, 52 (background), 83, 129, 130, 137, 159, 167, 169; 170; 195-6, 199-200, 216

Photos by Katlyn Simmons / Harpers Ferry Park Association: 186, 193, 198

Dennis E. Frye retired after serving twenty years as Chief Historian at Harpers Ferry National Historical Park and another dozen years as a supervisory park ranger at Harpers Ferry. For his trend-setting achievements in preservation, education and interpretation, he earned the highest honor in his branch of the federal government – the Department of Interior's Distinguished Service Award – along with a career commendation in the esteemed *Congressional Record* and a meritorious citation by the West Virginia Senate.

Dennis is the author of eleven books and 103 articles, and has been published in every major Civil War periodical. His *Harpers Ferry Under Fire* won acclaim and a national book-of-the-year award. Dennis has appeared in numerous network and television documentaries as a historian scholar, and he helped produce three Emmy-award shows on the subjects of John Brown, the Battle of Antietam and Maryland in the Civil War. Dennis is a nationally recognized leader in preservation as co-founder of renowned nonprofit organizations, including today's American Battlefields Trust, the Save Historic Antietam Foundation, and the Heart of the Civil War Heritage Area in Maryland.

Dennis is a life-long resident of the Harpers Ferry area, where his family roots go back more than 250 years.

Exploring Harpers Ferry's history has been Dennis Frye's eternal playground.

Catherine Mägi left the practice of law to pursue a childhood dream of living in an old house in the mountains and writing stories. Having fallen in love with Harpers Ferry from a train window as a kid, she returned as a grown-up to the Ferry, adopted an 1840s armorer's house which she has lovingly restored, and in 2017, joined the staff of the Harpers Ferry Park Association.

Catherine's career has been inspired by Thomas Jefferson's vision of "citizen lawyers," professionals who use their skills *outside of courtrooms* to guide, guard, and grow their communities in positive ways. She has spent nineteen years building a record of public service, including time with Maryland's Public Defender, domestic violence programs, and numerous archeology programs throughout Maryland and Virginia.

A product of the College of William and Mary and all things Colonial Williamsburg, Catherine's interest in history was perhaps inevitable. However, she credits her grandparents, refugees from Soviet-occupied Estonia, with transforming mere interest into passion, making America's long quest for liberty feel intensely immediate, relevant, *real.*